history
of the
franciscan brothers
of brooklyn
in ireland and america

For Niall Ó Ciosáin
Thank you for your
lecture!
Emmett Corry, OSF

emmett corry, o.s.f.
franciscan brothers and st. francis college
2003

Published by St. Francis College, 180 Remsen Street, Brooklyn, New York 11201 and Franciscan Brothers of Brooklyn, 135 Remsen Street, Brooklyn, New York 11201.

Corry, Emmett.
    History of the Franciscan Brothers of Brooklyn in Ireland and America / Emmett Corry.
    389 p. cm. — (St. Francis College and Franciscan Brothers).
    Includes bibliographic data and illustrations.
    ISBN: 0-9723703-0-7 (Paper: alk. paper)

Printed by H.R. Elliot & Co. Inc., New York.

This History of the Franciscan Brothers of Brooklyn is dedicated to the many Brothers in Ireland and America, and our religious and lay colleagues, whose work--as teachers, administrators and staff--has been an inspiration.

The cover illustration is the Franciscan Brothers' Roundstone Monastery, Co. Galway, Ireland, c. 1855.

CONTENTS

PREFACE

Who are we?" "Where did we come from?"

Rooted in the intrigue of the first fifty years of the Franciscan Brothers in Brooklyn, this work thoroughly investigates our roots and evolution as a lay religious institute. We are grateful to Emmett Corry for his capable and conscientious service in compiling the following historic data. He has examined original source materials, locally as well as in Ireland and Rome, carefully comparing and contrasting these materials in an effort to determine what did and what did not happen and where, how, and why it happened.

Remembering and re-telling the origin stories is part of our Celtic tradition and of our Judeo-Christian tradition. Reading our story reminds us that we have been shaped by all the past influences in our religious family story and that we are capable of creating a vision for the future when we have integrated our past, discovered its truths, and celebrated it.

The story of the Franciscan Brothers of Brooklyn is indeed a rich inheritance. We rejoice in the achievements of our Brothers and thank all those who were part of and supported us in our journey. And we thank God for being with us and bringing us to the present moment.

Brother Kevin Smith, OSF
December, 2002

INTRODUCTION

The Franciscan Brothers of the Third Order Regular trace their first founding to St. Francis of Assisi in the thirteenth century, when the Third Order Regular evolved from the Third Order Secular. The Irish Third Order Regular priests and brothers had forty-seven "monasteries," as their friaries were known, primarily in the West and North of Ireland. "The rapid spread through Connacht and Ulster of the 'Third Order Regular' or 'Third Order of Penance' was certainly a major event in the history of religion in Ireland. There was no comparable development in Britain and not much similar on the Continent. It was almost a uniquely Irish movement."[1] Their suppression in the "Troubles" of the Elizabethan and post-Elizabethan ages, came about because of the total restrictions on religious orders of the sixteenth and seventeenth century Penal Laws. [2]

The "global imperative" of spreading the Protestant faith was a "feature of the 1790s and early 1800s in Britain. Following the Act of Union of 1800, it became an article of faith among Evangelical Christians on both sides of the Irish Sea, that if the Catholic Irish could be "'brought over' to the Protestant faith, the problems which bedeviled Irish society such as economic backwardness, lack of respect for the law, and hatred of the Protestant establishment would be eradicated." [3] Although it is difficult in our current ecumenical age to appreciate the extent of the suspicion and fear Catholics had for Evangelical Protestant efforts to proselytize their children - and the opposite belief of these well-funded Evangelicals, that Catholic "Popery" must be opposed at all costs, much of nineteenth century religion in Ireland is suffused with this mutual animosity and suspicion.[4] The vigorous attempts of Protestant Evangelical Bible and Mission Societies to proselytize Catholic families and their children in the early nineteenth century, especially through the phenomenon of "souperism," before, during, and after the Great Irish Famine of 1847-1850, was one of the motivating reasons for the re-founding of the Third Order Regular and other religious communities in Ireland in the beginning of the nineteenth century.

The efforts of extremist Evangelical Protestants to convert the Catholics of Ireland had not been taken seriously by Catholic bishops, upper-class Catholics, nor the bishops of the Church of Ireland, until 1822, when William Magee, at his inauguration as the Church of Ireland's new archbishop of Dublin, called for the Church of Ireland to "shake off its reputation as a civil institution and underline its claim to the Apostolic succession and take up a 'Second Reformation'". [5]

> *Because of his stature as the head of the country's most important diocese, it appeared to contemporaries that he had not only invited open conflict with the Catholic bishops but placed himself and his church in the forefront of the crude anti-Catholic crusade of the Orange Order. Magee's sermon was seen as a turning point after which the highest echelons of the Church of Ireland came to be infected with the vulgar confrontational style of Orange supremacism.* [6]

Magee's claim, that the Church of Ireland was the only body in Ireland possessing a legitimate claim to apostolic-succession, met with a vigorous response from James Warren Doyle, the youthful Catholic bishop of Kildare and

Leighlin. In a long latter to the *Dublin Evening Post*, published two weeks later, Doyle challenged Magee's sermon and "lambasted him with unprecedented boldness, pouring scorn on the Anglican Church's claim to have preserved the apostolic succession of bishops. Magee, he wrote, had no more claim to be the successor of an apostle than he had to the dukedom of Leeds. Doyle did not attack abuses in the Establishment Church: he denied its right to exist. It was 'the scorpion's tail [which] is armed at all points and scourges the peasant through tithes and church rates till it draws his very blood'" [7]

The conflict between Doyle and Magee came to a notorious culmination that same year when a Catholic chapel in Ardee, County Louth, was desecrated with the clandestine placing of a calf's head on the altar, a symbol of insult and blasphemous ridicule. [8]

A more disturbing prospect for the Catholic clergy, however, was the strength of the Protestant response to Dr. Magee's proclamation of 'a glorious Second reformation in Ireland'. Before 1822, evangelical overtures to the Catholic population had not gone further than Bible and tract distribution and the enticement of children to schools run by one or another of the various societies. Between 1822 and 1827 this system was supplemented by more direct and blatant efforts to increase the number of converts from Catholicism. In line with Dr. Magee's manifesto that the established church was under a severe and immediate obligation to unfurl the banner of the reformation, the making of converts assumed pre-eminent importance and became the source of particularly bitter hostility between the two major religious groups. [9]

The evident need of the Irish Catholic church to counter the Protestant Evangelicals and the new, vigorous proselytizing of the Church of Ireland, was shown in the enthusiastic support of the Irish people to the emergence of a half-dozen religious teaching institutes. Among these was the Franciscan Brothers of the Third Order Regular which was re-founded in Dublin in 1818.

The Brothers were initially supported in their re-founding by their obedience to the Provincial of the First Order Franciscan Friars Minor at Adam and Eve's Friary in Dublin and the two Franciscan First Order priests, who were their superiors in two parishes in the Dublin Archdiocese. Although the Catholic Emancipation Act of 1829 had freed the secular clergy and Catholic laymen from many of the older Penal Laws, it did not remove the Penal Laws from the "regulars," religious such as the First Order Friars Minor Franciscans, whose major superior was outside the British Isles in Rome. As a community of Brothers obedient to these Friars, the Third Order Regular Franciscan Brothers could not receive novices or maintain a legal, corporate existence in Ireland.

In 1820, the brothers accepted the invitation of Christopher Dillon Bellew, a Catholic landlord, to establish a monastery in Mountbellew, County Galway. In 1830, at the insistence of Bellew, the Brothers successfully petitioned the Holy See to transfer their obedience from the Provincial of the Irish Province of the Friars Minor, to Oliver Kelly, their ordinary in the Archdiocese of Tuam, Galway, in the West of Ireland. This choice of diocesan status was a continuing source of difficulty for the Brothers through the nineteenth century, when some of their bishops were less than pastoral as their ecclesiastical superiors.

The "Interrupted Lives" [10] of most of the poor people of Ireland is one of the traumatic effects of the Great Irish Famine. The uprooting, separation and dispersal of families, the decimation of whole villages in the West of Ireland through banishment, death, and emigration, is a legacy the Irish Brothers brought to America from the West of Ireland. With other Irish religious institutes, founded before and after the turn of the nineteenth century, the Franciscan Brothers, as a non-clerical community, became a valued solution to the Irish and American bishops' need for religious to open and staff their Catholic schools and orphanages.

The Nativist, anti-Catholic violence experienced by the Church in America in the pre-Civil War generation of the 1840s and 1850s, reinforced a collective memory of the Brothers and influenced their response to the needs of the Church in Ireland and America through the nineteenth century. The emigration of two brothers and eight postulants to Brooklyn in the Summer of 1858, and the subsequent travel of the Superior, with five brothers and a novice to California in 1862, will be explored. The experience of the young community in the brief year they administered the Boys Catholic Orphanage, will show that the orphanage was totally unsuitable as a novitiate for the young brothers. In September of 1859, John McMahon opened a "Monastery and Select Catholic School at Nos. 22 and 24 Baltic Street, Brooklyn, which property has been purchased for this purpose. This is a desideratum long wanted in Brooklyn. Brother John McMahon is now engaged (with the approval of Bishop Loughlin) in collecting contributions for this purpose." [11] Less than a year later, St. Francis Academy would also be noted as conducting a "free evening school, for the instruction of young men whose avocations leave them no opportunity, during the business hours of the day, to acquire an education." [12] This free education for young men continued a centuries-long tradition of the Irish Brothers to educate young men in useful trades such as carpentry, barrel making, and stone cutting.

The experience of the brothers as educators in their own St. Francis Academy and College and their reputation as teachers of over 5,000 boys in almost a score of parish schools of Brooklyn, New Jersey, and Roundout, New York established their preeminence in the Brooklyn Diocese in the nineteenth century. The long history of the differing Rules and Constitutions which have evolved over the centuries of the Franciscan Brothers' history, reveals that the unique "monastic" character of the Irish community was changed to an exclusive teacher-only congregation in Brooklyn in the eight years between 1858 and 1866.

Leo XIII's 1897 Bull, *Felicitate Quadam,* which required the many Franciscan communities around the world to decide what they were and to join one of the four Roman Franciscan orders, prompted the Irish and American communities to seek to unite with the Roman Third Order Regular. The decade from 1897 to 1907, reveals the difficulties the brothers experienced with their diocesan bishops in Ireland and Brooklyn. An important part of the Irish Brothers' history will be their unsuccessful attempt, toward the end of the nineteenth century, to reestablish their "regular" status under the obedience of a major superior in Rome. Instead of the Provincial of the Irish Franciscan Friars Minor, to whom the brothers gave their obedience from 1818 to 1830, the brothers sought to join the Third Order Regular, under the obedience of the Roman Minister General of the Order in the ancient Basilica of SS. Cosmas and Damian in Rome. The unsuccessful attempt of the Brooklyn Brothers between 1904-1907, for the same unity with their Roman Third Order Regular confreres, would cause a painful split in the young Brooklyn community which would lead to the creation of the Sacred Heart Province of the Third Order Regular in America. Reluctant efforts of the Brothers to place their roots in America, instead of Ireland, where vocations had been sought for almost sixty years, promoted the creation of the two houses of formation in Smithtown, Long Island in the third decade of the twentieth century.

The creation and development of "The St. Francis Monastery of the City of Brooklyn" in 1868, as the legal corporation of the community, and its evolving relationship to St. Francis College and the other schools of the brothers, will be explored. The separation of the College Board of Trustees from the Monastery Board in 1957, will be examined and the fund-raising efforts of the Franciscan Brothers in 1922 and 1958, which directly benefited St. Francis College, will be discussed. Continuing efforts of the Community to return its schools to a Franciscan identity will be a theme throughout this history.

PUBLISHED SOURCES FOR A
HISTORY OF THE BROOKLYN COMMUNITY

Prepared for the Seventy-fifth Anniversary of the Community, the *Souvenir of The Diamond Jubilee of the Franciscan Brothers, Brooklyn, N.Y., 1858-1933*,[13] is a 128 page collection of the early history of the Community, remembrances of alumni, pictures of bishops, priests and brothers, illustrations of the schools and St. Francis Monastery, with advertisements from friends of the Franciscan Brothers.

Roger Nagle, O.S.F. completed a Master's Dissertation at St. John's University which devotes a section to the arrival of the Franciscan Brothers in St. John's, Nova Scotia, and their travels to other parts of the United States in the nineteenth century before their arrival in Brooklyn.[14]

Philip Harris, O.S.F. completed a 24 page pamphlet for the One Hundredth Anniversary of the Brooklyn Community in 1958. Along with pictures of brothers and some of the institutions of the Community, this pamphlet summarizes the public relations campaign created for the Centenary of the Brothers, directed by Brother Philip. [15]

The *Franciscan Brothers' Centenary Album*[16] was published to celebrate the one hundred years of the arrival of the Franciscan Brothers in Brooklyn. Each of the schools is described briefly, and professionally commissioned photographs of the brothers assigned to each institution in 1958 are included.

Over the last twenty years the Brothers' Newsletter contained many articles on the history of the Community written by Kevin Smith, O.S.F. *The Canticle*, sent to Brothers and Friends of the Community since the Winter of 1994, has also published a portion of the history of the Community in each issue, which has resulted in this publication.

MANUSCRIPT SOURCES

The history of the Irish Brothers has been revealed in the research of a number of Irish Franciscan Brothers. Bernardine Cowan's remarkable "The Story of the Irish Franciscan Brothers" was completed in 1955. This fifty-five page manuscript is a unique history, which makes use of the extensive Archives of the Brothers at Mountbellew,

Ireland. Brother Bernardine held many offices in the Irish Community, including Superior General from 1931-1937, and his earlier involvement in the process of seeking Pontifical Status, gives his "Story," a truly valuable place in the history of the Irish Community. [17]

Declan Fox continued the work of Brother Bernardine with his 1982, eighty-seven page draft manuscript, "History of the Irish Franciscan Brothers".[18] His gathering of the many papers of the Franciscan monasteries in Ireland, from the creation of Mountbellew in 1818 - to missionary work in Africa and the United States in the twentieth century, is recounted from the papers carefully filed in the extensive community Archives in Mountbellew, Ireland. Not only is Brother Declan's "History" exhaustive in its coverage of each of the Irish monasteries, but it lists where each of these collections of papers is filed in the Archives at Mountbellew. His creation of the Archives at Mountbellew has left us in his debt.

Vincent Jordan's "The Order of Penitents, The Third Order Regular of Saint Francis in Ireland," is a 1995 manuscript in draft form which continues the work of Declan Fox. Brother Vincent, who is the current Archivist of the community, brings the history of the Irish Franciscan Brothers closer to the present time. [19]

ARCHIVE COLLECTIONS

Among the many sources for the history of the Franciscan Brothers are the Archives of the Irish Franciscan Brothers in Mountbellew (AFBM) in County Galway. The Irish Brothers have preserved a great amount of their history in the papers of the individual monasteries from Clara in Kings County in the Irish mid-lands, to their

Monastery on Achill Island in the West of Ireland. The author was fortunate to have met the late Brothers Bernardine Cowan, O.S.F. and Declan Fox, O.S.F., who served as archivists of the Irish Community at Mountbellew. Their outstanding work is being currently well served by Vincent Jordan, O.S.F., who as Archivist has shared many aspects of the history of the Irish Franciscan Brothers.

FRANCISCAN BROTHERS ARCHIVES

The Archives of the Franciscan Brothers of Brooklyn (AFBB), consist of the minutes of chapters of the Brothers and meetings of the consultors of the Community. In an introduction to the 1878+ Minutes of the Council, a brief summary of the history of the Community was written by Paul Hill, who was the Secretary of the Community at that point. Celestine McGarry, who typed these hand-written Minutes in 1944, indicates that no Minutes had been compiled before 1878. [20] In addition, the nineteenth century financial records of the Community have proven to be very useful in tracing the close connections between the legal government of the brothers, which reposes in "The Saint Francis Monastery" Board of Trustees, and the governance of their schools. Only with the separation of St. Francis College from the government of "The Saint Francis Monastery" in 1957, by the creation of a separate Board of Trustees for the College, does it become evident how closely intertwined they were.

The Archives of the Brooklyn Diocese (ADB) are beginning to yield treasures from the records of John Loughlin, Charles McDonnell and Thomas E. Molloy. The Minute Books of the Roman Catholic Orphan Asylum Society have been particularly revealing in their coverage of the Society's responses to the disastrous fire of 9 November 1862, which destroyed the Male Orphan Asylum.

The Archives of the Franciscan Brothers (AFBB), and "The St. Francis Monastery" contain much correspondence from Thomas E. Molloy, who was a student of the brothers at St. Francis College. As the Ordinary of the Brooklyn Diocese, he was the President of both "The St. Francis Monastery" and the College Board of Trustees. His 1931 intervention in the governance of St. Francis College gave evidence of his concern for the survival of the College. His detailed suggestions for his Alma Mater's growth and preparation for Middle States Association accreditation will be examined in detail in Chapter Nine.

Responses to the correspondence (1858-1860s), of our brothers in the Archives of the Santa Barbara Province (ASBP) of the First Order Franciscans have been very helpful in establishing the dates of the travel of John McMahon, O.S.F., the first Superior of the brothers in Brooklyn and the leader of the five brothers who went to Santa Barbara, California in 1862, and eventually settled in the hills above Santa Barbara at the Santa Ines Mission. John McMahon became the principal of St. Mary's Free School for Boys in the basement of the Cathedral in San Francisco. Archival material from the Archdiocese of San Francisco (AASF), has been especially valuable for information from McMahon's correspondence with James Croke, the Vicar General of the Archdiocese.

The Archives of the Sacred Heart Province of the Third Order Regular (ATORL), which is now housed in St. Francis College in Loretto, Pennsylvania and the Archives of the Curia of the Third Order Regular (ACTOR), in Saints Cosmas and Damian in Rome, have been of great help in tracing the connections of the Brooklyn community and the creation of the Third Order Regular in the United States. The dedication of the late Bonaventure Kiley, T.O.R., as the long-time Archivist of the Sacred Heart Province of the Third Order Regular, is evident in the extraordinary depth and organization of these fundamental records. The author was privileged to work with Father Bonaventure when the Archives were at Bishop Egan High School before their transfer to St. Francis College in Loretto. He was also fortunate to have worked with the Archivist at the Curia of the Third Order Regular in Saints Cosmas and Damian in Rome.

PROPAGANDA FIDE ARCHIVES

Most of the correspondence to the Holy See from Catholic prelates, clergy, members of religious orders, and lay persons in nations such as Ireland and the United States, which were considered missionary countries because they were not ruled by a Catholic prince, are housed in the extensive Archives of Propaganda Fide (APF) in the Piazza di Spanga in Rome. These documents are extraordinarily valuable for research on Irish and American Church history and are wealthy sources of "civil, cultural and religious history of peoples in the domains of sociology, ethnography, glossology, and many other human sciences."[21] The great reference work, *United States Documents in the Propaganda Fide Archives, a Calendar*, published by the Academy of American Franciscan History between 1966 and 2002, is now up to twelve volumes. It is an extraordinarily important index and calendar of letters, documents, and petitions from the United States, Canada, and Middle America, and the responses of the Church to these documents. [22]

Many issues of *Analecta Hibernica* in which Henry

Fenning, O.P., J. Kennings and Benignus Millet, O.F.M. list and calendar Irish Archive materials. These are found in the Bibliography of the Kowalski - Metzler Inventory.[23] Brussels Manuscript 3947, which contains three pages on houses of the Third Order Regular in Ireland in Latin and Irish, was written between 1616 - 1618, in St. Anthony's College in Louvain, Belgium. [24]

THE HALIDAY PAMPHLET COLLECTION

The Haliday Pamphlet Collection in the Royal Irish Academy (HPCRIA), [25] is a remarkable treasure trove of about 30,000 eighteenth and nineteenth century pamphlets collected by physician and member Charles Haliday, and donated by his widow to the Academy in 1855. Organized and bound by the year of publication, these documents are accessed by a comprehensive index. Many unique pamphlets of the Hibernian Bible Society and other Evangelical societies' efforts to proselytize Catholic children are found in this collection.

RESEARCH COLLECTIONS

The newspaper collections in the New York Public Library, the Brooklyn Daily Eagle Picture Collection in the Brooklyn Public Library, the Brooklyn Historical Society, and the California newspaper collections in the Bancroft Library of the University of California in Berkeley, have been very useful in locating graphics and articles about the brothers and their schools in Brooklyn and California.

ACKNOWLEDGMENTS

Among the colleagues who assisted the author in researching the details of this history, is John Prior, CFC, who worked with the author as Research Intern from St. John's University. He was extraordinarily helpful in researching nineteenth century newspapers. His careful reading of the Account Books of St. Francis College and Academy revealed many details of persons and events which are discussed in the history. Brother John, who is organizing the Mission Archives of the Irish Christian Brothers in Peru, returned to his Mission after completing his Master of Library Science degree in May, 2000.

The late Bonaventure Kiley, T.O.R., the Archivist of the Sacred Heart Province of the Third Order Regular, was especially helpful in sharing copies of some of the documents of the Province which related to the Brooklyn Community. The two 1905-1906 pamphlets, advocating priesthood in the Brooklyn congregation and union with the Roman Third Order Regular, are invaluable to the history of the Franciscan Brothers of Brooklyn.

Vincent Jordan, O.S.F., Archivist of the Irish Franciscan Brothers and author of a history of the Irish Franciscan Brothers, has been very helpful in his reading and commentary on the manuscript.

Catherine Ann Curry, PBVM, Assistant Archivist of the San Francisco Archdiocese, was very helpful in sharing letters from John McMahon to James Croke, which filled in some of the reasons why the first superior of the Community left Brooklyn for California with five other brothers in 1862.

Joseph Coen, Archivist of the Brooklyn Diocese and his assistants Patrick McNamara and Shaun Martinell, have been very helpful in assisting this researcher to find documents relating to the Franciscan Brothers.

John Ridge, *"historien-extraordinaire"* of the Irish in New York City, past-president and now vice-president of the New York Irish History Roundtable, has kindly sent this researcher many items on the Brothers from nineteenth and twentieth-century Irish American newspapers.

Anna M. Donnelly, and Charles P. Livermore, Reference Librarians of St. John's University Libraries, have been especially helpful in answering the many questions which this researcher posed over the years this work has been in progress.

Monica S. Cupen (SFC Class of '02), Academic Counselor/Instructor with the Office of Freshman Studies at St. Francis College, assisted the author in formatting the manuscript for the printer.

The Franciscan Brothers, who encouraged and supported the research and writing of the author are thanked for their faith that the work would be concluded. In particular, Benilde Montgomery, Owen Justinian Sadlier, Thomas Grady, Edmund Holmes and Kevin Smith have offered their valued observations on the drafts of the manuscript. The author, however, assumes all responsibility for errors of fact and style.

ARCHIVES CITED

Archives Franciscan Brothers, Mountbellew, Galway, Ireland - AFBM

Archives Franciscan Brothers, Brooklyn, New York - AFBB

Archives Diocese of Brooklyn, New York – ADB

Archives Franciscan Fathers, Santa Barbara Province, California - ASBP

Archives Archdiocese of San Francisco, California - AASF

Archives Sacred Heart Province Third Order Regular, Loretto, Pennsylvania - ATORL

Archives of the Curia of the Third Order Regular, Rome - ACTOR

Archives de Propaganda Fide, Rome - APF

Haliday Pamphlet Collection, Royal Irish Academy - HPCRIA

Notes

[1] John Watt, *The Church in Medieval Ireland*, University College Dublin Press, 1998, p. 199.

[2] Patrick Quinn, T.O.R., "The Third Order Regular of St. Francis in Ireland," *ANALECTA, TOR:* XXIV/153 (1993), pp. 247-263.

[3] Irene Whelan, "The Stigma of Souperism," *The Great Irish Famine*, edited by Cathal Poirteir, Dufour Editions, 1995, pp. 135-154, pp. 136-137.

[4] Irene Whelan, "Evangelical Religion and the Polarization of Protestant-Catholic Relations in Ireland, 1780-1840," Ph.D. Dissertation, University of Wisconsin-Madison, 1994.

[5] Tanner, Marcus, *Ireland's Holy Wars: the Struggle for a Nation's Soul, 1500-2000*, Yale University Press, 2001, p. 208.

[6] Whelan, "Evangelical Religion . . . ., p. 381.

[7] Tanner, p. 233-234.

[8] Whelan., p. 389.

[9] Whelan., "Evangelical Religion, . . ." pp. 389-390.

[10] Kevin Whelan, "Born Astride of a Grave: The Cultural Effects of the Great

Irish Famine, " Lecture to the New York Irish History Roundtable, Fordham University, 8 April 1995.

[11] *The Irish American,* 17 September, 1859, p. 2.

[12] *The Irish News,* 2 June, 1860.

[13] *Souvenir of the Diamond Jubilee of the Franciscan Brothers , Brooklyn, N.Y., 1858 - 1933: Dedicated to Their Pupils Past and Present and to their Friends and Benefactors,* " The Woodhaven Press, Ozone Park, N.Y. 1933.

[14] Thomas Nagle, [Bro. Roger Nagle, O.S.F.] , "The Historical Growth and Development of the Franciscan Brothers of Brooklyn," Master's Dissertation, St. John's University, 1943.

[15] Philip Harris, O.S.F. "History of the Franciscan Brothers of Brooklyn," Franciscan Brothers, 1958.

[16] *Franciscan Brothers' Centenary Album: A Pictorial View of the Franciscan Brothers' Work in the Two Dioceses of Brooklyn and Rockville Centre on the Occasion if Their Hundredth Anniversary in America*, New City Printing Co. Union City, New Jersey, March 31, 1959.

[17] Bernardine Cowan, O.S.F., "The Story of the Irish Franciscan Brothers," Franciscan Monastery, Mountbellew, Co. Galway, Ireland, 1955.

[18] Declan Fox, O.S.F., "Irish Franciscan Brothers," Franciscan Monastery, Mountbellew, Co, Galway, Ireland, 1982.

[19] Vincent Jordan, O.S.F., "The Order of Penitents, The Third Order Regular of St. Francis in Ireland, "St. Francis Monastery, Mountbellew, Co. Galway, Ireland, 1995.

[20] "Oldest Minute Book of Saint Francis Monastery," 1878, p. 1 ["There is no evidence that Community records were systematically kept prior to the appointment of Brother Paul Hill as Secretary in 1878. The fact that Brother Paul began this book with an introductory summary of the early history of the Congregation in Brooklyn would seem to indicate that no earlier written document was extant" - Bro. Celestine McGarry, Secretary General, c. 1944], Franciscan Brothers' Archives.

[21] N. Kowalsky, OMI and J. Metzler, OMI, *Inventory of the Historical Archives of the Congregation for the Evangelization of Peoples or "De Propaganda Fide,"* Rome, 1988, p. 9.

[22] *United States Documents in the Propaganda Fide Archives, a Calendar,* edited by Finbar Kennelly, O.F.M., Academy of American Franciscan History, Washington, D.C., 1966 - 2002+, 12 volumes.

[23] Kowalski-Metzler, *Inventory. . . .,* pp. 118-123.

[24] Brendan Jennings, O.F.M., "Brussels Ms 3947: Donatus Moneyus, De Provincia Hiberniae S. Francisci", *Analecta Hibernica* , Including the Reports of the Irish Manuscripts Commission, No. 6 - November, 1934, pp. 12 - 138, [Third Order Regular material - pp. 102-104].

[25] The Royal Irish Academy, 19 Dawson Street, Dublin 2, Ireland.

CHAPTER ONE

FRANCISCAN BROTHERS ARRIVE IN BROOKLYN: SOME, *PRO TEMPORE*, 1858-1862

John Loughlin happily reported the arrival of ten Irish Franciscan Brothers to his Brooklyn Diocese in the late Spring and Summer of 1858 in a news-filled letter to Cajetan Bedini, the Pro-Prefect of Propaganda Fide in Rome. In his chatty letter [1] Loughlin asks for the admission of two students, Francis Freel and Peter Foote to Propaganda Fide College in Rome, reports on the state of his new diocese (created five years earlier in 1853) - ten new churches, two restored and two enlarged, the opening of a new orphan asylum for boys, and mentions that he has recently obtained four religious orders to work in Brooklyn:

I have introduced the Sisters of the Visitation for the education of what is termed the more respectable portion of the community, and for the purpose of uniting most intimately both parents and children by the acquaintance formed at the school. I have also secured a community of the Sisters of Mercy to attend to the duties of their Institute, a community of the Sisters of St. Joseph for the female parochial schools - **and for the male parochial schools some brothers of the Third order of St. Francis. They were but three when they arrived from Ireland, now they are ten. At present they have charge of a new Male orphan Asylum, finished a few weeks since, and containing one hundred and sixty boys, though capable of accommodating over three hundred.**

We know the names of only the two professed brothers, John McMahon and Vincent Hayes, and one unknown postulant, who emigrated from Roundstone, County Galway, Ireland and arrived on Monday, 31 May 1858. [2]

Seven more anonymous postulants arrived later that Summer, before Loughlin's letter of 23 August to Bedini.

Travel conditions on the Atlantic crossing may have been slightly better in 1858 than in the Great Irish Famine period from 1847 to 1852. Before the Famine period, however, passengers were safeguarded by the 1842 British Consolidated Passenger Act which legislated that:

> *Emigrant vessels bound for North American posts could carry only one passenger for every ten square feet of deck surface or three passengers for every five tons of ship weight; at least six feet must separate the upper and lower decks; only two tiers of bunks were permitted, each berth to be nine square feet in area; every passenger had to be issued three quarts of water daily and seven pounds of bread, oatmeal, flour or rice weekly, half of it in bread and biscuit; each vessel had to carry medicines and lifeboats; sailing tickets had to be drown up in a prescribed form and passengers who did not receive the passage contracted for had to be maintained at the ship owner's expense until they sailed.[3]*

Although these minimal requirements of food, berth space, and safety were mandated on emigrant ships in 1842, they were soon abandoned by the ship owners when the large-scale emigrations of famine-stricken Irish to North America began in 1847. Conditions aboard these ships became so bad that:

Between January 1 and June 30, 1847, 81,954 passengers arrived in New York. The ships' captains reported a total of 947 deaths on board before arrival in port--and 2,750 of those who did land were subsequently confined to the Quarantine Hospital. Thirty of these died from the effects of the voyage within 24 hours of being quarantined on Staten Island. [4]

IRISH EMIGRANTS LEAVING HOME— THE PRIEST'S BLESSING, C 1851[5]

Despite new statutes enacted by the British Parliament in 1848 and 1849, which attempted to improve conditions on these ships, the Liverpool ship owners flouted these laws by not providing the cooked food, berth space, sanitation, and medical attention the laws required. Passengers who could not cook their food were reduced to eating raw flour and water. A berth of six feet by 18 inches was all the space provided for each passenger.[6]

We do not know the exact conditions the brothers endured when they traveled from Ireland, but we do know what they found when they arrived in the summer of 1858. Although John Loughlin was happy to report the arrival of these ten brothers in his letter to Bedini, he does not report that he was unable to give the brothers suitable housing until October of that year. The ten newly arrived brothers were imposed guests of the De La Salle Christian Brothers for four months that hot summer, living in the basement of their small house at 256 Pearl Street, three blocks from the East River, [7] until they could move into their own residence in the newly built Boys' Catholic Orphan Asylum on Bedford and Willoughby Avenues in the Clinton Hill section of Brooklyn. This lack of suitable housing for the Brothers during their first four months in Brooklyn, and later, from 1859 to 1862, when they lived in the "damp cellar" of St. Francis Academy in Baltic Street for three years,[8] was in sharp contrast to the spacious Roundstone Monastery they had left in the Spring and Summer of 1858. These hardships would be remembered by them when they negotiated living accommodations in the "California constitutions" they would write in 1863 and 1868 in Santa Ines, California for Joseph Sadoc Alemany, O.P, Archbishop of San Francisco and Thaddeus Amat, C.M., Bishop of Santa Barbara.

FRANCISCAN MONASTERY IN ROUNDSTONE, GALWAY, c. 1855   Sketch by M. Carroll

The brothers who arrived in Brooklyn from Roundstone in the Summer of 1858 were just in time for an oppressive heat wave in New York City, Brooklyn and the whole Eastern seaboard. The torrid heat in Brooklyn that summer was in strong contrast to the brothers' Roundstone Monastery, next to the sea in Galway, Ireland, which they had left in April or early May. Roundstone is described as having "air so bracing that the route has been nicknamed the 'Brandy and Soda road'". [9] The Roundstone Monastery was borrowed for a day each summer by the Canon from Clifden to entertain Archbishop John MacHale and the local clergy:

> *Before the Presbytery was built in Clifden the Archbishop (John MacHale) and priests always held Conferences at the Roundstone Monastery and dined there. In order to accommodate them more comfortably the Brothers built a new wing which contained a large dining room. The Brothers had not to provide anything as the Parish Priest of Clifden sent beforehand a superabundant supply of all things necessary (which the brothers enjoyed through "half the Winter").[10] They also erected a small house near the Monastery furnished with all fittings necessary for hot and cold salt-water baths.* [11]

Vincent Jordan, the Archivist of the Franciscan Brothers in Mountbellew, notes that this special bath house (a kind of sauna), built for the Archbishop's use, was still in existence in 1939. [12]

The Roundstone Monastery was founded on 11th November, 1835, for "the extension of education and the benefit of the poor," by brothers from Mountbellew.[13] With the support of John MacHale, the brothers leased a small two-story house, which served them until they were able to build a larger Monastery about 15 years later.

ROUNDSTONE MONASTERY IN 1836

The carved stone inscription on the little rented house was transferred to the Monastery and is still to be seen above the door on the old Monastery Bell Tower. Ship captains, who use the tower as a navigation mark, would not allow it to be demolished when the Monastery was sold to the Irish Government in 1974 and razed for apartments and a crafts center.

**MONASTERY BELL TOWER, ROUNDSTONE
(NOW A CRAFT SHOP)**

The inscription, which the English writer Thackeray found so offensive as to comment upon it in his *Irish Sketch Book of 1842,* read:

"Deus Meus et Omnia"

"This monastery was founded by the religious Brothers of Mountbellew of the Third Order of St. Francis, by the Sanction and Approbation of His Grace the Most Reverend Dr. MacHale, Lord Archbishop of Tuam, and dedicated to the Blessed Virgin and our Holy Father St. Francis, to the greater glory of God."

Thackeray found fault with calling John MacHale, "**Lord** Archbishop of Tuam," but he admired the brothers in Roundstone and wrote:

[There is] a sort of lay-convent, being a community of Brothers of the Third Order of Saint Francis. They are all artisans and workmen, living together in common, and undergoing a certain religious regimen. Their work is said to be very good, and all are employed upon some labour or other. [14]

When the Franciscan Brothers were invited in 1837 to take over the National School by Peter Curran, who was the Parish Priest of Roundstone and Manager of the School, a marked increase in the number of students was recorded. In 1836, only 56 pupils attended (44 boys and 12 girls). When the brothers became the teachers, the numbers increased in 1837 to 190 pupils (120 boys and 70 girls), and in 1838, to 217 students (135 boys and 82 girls).[15] When the Protestant Bible Society found out that Franciscan Brothers were in charge of a National School, they wrote to Dublin complaining that "Monks were teachers in a National School". This controversy continued until the school was removed from the National School System in 1840 and was renamed the "Roundstone Roman Catholic School". Accounts published about the state of religion in the Archdiocese of Tuam in 1843, stated that the brothers' school:

> *"was filled to the door with children from the town and surrounding districts". Not only were the Brothers teachers in the school but some were skilled tradesmen who had been trained in Mountbellew. They plied their trades in Roundstone, and their "work was excellent. They taught their trades to the boys of the neighborhood-the three most common were: coopering (barrel-making), carpentry, and stone-masonry or house-building. There was great emphasis on coopering because the place was a centre of the fishing industry."[16]*

Memories of the Roundstone Monastery are still recalled. John Fallon's nostalgic column in a recent *Irish Times* traces the history of the Franciscan Brothers in Roundstone, and narrates their role as John MacHale's bulwark "against the insidious activities of the Bible societies along the western seaboard." He remembers with affection his vacations as a schoolboy at the old Monastery: "Languid days and the world was all before us, as we spent days boating, swimming, mountain-climbing and at night listening to Br. Alphonsus playing the mandolin" -- but he laments the destruction of the old Monastery for a crafts center. [17]

FRANCISCAN BROTHERS RESPOND TO THE GREAT FAMINE

During the Great Hunger (1847-1851) the Franciscan Brothers of Roundstone and their other monasteries in the West of Ireland, were very responsive to the terrible disaster which had been caused by *Phytofhora infestans*, the potato-blight. Brother Michael was sent to England to beg for money to assuage the hunger of the children who came to their school and their parents. In 1848, a letter [18] appeared in *The Tablet* in London:

June 20th, 1848

Sir,

Feeling a deep interest in the success of Brother Michael, O.S.F., who is now in London soliciting contributions for his Monastery, in Roundstone, Connemara, I beg to impress on the Catholic public the great service they would be rendering to religion by contributing towards the support of those worthy sons of St. Francis. I have visited their institution and can bear witness to the immense good they are doing in that destitute and plague-stricken locality. The number of their pastors is totally insufficient for the wants of the extensive and widely spread population, and were it not for the unremitting labours of these holy men, the rising generation would be left totally destitute of schools or religious instruction. Their door, too, is ever open to the relief of their starving fellow-creatures.

An Englishman

The Society of Friends (Quakers) also assisted the starving people of Clifden and Roundstone. From notes found in the Archives of the Brothers in Mountbellew we read:

In the autumn of this year (1847) James T. Tuke of York undertook a journey through Connaught, Galway and Mayo in company with William Forster. [They report]:

Clifden 13th March 1847. *I have spent 5 hours with relief committee. There is much distress. The deaths from starvation on average 20 per day. Dysentery and low fever, no preparation to sow crops or seed to plant. People are depressed and heartless. Whole families have died. Turnips cost 2 shillings 3 pence per cwt.*

This is one of most distressed areas we have visited. Also the district of Ballindoon. We estimate the number of destitute at 4,000. Meal at 2 shillings and four pence a stone. It costs 16 to 17 per day or 125 per month. Most of the landlords are absentees and have not contributed any funds. Toward the end of this year

[1847], we established fishing stations in Ballinskill Bay near Clifden, Achill Sound and Belmullet in Co. Mayo. After a year the stations at Clifden and Achill Sound were closed for want of interest as the poverty deterred people in their efforts.

Roundstone 29th March 1847 There have been some deaths from want, yet conditions are better. We saw many cattle also some pigs and poultry. It is impossible to induce these people to go out fishing, although there is a curing house, which gives a certain market. [19]

SOCIETY OF FRIENDS (QUAKER) SOUP HOUSE[20]

From the Kilmoylan Monastery in Brooklodge, Joseph Griffin, the Superior, in twelve letters to the Society of Friends, graphically describes the terrible conditions of poverty afflicting the people in their district of Galway. In the first of these letters he writes:

May 29th 1847

Gentlemen,

With diffidence & the greatest respect we, the Monks of Kilmoylan presume to address your honorable and humane society through the bearer Br. Peter Kivelahan, who is one of our numbers, on behalf of the fever-stricken and starving population by which we are surrounded, in the hope that your honorable society will enable us to continue to give relief to the hundred walking skeletons in the shape of human beings, whose wild cries are to be heard daily around the doors of our monastery, supplicating us, aye, even for a single mouthful of food to save them from death. . .

We have given relief to the average number of eighty poor persons per day up to the present from our own funds which are now exhausted, and, unless aided by some charitable society, we will be obliged to abandon them to their fate. We beg leave to draw your attention to the extreme sufferings of these truly destitute people for which our representative awaits your kind answer. Pardon, gentlemen the liberty we have taken and we beg to subscribe ourselves,

The Monks of Kilmoylan,-Superior, Br. Joseph Griffin, Dangan Reference: Rev. John O'Grady, P.P. Abbey Knockmoy.[21]

Declan Fox, comments on the substance and style of these unique letters:

They were written in reply to letters from the Society of Friends in Dublin whose help Br. Joseph had secured while questing funds in Dublin for the starving people around Brooklodge. Altogether this Society sent a hugh tonnage of foodstuffs, along with clothing, to be distributed at the Monastery. Each letter is a masterpiece of English, giving a detailed account of the distribution of the recent consignment, and while the gratitude expressed is fitting and sincere, one can read into it a "lively sense of favours to come". [22]

The brothers in Mountbellew were also very active in assisting the poor people at this time. Declan Fox's same History tells of their efforts:

> *During 1847 and 1848 the Great Famine came and during these years the Bellews and Franciscan Brothers fed daily and clothed 200 poor people and sometimes many more. The cholera followed the famine and corpses of stricken people were strewn on the roads around Mountbellew. Two Brothers were told off [assigned] to attend the cholera patients and to bury the dead. One of these, Brother Jerome Ryan, famous for his heroism and charity, lived until 1883. Brothers were sent to America to quest for funds and they sent home hundreds of pounds to buy food. Other Brothers went with jennets and carts often a distance of 30 or 40 miles to collect food for the people who were starving. [23]*

The Bellews, who were very responsive to their starving people during the Great Famine, were among the more successful Catholic gentry families of eighteenth-century Ireland, and became the patrons of the Franciscan Brothers in Galway about 1820. Michael Bellew was able to build a substantial country house and purchase additional lands before the repeal of the Penal Laws restricting Catholic ownership in 1829. However, because of these Penal Laws, the Bellew family was never completely secure, and the transfer of lands from one generation of Bellews to another required at least a minimum of care and circumspection. Whelan estimates that about 20% of the land, especially in the West of Ireland, remained in the hands of Catholic gentry in the eighteenth century. [24]

The Bellew sons were educated outside Ireland - a career in the military meant service abroad, in the armies of France, Spain or Austria. Higher education, either clerical or lay, also required residence on the continent, often in the Irish colleges in St. Omer and Douai in France, or Salamanca, Spain. Christopher Dillon Bellew, who invited the Franciscan Brothers to Mountbellew, and three of his four brothers, were educated in France. [25]

John MacHale best summed up the disastrous response of the English government to the Great Irish Famine, when he predicted that "the people's bones, piled in cairns more numerous than the ancient pyramids" would remind later generations of "the ghostly triumphs" of Lord John Russell's "brief but disastrous administration."[26]

In a lecture, "Born Astride of a Grave: The Cultural Effects of the Great Irish Famine," Kevin Whelan, quoted the Australian poet Vincent Buckley:

> *Every generation of the Irish has had as one of its chief signs the phenomenon of **interrupted lives**, and hence interrupted memory transmission. Families became dispersed, like leaves at the end of autumn; the 'family' remains, it is true, but as a denuded tree-stump, full of stay-put melancholy.* [27]

Whelan believes that The Great Irish Famine scarred its survivors and quotes Malachi Horan, who observed that its main effect had not been to create poverty - 'they were used to that' - but to make people 'so sad in themselves' that 'it made many a one hard too'. He quoted Edith Martin (the Galway half of "Somerville and Ross," Anglo-Irish novelists) who concluded that 'the Famine yielded like the ice of the northern seas; it ran like melted snow in the veins of Ireland for many years afterwards'.

Not only was the loss of the potato as a food source one of the causes of the Famine, but Whelan believes that the destruction of the Irish Clachan system of small-village life and the Rundale agricultural system were contributing factors to the disaster of the Great Irish Famine. The Clachan/Rundale system of village living and agriculture, which sustained mutual aid in a close-knit horizontal landscape, concealed, rather than revealed social distinctions. To the Anglo-Irish landlord, the Irish peasant in this Rundale landscape, which was flexible in response to the varying needs of each family, signified a disturbing democracy, rather than a recognizable hierarchical landscape. Surrounded by their small, thin strips of arable potato "lazy-beds," and the "grass of one cow" on a common green field, the Clachan/Rundale system appeared as a disheveled, slovenly settlement surrounded by small fields which lacked any stable, individual entity.

VILLAGE OF DOOGORT, ACHILL ISLAND, WITH LAZY-BEDS IN THE FOREGROUND, c. 1855[28]

Post-Famine changes had a profound impact on Clachan culture. In pre-Famine times, inhabitants were 'front-door neighbors,' who lived so close to one another that men would chat from house to house without ever coming to the half-door. The earlier, informal networks of the Rundale system were replaced with a legal landscape, abstract, dehumanized, a world of numbers, where land was valued in terms of property, power and money. By contrast, the Irish poor inhabited a landscape, a world of family, community and memory, in which invisible but powerful filaments of tradition, kinship and occupation linked them to a living, not a legal landscape.[29] The landlord's 'paper and parchment' landscape did not supersede the tenant's prior moral claim, even when backed by Penal Law and coercion. The landlord **owns the land**, but the tenant **occupies the soil**. In the fissure between land and soil, in the gap between external and intrinsic value, The Great Irish Famine fell between landlord and tenant, exposing the asymmetrical relationship between eight thousand landlords and eight million tenants.

The cohesive quality of Clachan life, with its communal, customary and contextual modes of organization, the vivacity and gaiety of the society, as well as its famous hospitality, was commented on by pre-Famine visitors. An incident from Mayo in the 1830s illustrates this: A deserted child in the Ballina area was passed by consent from house to house, being looked after for a month at each in turn 'as they agreed among themselves, until it came to a married couple, who, having no children, adopted it and have since reared it as their own.' [30] In an earlier article on the same subject, Whelan writes that the:

[U]nprecedented attack of Phytophora infestans,
destroyed one-third of the potato crop in 1845; the
combined impact of blight and the failure to sow the
crop led to the yield being lower by three-quarters in
1846 and 1847, and one-third in 1848. Massive
mortality and emigration ensued: one million died and
two million emigrated in the next two decades cruelly
paralleling the three million 'potato people,' who were
totally dependent on the now fickle tuber in the
immediate pre-Famine period. These deaths were
disproportionately concentrated in the areas of new
settlement dominated by rundale and clachan, and the
lumper potato. [31]

Although blame for the neglect of the poor in the Great
Irish Famine has traditionally been assigned to the British
government's mid-nineteenth century laissez faire attitude
toward permitting a free economy to prevail, revisionist
historians in *Irish Historical Studies* have tried to rewrite
Irish nationalist interpretations of British imperialism and
Protestant sectarianism. In 1989, Brendan Bradshaw
published a famous 'anti-revisionist' article[32] in which he
charged the revisionists had used a kind of scientific,
objective, value-free examination which filtered out the
trauma of the catastrophic episodes of Irish history, such
as the English conquest of the sixteenth century, the great
rebellion of the 1640s, and the Great Famine itself.[33] The
controversy over the Great Irish Famine continues in
America in the classrooms of elementary and high school
students in New Jersey and New York State's schools with
the recently mandated *The Great Irish Famine Curriculum*,
which will hopefully, examine the **"interrupted lives"** of
the Irish over the last century and a half.[34]

LOUISVILLE, KENTUCKY

John MacHale's strong support for the religious teaching communities in his Province in the West of Ireland was well known to many of the Irish-born Bishops in America. The first school opened by the Irish Franciscan Brothers in America was at the request of Martin John Spalding, the Vicar General of Louisville, Kentucky, later coadjutor and successor to the enfeebled Benedict Flaget.[35] Just before the Great Famine, MacHale sent two brothers from Tuam to teach in Louisville in August, 1847:

> *A free school for boys is about to be organized at Louisville, Kentucky, under the direction of the Brothers of St. Francis. Two members of this Order from the Archdiocese of Tuam in Ireland have reached Louisville for that purpose. "Catholic Free School for Boys:" This institution under the management of the Brothers of St. Francis, Louisville, was opened Monday morning last at 307 Market Street... Already about 60 boys have been enrolled as pupils, and from the zeal thus far manifested by the Catholics of the city, we doubt not that the worthy Brothers will receive every encouragement in their laudable enterprise. [36]*

The "worthy Brothers" did not receive the encouragement the *U.S. Catholic Magazine* foretold - after a year's absence, the Jesuits returned to Louisville, and replaced them, "opening a spacious edifice as a college adjoining the free school". [37]

ST. JOHN'S, NEWFOUNDLAND

The second community of Franciscan Brothers in North America also arrived in 1847 in St. John's, Newfoundland, Canada. Michael Anthony Fleming, O.F.M., a Franciscan Friar Minor of the Irish Province requested some brothers from Dr. MacHale, who responded:

> *Whatever may be your own necessities, and they are great in consequence of our unalterable purpose to assert the complete freedom of education, I cannot refuse to comply with your desire. I therefore freely release from his obedience for a time, Brother John Hanlon, a young man of most excellent character, well-fitted to instruct youth and to mould their pliant hearts to virtue, in order that he may place himself under your jurisdiction.*

Bishop Fleming must have been very persuasive. He eventually succeeded in receiving four brothers of superior qualifications, some of whom had been selected to establish several schools in Ireland. "Dr. Fleming is now arrived here [Dublin] with the monks and has taken passage for them on the brig '*Mary*' to leave next week."[38] The four brothers arrived in St. John's on 7 September 1847 and began operation of an orphan asylum and school with the financial backing of the Irish Benevolent Society. However, by 1852, "friction" with local officials was interfering with the brothers' operation of their school. As the Irish Brothers' Archives note: the "friction arose from a new system of education involving right of entry and supervision established by local officials whose prejudices against Catholic Education were well known." Two of these brothers, John Hanlon and Bernardine Rogers left Newfoundland for Ireland, but ultimately went to Loretto and died in that community.

LORETTO, PENNSYLVANIA

The third community of Franciscan Brothers, which emigrated to North America, was more successful. Invited by Michael O'Connor, the first Bishop of Pittsburgh:

> *Six Brothers of the Third Order of St. Francis, three from the communities of Clifton* [sic] *and Roundstone, and three from Newfoundland, came over in 1847 and began their labors in Loretto. Here, on the 27th of August, 1848, the corner-stone of a suitable monastery was laid by the Bishop, and on its completion an academy was opened. The Brothers proved themselves able instructors. Their community prospered, the academy was incorporated as a college* [primary and secondary levels], *in 1854, the Brothers continued to do good service in parochial schools.* [39]

The signatures of these six brothers are found on their petition for a rescript to establish a monastery and transfer their obedience to Michael O'Connor, Bishop of Pittsburgh. [40]

This community would eventually become a province of the Third Order Regular in the twentieth century, when 27 brothers from Brooklyn, eventually joined them between 1907 and 1910.

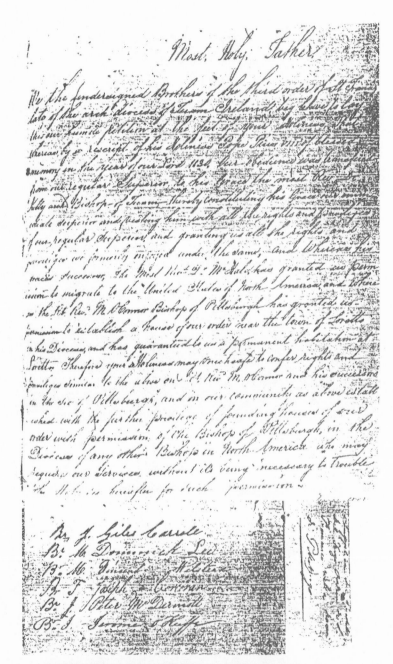

LORETTO BROTHERS' PETITION

BROTHERS FOLLOW THE IRISH
TO BROOKLYN, NEW YORK

The brothers must have longed for the cool air of Roundstone when they met the oppressive heat of New York City and Brooklyn in the summer of 1858.

"MORE DEATHS FROM SUN STROKE"

The Coroners had another busy day yesterday holding inquests in the following cases of death caused by sunstroke:

John Murphy, laborer, employed the iron foundry No. 36 Bank street, was suddenly overcome by the excessive heat, drank a glass of ice-water and fell dead. He had been employed but three days at the foundry. He was about 35 years of age, and has family living in Pennsylvania.

Margaret Hammond, a native of Scotland, was overcome by the heat while passing through Tenth-avenue, near Forty-fifth Street. She was taken into the nearest drug store, but died in a few minutes.

On that same day, the article lists six more persons as dying from sun-stroke, and six others who collapsed from the heat, but later recovered. [41] Two days later the *Times* reports:

"THE RECENT HOT TERM"

We have just had a remarkably hot period, following heavy rains. In the Middle and New-England States, where neither the grain nor the grass were far advanced, the heat of the past fortnight has done wonders. . . . But a temperature of 99° upon a saturated soil, quickened vegetation like the working of magic.

A letter to the *Times* Editor comments:

Why is it, Mr. Editor, that we who do business in the vicinity of the Park are deprived of even the "sight of water" in the fountains? As for a jet d'eau, there is none, the poor Croton having, since yesterday, declined from stagnant lymph to airy nothing in this torrid weather.[42]

Walt Whitman, the poet and editor of the *Brooklyn Daily Times* also suffered a sun-stroke" in that hot summer of 1858.[43]

The large number of Irish who arrived in New York after the Great Famine eventually settled in Brooklyn which was just across the East River from Manhattan and connected by five ferries operated by the Union Ferry Company before the completion of the Brooklyn Bridge in 1869:[44]

In Brooklyn, "Irish Town" [the Fifth Ward], *referred chiefly to the substantial enclave around the Navy Yard, but there were others. Brooklyn Irish laid out Bedford's streets and horsecar lines, then stayed as residents (immigrants constituted 70 percent of Bedford's population in 1855, and three-fourths of these were Irish). Red Hook housed the Irishmen who built and worked its docks, brickyards, distilleries, warehouses, and factories. By 1855, out of Brooklyn's total population of 205,250, roughly a hundred*

thousand were foreign born, and of these, fifty-seven
thousand were Irish, twenty-six thousand German, and
eighteen thousand English.[45]

In that same year, Bayor and Meagher give the
Irish-born population of Kings County, the present
borough of Brooklyn, as 59,308, which was 27.4% of the
total population of 216,355. The wards with the largest
percentage of Irish-born were: the 7th Ward, Southeast of
the Navy Yard, with 6,471 or 51.7%; Red Hook, the 12th
Ward, with 3,332 persons or 47.7%; Fulton Ferry, the 2nd
Ward, with 2,967, 35.4%; Brooklyn Heights, the 1st Ward,
with 2,227, 35.2%; and the aptly-named Irishtown, East of
the Navy Yard, the 5th Ward, with 5,629 Irish-born, which
was 34.4% of the 16,352 non-Irish-born population of that
district. [46]

By 1875, the total Irish-born in Brooklyn rose to 83,069,
which was 16.3% of the non-Irish-born population. But this
figure does not account for the many American-born
children of their Irish-born parents. An estimate of 200,000
Irish-born and first-generation Irish-Americans would
raise the number of the Irish-connected population in
Brooklyn to about 40% of the total of 509,154 persons listed
above.[47]

The newly arrived brothers had great work to
accomplish for the children of the many Irish immigrants
during their first years in Brooklyn:

Between 1847 and 1851 a total of 1.8 million immigrants disembarked in New York, of whom 848,000 were Irish women and men and the rest mainly German. Between May and December of 1847, the number from Ireland who landed in New York totaled 52,946, which was more than from any other place. Few newcomers had the resources to go beyond New York and therefore stayed for negative reasons: most, although not all, had no other options. Yet, as more and more Irish settled there, creating within the metropolis, dense, throbbing Irish enclaves, replete with formal and informal institutions that sustained communal life, New York became an increasingly attractive destination. A French visitor to New York summarized it best when he commented: "Emigration will soon cause it to be said that Ireland is no longer where flows the Shannon, but besides the banks of the Hudson River."[48]

Although many New Yorkers considered Brooklyn a backwater, a decade after the brothers arrived -

"It was the third-largest city in America, larger than Boston, Chicago, St. Louis, and San Francisco. Brooklyn had nearly eight miles of piers, dry docks, grain elevators, and warehouses. The new Atlantic Basin, on Buttermilk Channel, was forty acres in area. More ships tied up in Brooklyn than New York and Hoboken combined. From the East River the city looked as though it were enclosed behind a protective screen of ship masts and rigging. The sea- lanes of the world ended at Brooklyn. Gulls wheeled and cried over the housetops. Sailors mingled with the evening crowds along Fulton Street. The sea air, reputedly, was "pure and bracing wafted from a thousand miles seaward." [49]

Brooklyn was a larger seaport than New York and a major manufacturing center for glass, steel, tinware, cordage, whiskey, beer, and, as any who lived in Greenpoint could testify, a producer of pungent glue.

**BROOKLYN NAVY YARD, LOOKING SOUTH
WITH MANHATTAN TO THE RIGHT, 1855** [50]

However, the Brooklyn of the mid-nineteenth century was not the same as today. Kings County had a number of villages and towns poorly connected by muddy roads. To the East and South of Brooklyn Village the towns of Flatbush, New Utrecht, Gravesend and Flatlands were primarily farming villages.[51]

Although most of the Irishmen who arrived as post-famine immigrants in the 1850's were laborers, a surprising number were counted as farm laborers. In the 1860 Decennial Census, 63 % of rural Kings County residents who said they were farm laborers were from Ireland, 15 % were from Germany, while another 12 % were U.S. blacks.

However, by 1870, the Irish share had fallen to 38%, and by 1880, the number of native-born Irish in farm work had declined to 27 %. [52] The decline in the number of Irish in farm work may indicate that, as better employment opportunities became available, the Irish moved away from the work which would have painfully reminded them of the "impoverished potato patches" they had left during the Great Irish Famine.

The Franciscan Brothers who came from Roundstone in rural Ireland may have remembered with nostalgia their farm and the dairy cows attached to their Irish Monastery. However, the City of Brooklyn, near the ferries to Manhattan, had few farms. As Bayor and Meagher report above, most of the emigrant Irish population was crowded close to the piers of Red Hook and the Fifth Ward surrounding the Brooklyn Navy Yard. The brothers shared this crowded experience in the Summer of 1858, when they were guests of the Christian Brothers for four months in the basement of their small house at 256 Pearl Street near the East River.

By 1859, the brothers were teaching in their own St. Francis Academy and began to teach in many of the parish schools which served the children of these recent emigrants. They walked daily from St. Francis Monastery at 41 Butler Street to their schools in Brooklyn Heights, Red Hook, the Navy Yard, Williamsburgh, and, for a time, rode on the street car to Greenpoint. In that same year, the brothers requested the Papal Rescript which would approve their new foundation in Brooklyn and place them under the obedience of John Loughlin. John McMahon's Petition to Pope Pius IX mentions the two previous Petitions of Franciscan Brothers to Rome asking that the Mountbellew community be placed under the obedience of Oliver Kelly, Archbishop of Tuam, in 1830, and that the

Loretto community be assigned to the obedience of Michael O'Connor, the Bishop of Pittsburgh, in 1848. In both of these Petitions the term *"Pro Tempore,"* was inserted to allow them to "make new foundations, when the competent authority approves." John McMahon's 1859 Petition, on two small pages of light-blue onionskin paper, was found in the Archives of Propaganda Fide in 1986:

BROTHER JOHN'S PETITION TO POPE PIUS IX[53]

John McMahon, who was the superior of the young Brooklyn community for its first four years, entered

Cummer Monastery, County Galway, on 1 January 1848, aged 19 years. He received the Habit on 12 February 1849 and was professed on 25 July, 1850. In 1856, at the young age of 27, he was elected Master of Novices in Mountbellew Monastery.

A legend in the Irish community tells the story that a brother was deputed to quest for funds for the purchase of a site and the erection of a monastery at Cummer. As he was in the North of Ireland a young man presented himself to him and asked admittance to the Order. Bonaventure Burke, the Superior, knew by inspiration what was transpiring many miles away and at that very hour wrote to the brother to encourage this young man to come along and said that one day he would do great work for the Order. On the day of the interview the brother moved on to another town many miles distant, yet Bonaventure Burke sent this letter to his new address. The brother went back and interviewed the postulant, who ten years later became the founder of the Brooklyn Monastery.[54]

In addition to the Petition to Rome, seeking to be under the obedience of John Loughlin, other correspondence has surfaced from the Archives of the Archdiocese of San Francisco, reflecting John McMahon's life in California on the Mission Ranch in Santa Ines in the hills above Santa Barbara. He was trying to organize a college in Santa Ines and wrote to James Croke, the Vicar General of San Francisco. McMahon eventually went to San Francisco and was the principal of the School for Boys in the basement of St. Mary's Cathedral. He was naturalized as an American citizen on 6 April 1867, and was registered, aged 58, on 17 October 1888, in Precinct District 15, as listed in the Great Register of San Francisco Voters. [55]

Vincent Hayes, who arrived in Brooklyn with John McMahon on 31 May 1858, entered Tourmakeady Monastery, County Mayo in 1848. He received the Habit on 21 July 1849 and was professed in April of 1853. He left Brooklyn for the First Order Franciscans in Buffalo, New York before the end of 1858. In November 1863, he was ordained a priest with the status *Titilum Missionis*, because he was attached to, but not solemnly professed, in the First Order.

In 1866, when he learned of the impoverishment of his sister's family in Ireland because of the death of her husband and son, he wrote three poignant letters to Propaganda Fide in one week, two requesting secularization; and, when the Guardian assured him that the College would send money to his sister in Ireland, a third letter asking that the first two be ignored. However, he eventually left the Franciscan College in Buffalo and was accepted into the Diocese of Dubuque, Iowa as a secular priest in 1869. As an assistant pastor in Keokuk, Iowa, he was able to earn a regular salary to send money to Ireland for their support. [56]

Reasons for the departure of the Superior and half the young Community for California, without the permission of John Loughlin, is a continuing mystery in the history of the Brooklyn Brothers' first four years in the young diocese. They may have been unhappy with some aspects of their living accommodations, with possible interference of the Bishop in transferring brothers, or with efforts of John Loughlin to change their monastic, inclusive Franciscan charism to an exclusive community, admitting only young men able to teach. Little did Loughlin know when he wrote to Bedini on 23 August 1858, that five of these brothers, led by John McMahon, their Superior, would seek to go to California in 1859, and actually depart in 1862. They tried to establish a college in Santa Barbara with the First Order Friar Minor Franciscans, taking the phrase, Pro *Tempore,* in their Papal Rescript, at its literal meaning. [57]

Notes

[1] Propaganda Fide Archives [PFA], *Congressi, America Centrale,* Vol XVIII, fols 337 rv and 338 rv .

[2] Six ships arrived from Southhampton or Liverpool at New York City piers that day. However, research in the microfilmed Passenger Lists of these ships in The New York Public Library has not revealed the two brothers' names on any of the passenger lists of these six ships. Colleagues who are familiar with immigration arrivals from Ireland at that time, suggest that they might have sailed directly from Galway to Boston, and then traveled by a smaller coastal boat or the railroad to New York. It is believed that the eight unnamed brothers were postulants, because John McMahon tried to open a novitiate in the orphan asylum, but soon decided that it was unsuitable for that purpose.

[3] *5 & 6 Victoria cap. 107, sect. 2, 3-6, 8, 13, 22 [1842].*

[4] John Ridge, "The Great Hunger in New York," *New York Irish History,* Vol. 9, 1995, p. 9.

[5] *The Illustrated London News,* 10 May 1851.

[6] Emmett Corry, O.S.F., "Immigration in the Age of Sail," review of an exhibition in the South Street Seaport Museum, " The Irish Family History Forum Newsletter," November, 1995, p. 1, "To appreciate the size of this "berth" the reader might use a piece of chalk and measure this out on the floor, as was done in the Museum's Exhibition, and then try to lie down in the space!"

[7] The original Christian Brothers house at 256 Pearl Street, four blocks from their school at St. James, no longer exists - it was replaced by one of the piers of the Manhattan Bridge in 1909.

[8] *Souvenir of the Diamond Jubilee of the Franciscan Brothers, Brooklyn, N.Y.,*

1858-1933, p. 24

9 *Ordnance Survey Leisure Guide of Ireland,* Purnell Book, 1987, p. 105.

10 Conversation with Declan Fox, O.S.F., Archivist, Irish Franciscan Brothers.

11 Declan Fox, O.S.F., "Irish Franciscan Brothers," Mountbellew, 1983, p. 19.

12 Vincent Jordan, O.S.F., Letter to the author, 15 November, 1996.

13 *Irish Catholic Directory*, 1836, p. 141.

14 William Makepeace Thackeray, *Irish Sketch Book of 1842,* in *The Complete Works,* Vol 18, Crowell, 1904, p. 239.

15 Bernard Mac Uaid, O.S.F., "The Brothers of the Third Order Regular in the Diocese of Tuam," *ANALECTA TOR,* XVI /137, 1983, p. 374.

16 Mac Uaid, p. 376.

17 John F. Fallon, "An Irishman's Diary," *The Irish Times,* 26 February 2000, p. 17.

18.Franciscan Brothers Archives (FBA), Mountbellew, Galway.

19 FBA, Mountbellew, Galway.

20 *The Illustrated London News,* 16 January 1847.

21 FBA, Mountbellew, Galway

22 Declan Fox, O.S.F., "History of the Irish Franciscan Brothers", p. 25.

23 Declan Fox, O.S.F., "Irish Franciscan Brothers", 1982, p. 8.

24 Kevin Whelan, *The Tree of Liberty: Radicalism, Catholicism and the Construction of Irish Identity, 1760-1830,* University of Notre Dame Press, 1996, p. 6.

25 Karen Harvey, *The Bellews of Mount Bellew, A Catholic Gentry Family in Eighteenth-Century Ireland,* Four Courts Press, Dublin, 1998, pp. 175-178.

26 Cormac O Grada, *Black '47 and Beyond: the Great Irish Famine in History, Economy, and Memory,* Princeton University Press, 1999, p. 78.

27 Kevin Whelan, "'Born Astride of a Grave': the Cultural Effects of the

Great Irish Famine," Lecture to the New York Irish History Roundtable at Fordham University on 8 April 1995. Whelan is a Professor and Director of the Notre Dame Program in Irish Studies at University College Dublin and a Member of the Royal Irish Academy.

[28] John Eliot Howard, *The Island of Saints, or Ireland in 1855*, London, 1855.

[29] Tom Yeager, "What was Rundale and Where did it come from?", *Béaloideas, The Journal of the Folklore of Ireland Society*, Dublin, Vol. 70, 2002, pp. 153-186

[30] Kevin Whelan, Lecture . . . . 8 April 1995.

[31] Kevin Whelan, "Pre and Post-Famine Landscape Change," *The Great Irish Famine*, edited by Cathal Poirteir, Dufour, 1995, pp. 19-33, p. 27.

[32] Brendan Bradshaw, "Nationalism and Historical Scholarship in Modern Ireland," *Irish Historical Studies*, xxvi, no. 104, (Nov. 1989), 329-51.

[33] James S. Donnelly, Jr., *The Great Irish Potato Famine*, Sutton Publishing, Gloucestershire, 2001, pp. 12-13.

[34] *The Great Irish Famine Curriculum*, Maureen Murphy, et al, editors, New York State Education Department, 2001.

[35] John Gilmary Shea, *History of the Catholic Church in America 1844-1866*, Vol IV, 1892, pp. 188-192.

[36] *U.S. Catholic Magazine*, Vol. VI, 1847, p. 49.

[37] *Catholic Encyclopedia*, Vol. IX, p. 388.

[38] Hon. L. O'Brien, President, Irish Benevolent Society, Letter to Patrick Keough, the Vice-President of the Society, August 3, 1847, in *Centenary Volume of the Benevolent Irish Society of St. John's Newfoundland*, 1806-1906, p. 130.

[39] Shea, Vol. IV, pp. 75-76.

[40] PFA, Udienze di N.S. 1848, P. II, Vol. 109, fols. 950 (a) rv , 950 (b), rv. 4 June 1848.

[41] *The New York Times*, July 1, 1858.

[42] *The New York Times*, July 3, 1858.

[43] David S. Reynolds, *Walt Whitman's America, a Cultural Biography,* Knopf, 1995, p. 375.

[44] David McCullough, *The Great Bridge,* Simon and Schuster, New York, 1982, p. 105

[45] Edwin G. Burrows and Mike Wallace, *Gotham: A History of New York City to 1898,* Oxford University Press, 1999, p. 746.

[46] Ronald H. Bayor and Timothy J. Meagher, editors, *The New York Irish,* Johns Hopkins University Press, Baltimore, 1996. [Appendix I, Statistical Table], pp. 554-555.

[47] David Noel Doyle, "Cohesion and Diversity in the Irish Diaspora," *Irish Historical Studies, vol.* xxxi, no. 123, (May 1999), pp. 411- 434.

[48] Hasia Diner, "The Most Irish City in the Union: The Era of the Great Migration, 1844-1877," in Ronald H. Bayor and Timothy J. Meagher, *The New York Irish,* Johns Hopkins University Press, 1995, p. 91.

[49] McCullough, The Great Bridge, pp. 104-106.

[50] Ellen M. Snyder-Grenier, *Brooklyn! an Illustrated History,* Temple University Press, Philadelphia, 1996, p. 141.

[51] Marc Linder and Lawrence S. Zacharias. *Of Cabbages and Kings County: Agriculture and the Formation of Modern Brooklyn,* University of Iowa Press, 1999, p. 20.

[52] Linder & Zacharias, pp. 90-91.

[53] PFA, Vol. 985, Fol. 2430rv, 2431,r., 25 October 1859. [John McMahon signs his name with the letters *3rd O.S.F.* to distinguish that he is a Franciscan religious of the Third Order Regular].

[54] Bernardine Cowan, O.S.F., "Memoirs," from FBA, Mountbellew, in a letter from Declan Fox, O.S.F., Archivist, to Austin Gill, O.S.F., 11 January 1984.

[55] Catherine Ann Curry, PBVM, Assistant Archivist, Archives Archdiocese of San Francisco, (AASF), Letter to the author, 12 July 1996

[56] Letters of Vincent Hayes, O.S.F., 24 February, 1 March and 3 March 1866, PFA, *Scritture riferite nei Congressi, America settentrionale. Canada* [sic], Vol 9, fols 55r, - 64rv , 1866-1867.

[57]"In an audience with his Holiness, held on the 15th day of December, 1859, our most Illustrious Lord, Pius IX, by Divine Providence Pope, through me the undersigned Cardinal, Prefect of the Congregation de Propaganda Fide, graciously granted the Bishop of Brooklyn the necessary faculties, in accordance with the petition. . . . . .Al Barnabo, Prefect" *Franciscan Brothers' Constitutions, 1924.*

CHAPTER TWO

MALE CATHOLIC ORPHAN ASYLUM
BROTHERS' FIRST BROOKLYN ASSIGNMENT

There was a ready population of students needing the Franciscan Brothers' teaching ministry in Brooklyn, but by the mid-nineteenth century, the number of Catholic children requiring public welfare support was also steadily growing. Bishop John Loughlin assigned the two brothers and the eight postulants who arrived in the summer of 1858 to the newly opened Male Catholic Orphan Asylum at Bedford and Willoughby Avenues in the Eastern District of Brooklyn.

The creation of Catholic orphan asylums, as an answer to the Protestant "New York System" of public support for indigent and neglected Catholic children, was a phenomenon, which the New York diocese responded to in the early nineteenth century. The Catholic orphanages in New York City, and the creation of The Brooklyn Catholic Orphan Asylum Society in 1830, were accomplished with the assistance of the philanthropist Cornelius Heeney.

The "New York System" of child welfare provided public support through voluntary associations such as the Association for Improving the Condition of the Poor, the American Female Guardian Society, and the Children's Aid Society organized by Charles Loring Brace. Created in 1853, the Children's Aid Society was organized with the primary aim of "sending children to foster homes in 'the West' where fresh air, hard work, and Protestant religion might transform street urchins into yeoman farmers". The

Society's 1875 Annual Report claimed that over 40,000 poor children were saved as a result of its efforts over three decades. What the Children's Aid Society did not report was that the majority of these children were Irish and Catholic. Reacting to these "pernicious rescue efforts," Catholics became alarmed and began a much more aggressive approach by creating their own child-care institutions.[1]

The development of the Catholic Church's extensive welfare system in New York City and Brooklyn was a direct response to the efforts of Brace and other Protestant reformers to control the children of the poor Irish who were arriving in great numbers in the post-Irish Famine period:

> *The hundreds of thousands of Famine survivors who landed in New York City were not only terribly poor, sick, and traumatized, but also represented for middle-class Americans the first large-scale influx of profoundly impoverished people into American cities. Reformers, consisting mostly of the native-born and Protestant elite accustomed to running the affairs of the city, considered poverty to be a mark of moral failings. Individuals who did not work hard, save money, and discipline themselves properly, became poor and stayed poor. Their children, theoretically innocent of their parents' fallen nature, were particularly at risk. As early as 1853, legal mechanisms enabling Protestant reformers to remove children from poor parents were officially in place.*

> *The truancy law, for example, allowed for any citizen or police officer to arrest a child who was on the streets during school hours. If parents were found, however, they could retain custody by promising to keep the child in school. If they were not found, or if a child was*

arrested a second time, the child would be committed for the entire length of his or her childhood to a Protestant institution, such as the Children's Aid Society. Children, once taken from parents, were placed out in a "Christian home". The practice of sending urban poor children out to rural Protestant homes in the Midwest - a process often referred to as "riding the orphan train," rested on the belief that the American Protestant nuclear family, guided by the maternal devotion of the American woman, was the only proper setting for child-rearing in the American republic. No placing-out society run by Protestants in New York would agree to the option of placing a Catholic child in a Catholic home until the turn of the century. This Protestant "home" and family care were to serve as the setting, and Protestant women as the redemptive agents, in poor immigrant children's reform, and "the family as God's reformatory," became the rallying cry of the Protestant "child-savers" throughout the century. By the mid-1870's, Catholics estimated the number of children who were taken from parents and shipped to the mid-west to be ten thousand per year from New York City alone. [2]

Fitzgerald summarizes the efforts of the dominant culture to control the newly arrived immigrants, especially by taking their children away from Irish-Catholic immigrants:

Brace articulated the state's interest in demanding that poor immigrant children's ties to, and conceptions of family, community, and church be forcibly reconstructed to correspond with those of the dominant culture. In doing so he set the terms of the debate between Protestant and Catholic child-care workers for the rest of the century.

The two primary social control movements conducted by 19th-century Protestant reformers, and directed at controlling Irish-Catholics in particular, were the Common Schools [which will be examined in Chapter Three], and "child-saving" movements. Fear of Protestants, and of religious and cultural assimilation, encouraged resistance to these movements and prompted Catholics to support and construct systems by which educational and social services were provided under Catholic auspices.

Fearing the potential reproduction of Irish-Catholic "paupers," and thereby the creation of a permanent dependent class in the city and throughout America, Protestant reformers concentrated on two methods to insure that poor immigrant urban children would be socialized according to the values of the Protestant native-born culture. First, through child removal policies, Protestant reformers were able to deny poor people's parental control and rights over children. Second, Protestant reformers put immigrant children directly into the homes of Protestants throughout the mid-west. There was nothing subtle in these policies; mothering was directly transferred from poor immigrant women to American Protestant women, the latter responsible for socially reproducing an American citizen with values of and allegiances to the Protestant community. [3]

**ILLUSTRATION FROM A
CHILDREN'S AID SOCIETY ANNUAL REPORT** [4]

Catholics in the City of Brooklyn had anticipated the need for Catholic orphan asylums more than a generation before the creation of the Brooklyn Diocese in 1853. When John Loughlin arrived in his new see, which had been part of the New York Archdiocese, the Sisters of Charity, supported by the Roman Catholic Orphan Asylum Society, were conducting girls' and boys' orphanages in St. Paul's Parish, south-west of Brooklyn Heights. [5] Joseph W. Carroll writes that the creation of these orphanages came about:

> [A]t a numerous and respectable meeting of the Roman Catholics of this village, convened in the Schoolroom attached to St. James' Church, on Thursday evening,March 25, 1830, for the purpose of establishing a Roman Catholic Orphan Asylum in the Village of Brooklyn. [6]

At this meeting a society was formed which would eventually be the nucleus of all the welfare institutions of the Catholic Church in Brooklyn.

> The charter was applied for at this time, to enable the Society to receive a legal transfer of a house and lot from Rev. John Walsh, who had previously offered said house and lot to the Society; to enable them immediately to open an Orphan Asylum; the house being, at that time, the residence of the Sisters of Charity. . . . In pursuance of this act the first Asylum was opened at 188 Jay Street, and placed under the care of the Sisters of Charity. [7]

From its beginnings the Roman Catholic Orphan Asylum Society would be concerned with money, trying to persuade John Hughes to permit it to raise funds by sponsoring charity sermons at specific times in the Brooklyn churches of the New York Diocese. Although, by long-standing custom, the Christmas and Easter collections in the parishes were allocated to the orphan asylums, these funds were never enough to support these institutions through the long months of summer and fall. The Committee wrote to the Bishop requesting one charity sermon in each parish spaced through the year:

> *They requested, and I quote: that [I]n the Church of the Assumption some Sunday in June, in the Kent Avenue Church [St. Patrick's], some Sunday in July, in St. James's Church in September, and in St. Paul's Church some Sunday in October....(end quote) The Bishop took exception to the presentation of the letter, refused to recommend that a charity sermon be preached in such a church at such a time, advised the committee to call on the priests in a friendly way to state the conditions of the asylums, ask their advice as to what had best be done for its support, coax them instead of presenting resolutions, and thus they could hope to succeed.* [8]

Cornelius Heeney is briefly mentioned in Carroll's article,[9] but his munificent support of the fledgling Catholic Church in New York City and his love and financial support for orphans, must be acknowledged. Heeney was an Irish immigrant from Edenderry, County Offaly who arrived in America in 1784. He lived for a short time in Philadelphia, but spent the rest of his life in New York City where he met John Jacob Astor and formed a partnership with the German emigrant in the fur trading business. Differences in temperament, however, eventually dissolved the partnership and the young Irishman continued in the fur trading business, amassing a fortune which he gave with great liberality to the Church, to orphans and the poor.[10]

Heeney's creation and financial support of Catholic orphan asylums in New York and Brooklyn was a continuing concern throughout his life. He invited the Sisters of Charity to New York to take charge of the Orphan Asylum on Prince Street next to the old St. Patrick's Cathedral, which he had built for them with a donation of $18,000.

Later, in order to establish two orphanages in St. Paul's parish in Brooklyn:

> "*Mr. Cornelius Heeney generously donated to the* [Brooklyn Catholic Orphan Asylum] *Society ten lots of ground on Congress street,*" which "*enabled the Society to build their first asylum, that fronting on Congress street, for male children, and the one fronting on Clinton, on the same lots, for females.* [11]

In 1826, Heeney invited the Sisters of Charity to Brooklyn to assume responsibility for the Catholic Orphan Asylum at 277 Fulton Street. Sister Rose White, with three other Sisters, were sent from Emmitsburg by Mother Seton, a personal friend of Heeney's. In 1839 the Sisters moved into their new residence at 202 Congress Street in a house built for them by Heeney on land he donated from his seventeen-acre farm in the City of Brooklyn which he purchased in 1805 for $7,500. For the rest of his life he lived in the mansion on this extensive farm overlooking New York Harbor. [12]

"Bounded by the present Congress, Amity, and Court Streets, and the East River, his house stood on a slight hill about the line of the present Amity Street between Hicks and Henry Street. It faced south. From its windows a splendid panorama of the waters of the East River, the distant shores of New Jersey, the faint outline of the Orange Mountains, the Battery, and the spires, roofs, ships and docks of the growing Metropolis could be seen." [13]

Cornelius Heeney's early benefactions to support the Catholic orphan asylums were continued with his creation of the Brooklyn Benevolent Society in March of 1843, five years before his death. His "Last Will and Testament" of 11 March 1843, named a number of relatives, and the Roman Catholic Orphan Asylum Society in Brooklyn, directing that: "All the rest, residue and remainder of my Real Estate in the City of Brooklyn" would be administered by the Brooklyn Benevolent Society which he had created by charter in Albany and established in Brooklyn for that same purpose.[14] After his death on 3 May 1848, the benefactions of the Society continued into the nineteenth, twentieth and twenty-first centuries, [15] and are still being donated annually to the Catholic Charities of the Diocese of Brooklyn.

NEW MALE CATHOLIC ORPHAN ASYLUM

Finding the boys' orphan asylum on Clinton Street to be too small to house its 120 children, John Loughlin decided to "erect another building for them and to use the old one for a house of industry for the orphan girls at Congress Street."[16]

Loughlin purchased a 14-acre plot at Bedford and
Willoughby Avenues for a boys' orphanage, "three stories
high, 125 feet long, with two wings, 70 feet deep," which
was "completed" with a three-day fair on June 6, 1858.[17]
The Brothers' history, however, indicates that it was not
ready for occupancy by them until October of that year.

Funds for this building were raised in the churches of
the Diocese. Sharp records that $4,047.56 was collected by
James Harper of St. Paul's between October, 1856 and
October, 1857.[18] The building and grounds cost a total of
$40,328, and Sharp records that all but $11,000 was paid by
the spring of 1858.[19] Contemporary newspapers note the
opening of the new orphanage:

*New Orphan Asylum - The new Roman Catholic
Orphan Asylum building, recently erected on Bedford
Avenue, will be formally opened today. The building,
and ground upon which it stands, cost about $40,000,
all but $11,000 of which has been paid.* [20]

However, funds were still being collected in the fall of
that year:

*The Bishop of Brooklyn, Dr. Loughlin, assisted by his
clergy, has commenced the collection of a fund for the
purpose of erecting a building in the eastern part of the
City, as an asylum for male orphans, where they will
receive a moral and religious education, and where they
will be taught trades.* [21]

Although Loughlin's effort to build a larger orphan
asylum for the male children of his diocese was successful,
Fitzgerald believes that:

Catholic rhetoric in support of institutionalization never suggested that institutions were the best places to raise children, but instead focused on their strategic necessity against child-removal policies, and defense of poor parents' rights to retain legal control over their children. Through the 1890's, Protestant placing-out advocates continued to concentrate on children's rights only, and portrayed the "home" into which children would be placed as the only proper setting for dependent children. . . . Protestant placing-out advocates did not consider "parental rights" as important in their policy discussions. Catholics, on the other hand, did not separate parental and children's rights historically, but saw them as linked; indeed, the severing of ties between poor Catholic children and parents had been and continued to be the most objectionable strain of Protestant "child-saving" work, considered an assault on the very foundations of the Catholic community.

Protestant social reformers in the years following the Great Irish Famine, were overwhelmed by the number of Irish immigrants and their relative destitution:

For New York's reformers dedicated to eliminating widespread dependency and working to somehow stop the creation of a permanent dependent class in America, ... the Irish as a group loomed as the most frightening specter on the American landscape. Robert Hartley, the leader of the Association for the Improvement of the Condition of the Poor, warned that New York City's unique position as the hub of European immigration, has brought with it, "not only wealth, and skill, and labor which we want, but also a vast amount of impotent and thriftless poverty we do not want." [22]

About Irish immigrants' propensity to stay in New York City, (Fitzgerald quoting Hartley):

> *[A] large number of Irish immigrants, . . . are but little disposed to change their thriftless habits with a change of country. They are prone to stay where another race furnishes them with food, clothing and labor. Unlike immigrants of other nationalities, they have a disrelish for migration into our new country, especially the 'far west'.[23]*

McCaffrey offers another view of the reason for the Irish to settle in cities rather than the Mid-West:

> *Portions of the Irish Catholic Diaspora came from cities and towns, but for the most part it was composed of country people. A large number of Irish Catholic emigrants who went to Canada and later Australia and New Zealand did settle in rural areas, but in the United States they collected in cities, scorning the vast, inexpensive, fertile acres of the Midwest. In 1870, 72 percent of the American Irish were concentrated in seven urban, industrial states - Massachusetts, Connecticut, New York, New Jersey, Pennsylvania, Ohio, and Illinois - usually residing in communities exceeding 2,500. About 85 percent of Irish-American Catholics were engaged in the industrial or transportation sections of the American economy, but only 15 percent were involved with farming. [24]*

However, the 15% in farming was a significant number as reported by Linder and Zacharias. In 1860, 63% of rural Kings County residents who said they were farm laborers were from Ireland, 15% were from Germany, and 12% were U.S. Blacks. [25]

BROTHERS SUPERVISE
RELUCTANT ORPHAN BOYS

Orphan asylums were places where children and young teenagers were placed by orders of the courts because of their truancy, delinquency, or the inability of their parents to care for them. This was a new experience for the brothers from Ireland. Bible schools and orphanages for Catholic children in Ireland, especially in the West, were operated by Protestant Bible Societies as a means to proselytize the children. A Catholic Defense Association, formed by leading Catholic churchmen and laity in August 1852, had as one of its objects the protection of the poor from 'pecuniary proselytism'. [26] However, most of the boys in the new Brooklyn orphan asylum assigned to the brothers would have been placed there because of evidence that they were living in the streets, "without education, religious instruction, a home as 'haven,' or parents themselves". Many would have been "poor children (who) contributed to their family income or managed their own survival through scavenging, huckstering, rag-picking, and begging." [27] The brothers would have found that most of these boys were in the asylum against their wills. Indeed, the nature of these child-caring institutions in the mid-nineteenth century - as solutions to the social ills which identified these children as poor, undisciplined examples of their parents' neglect - would have tested the talents of the best of men.[28] It would soon become evident that the brothers were unsuited to the task of "mothering" these children. We read that, by 1860:

At a meeting held September 24, 1860, it was moved, seconded and carried: "That the Visiting Committee [of the Society] have power to employ and pay two women under the direction of Ann Kerrigan, to go into the male asylum at 7 o'clock A.M., wash and comb children, and then attend to cleaning dormitory, and particularly look after the beds, and then wash and mend all the clothes." [29]

More revealing is the information about the salaries paid to the teachers and a comment on the Society's financial priorities:

On February 4, 1861, a committee of one was appointed "To employ a washer woman at wages not to exceed $12 per month, which, by the way, was the salary paid to an **assistant teacher** *[author's emphasis] except that he had his lodging thrown in"* .... *The board was evidently economical as to washer women and teachers, but liberal in its patriotism, for we read that "the Fire Works Committee was empowered to draw on the Treasurer for $25 expended for a band, etc., on the Fourth of July, 1861". Again, at a meeting held April 22, 1862, "the Visiting Committee reported that they had discontinued lunch to the boys."* [30] *Some time in the year 1857 [sic] the total separation of the boys and girls took place, the boys going to the asylum on the corner of Bedford and Willoughby avenues,* **for a time in charge of the Franciscan Brothers,** *[author's emphasis] and girls remaining in Congress Street.*

How long the brothers were in charge of the Male Orphan Asylum is not known directly, but evidence suggests that they were there only until they opened St. Francis Academy in Baltic Street in September of 1859. [31] That the brothers were not long in the orphanage is seen in the decision of John McMahon not to use it as the novitiate for the eight young postulants who arrived in the summer of 1858 from Ireland. The history of the Community records that he found the orphanage "unsuitable" because the nature of the institution permitted little privacy for the brothers. Supervision of the boys, as well as teaching, allowed little time for their communal meals, prayers and recreation, which were part of their understanding of religious life. Even though the brothers were lay friars, not monks, the cloister they were accustomed to in their "monasteries" in Ireland, would not have been possible in the orphan asylum. In addition, the presence of women in the institution, noted above, and the presence of fourteen Sisters of Mercy, would further complicate their attempts to create a monastic life at Bedford and Willoughby Avenues. However, a traditional history of the Brothers places them at the orphanage until the disastrous fire in the early morning of Sunday, 9 November 1862:

> *With a calmness feigned to avert panic, the brothers were able to lead out all but three [sic] of their charges to safety. The building was a total loss, and the death of the three boys was a terrible shock to the brothers. The brothers, after this terrible night of destruction, placed the survivors in other homes, and joined their confreres in their monastery lately opened on Butler Street.*[32]

The 1958 *History of the Franciscan Brothers* also continues this tradition when it claims that the brothers showed "heroic courage" during the fire:

> *The first mission assigned to the Brothers was the Roman Catholic Orphan Asylum for Boys on a fourteen-acre plot at the corner of Willoughby and DeKalb Avenues. This first foundation was successfully conducted until tragedy struck in the form of fire in 1862, which destroyed the orphanage. Throughout the horrifying experience, the Brothers displayed heroic courage and unselfish devotion. While the saddening event did not down the spirit of the new pioneers, it did cause the Brothers to give up the supervision of institutions of this type.[33]*

Current research, however, does not agree with these early versions of the Brothers' history. More compelling sources of evidence indicate that Franciscan Brothers were **not in charge** of the Boys Orphanage in 1862. All the contemporary New York and Brooklyn newspaper articles and the Minutes of the Roman Catholic Orphan Asylum Society, which discuss the details of the disastrous fire, which took the lives of two boys and destroyed the building during an early blizzard on the night of Sunday, 9 November 1862, fail to mention the presence of brothers. A lengthy, detailed article [34] written by a "stringer" reporter appeared in *The New York Times, The New York Daily Tribune* and *The Brooklyn Daily Eagle* on 10 November, the Monday following the fire:

TERRIBLE DISASTER
Destruction of the Brooklyn Roman Catholic Orphan Asylum by Fire
TWO CHILDREN BURNED TO DEATH
Several Hundred Turned Into the Street –
Meeting in Behalf of the Unfortunates, &c.

About 2 1/2 o'clock, Sunday morning, a fire broke out in the extensive building on Bedford-avenue, between Willoughby and DeKalb Avenues, Brooklyn, occupied as an Asylum for Roman Catholic orphan boys, and resulted in its complete destruction, together with the loss of two lives. The structure is of brick, 150 feet front by 100 in depth, and five stories in height. The grounds attached comprise fourteen lots, and extend from Bedford-avenue to Spencer-street, affording ample space for exercise in fine weather. About 150 feet in the rear is a wooden shed about 30 by 75 feet in extent. Which was designed for a play-house in inclement weather. The main building is divided into apartments for the accommodation of the Superintendents and Assistants, and conveniences are provided for 350 children. The second, third and fourth floors were used as sleeping apartments. Heat was furnished by means of furnaces, two of which were located in the basement under the north wing, and two under the south wing. The main entrances in front and rear of the centre building, the halls and stairways were all of wide dimensions, and to this feature, together with the presence of mind and the activity displayed by those in charge, it is mainly owing that the conflagration did not result more disastrously -- for, as near as can be ascertained, two children only, out of 248, lost their lives.

The fire was caused by the overheating of a flue leading from one of the furnaces of the south wing. The floors and other wood inside, being of pitch pine, ignited with great rapidity and the flames speedily extended upward until the whole was enveloped.

The teachers were aroused from their slumbers by one of the lady assistants, and immediately proceeded to save the children. In this they were fortunately most successful, having, in a very short time thereafter, conducted them to the play house. It was supposed at the time that no one was missing, and the police and firemen were so informed. The efforts to suppress the flames were then redoubled, but without avail, and the firemen were compelled to leave the building to its fate.

Some two hours thereafter Mr. James Gill, of Hose Company No 13, discovered the crisped body of a child on one of the upper floors, and Messrs. Brady, of Engine No. 9, and Waldron, Start and Colyer, of Truck No.3, found another, and conveyed them to the Ninth Ward Station-house. The children had doubtless become bewildered, and ascended to the upper floors, instead of coming down stairs. Nearly all the books and papers were consumed. A record of the names of the children was saved, and, on calling the roll, all answered but two, named Michael Carrick and Daniel McMann.

At the time of the fire the wind was blowing strongly from the northwest, and the rain was falling in torrents. The ground was covered in snow and slush, and through this the children were compelled to wade, barefoot and in their night-clothes, to the play house on Spencer Street, which provided a temporary place of refuge from the elements. Subsequently they were conducted to the neighboring residences, and everything possible was done by all to relieve the little ones of their sufferings.

In consequence of the early hour and the disagreeable state of the weather, comparatively few citizens gathered about the scene of disaster. The duty of saving the inmates therefore, devolved almost exclusively upon the Superintendent and his assistants. The President of the Brooklyn City Railroad Company placed the cars on the several routes, as well as all the old stages, at the disposal of the officers of the institution. The children having all been provided with shoes by Mr. McNally, who keeps a store on Myrtle Avenue, near Bedford, were collected together and conveyed to the Roman Catholic Orphan Asylum in Congress Street, where they will be provided for until other arrangements can be made.

The Roman Catholic Orphan Asylum for Boys was erected in 1856, at a cost of $25,000. Last year some necessary improvements were made at an expense of $5,000. The loss, including contents, amounts to about $35,000, upon which there is an insurance of $15,000 in the Montauk, Lafayette, Firemen's, Mechanics, Brooklyn, and Nassau Companies.

The Institution is in charge of the Roman Catholic Orphan Asylum Society of the City of Brooklyn, of which the Right Rev. Bishop Loughlin is President. It is supported by contributions collected in the different city Catholic Churches.

Those in immediate charge are Mr. Thomas Brady, Principal; Alexander J. Rooney, James P. Barry, Walter Hoyle [none of whom were Franciscan Brothers], *and fourteen female assistants - Sisters of Mercy.*

The fact that the building was on fire was discovered by a little boy seven years of age, who is sick with intermittent fever. He went to the bedside of one of the Sisters and told her he could not sleep as he was sure there was fire somewhere. She ordered him back to bed and then took the precaution of looking out into the hall, and was made aware of the fact that but little time remained to save the inmates. Every one was aroused, and all, with two exceptions, saved. . . . It is understood that the children will be transferred to the Convent, corner of Willoughby and Classon Avenue [Sisters of Mercy Convent], *in a day or two.* [35]

ORPHAN ASYLUM SOCIETY MEETING

The immediate response of the Roman Catholic Orphan Asylum Society can be seen in the minutes of their meeting held on Sunday 9 November 1862, on the afternoon of the fire: "a large attendance of members araising":

> *The Chairman called the attention of the members to the destruction of the Male Asylum on Bedford Ave which was destroyed by fire this morning, leaving 242 children thrown destitute upon the Community.*

The immediate response of the Society's Board was to approve the appointment of a committee to make arrangements for a public lecture to raise funds at the Academy of Music "at as early a moment as the building can be obtained . . . and that the Committee invite Mr. Richard O'Gorman to deliver said lecture." [36] On the next day, the Society met and the "Chairman stated subscriptions were solicited on behalf of the orphan children when the sum of $2,292.87 was handed to the secretary."

Previous to adjourning, a vote of thanks was passed to the Brooklyn City Rail Road Co. . . . .the Fire Department's J. S. Douglas, and to ask those who aided at the time of the fire and thereafter, but whose names the man is unable to obtain. [37]

In response to a request of Mr. Carroll at the Meeting of November 30th, which seems to arise from criticisms against the Society for too slow a response to the tragedy of the November 9th fire, the Board of Directors was asked to report at its next Meeting "what actions they have taken and they intend doing in relation to the Male Asylum." [38]

The Board of Directors, in answer to the Resolution of November 30/62, inserted the following: It is painful to go back, even in thought to that fatal Sunday morning when the poor orphans, so kindly cared for by this Society, were suddenly aroused from their slumbers by the fearful cry of fire. It is sad to recall the picture of terrified children, bewildered, and almost naked, hurrying out into the frightful storm, which at this early hour of the night, raged with a fury only to be excelled by that other storm of fire, which was then devastating and laying waste the home of these poor children, who were driven homeless into the streets, deprived of the Asylum and shelter which the charity of the Catholics of this City provided for them. . . . [A]s guardians of the Orphans, placed there by your suffrage, they were not abroad when duty called them, and did not rest till a late hour that afternoon, they saw the Orphans comfortably settled in the Female Asylum under the care of the good Sisters of Charity.

Their next care was to provide a temporary home till such time as the new asylum should be built; various large buildings were examined for this purpose, their size and capacity considered , negotiations entered into with the owners or occupants. When it is considered that the wants of 250 human beings have to be provided for, that even with the capacity of the late Asylum there was much inconvenience for room experienced, and everything being lost at the fire, it will be readily conceived the great difficulty attending this subject.

In an interview with the R.R. Bishop Loughlin, he mentioned the Convent on Jay Street, from which the Sisters were about removing, as likely to suit our orphans. On examination, we found that by occupying the Schools opposite and erecting a temporary building on the vacant lot adjoining we might provide the necessary accommodations till the erection of the new Asylum. Arrived at this conclusion, we at once entered into an agreement for putting up a building as soon as possible, that would suit all the requirements of the children during their temporary occupation.

And here the Board have to claim the Society's kind indulgence, not for being too slow, but for being with [the] matter of new buildings, too fast, for in their haste to get the orphans settled they neglected to obtain the required sanction, an omission they trust you will overlook, considering the occasion and by a vote of this meeting give legal sanction to our action.

*Besides the time and labor required for the above, there was the ordinary providing [of] food, clothing, etc. For the children, there was the securing of old beds, iron, and other valuables buried under the ruins, **the careful seeking among the rubbish that perchance other remains may be lying there, as our utmost exertions have been unavailing in finding one small boy, although several of his companions testify to having seen him enter the asylum after the fire.** [39]*

The question of the number of boys (two or three) who died in the fire is continued by this last sentence, because no mention is made in the Society's Minutes of the bodies of the two boys (Michael Carrick and Daniel McMann), reported as being removed by the firemen in the newspaper account above.

The Board further reports that: *for fitting up of the late Convent, we have masons, carpenters, plumbers, and servants exerting themselves to the utmost in preparing the Convent and schools for the boys. In taking possession of the building we found there was neither hot water pipes through the house, wash tubs, water closets, or means to wash the children, is just not at all suitable for the health, or comfort of so many orphans as will soon find shelter under its limited roof.*

We have just received 150 iron bedsteads made to order and bedding to correspond, all the furniture, cooking utensils are being specially furnished, and at the end of this week we hope to be able to have the boys comfortably settled in their new home where you will be able to see the great work you are solicitous of having completed.

We have advertized for proposals for removal of the ruins of the late asylum and intend securing the bricks, timbers, iron, or other materials likely to be used in the new Asylum, leaving the grounds ready to be rebuilt on or otherwise as may be hereafter determined.

In reference to rebuilding, the Board has taken no action whatever. The funds collected are carefully secured and placed at interest in the joint account of the R.R. Bishop Loughlin and the Treasurer and are on call, so that no delay will arise as to the immediate withdrawal of all or any part of it when called for.

The Board will, as soon as the Orphans are settled in their new home, prepare a statement which will be the whole matter of the contemplated building of the Asylum and matters connected therewith in as tangible shape before you, as no action can be legal but by the sanction of at least two thirds of the Society in meeting assembled.

In the meantime, the Board beg the assistance of any members who may wish to give the benefit of their views on this important matter.

In conclusion, the Board beg to assure the Society that they are fully alive to the position in which they have been placed, and they trust their decisions on their duty fully and faithfully will not be underrated. Many things may be done which perhaps might be better done, but it would not be fair to expect so much while demanding that the Board shall not do too little; in any case, the directors hold themselves responsible to the Society for their actions as officers, so duly ask the confidence and encouragement of those who have placed them in office, as this will lead them to work with vigor and cheerfulness in behalf of the little ones who are placed by Providence under your care.

All of which is respectfully submitted.

On motion of Mr. O'Mahoney, the report was seconded, and the action of the Board was confirmed.

On motion of same, the Board was directed to give the servants such sums as they (the Board) may think proper as a recompense for their losses by the burning of the Asylum.

In what is a very thorough report of the Board to the full Society, no mention is made of the presence of Franciscan Brothers.

This remarkable picture of the fire at the Orphanage was published in the *1863 Manual of the Brooklyn Common Council.*

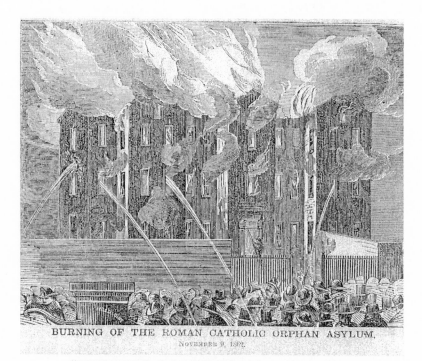

BURNING OF THE ROMAN CATHOLIC ORPHAN ASYLUM,
November 9, 1862.

"BURNING OF THE ROMAN CATHOLIC ORPHAN ASYLUM" [40]

The *Manual of the Common Council* also describes the Asylum building and the disastrous fire of the previous November:

> In 1858 a new building was erected on Bedford Avenue, . . . at a cost of about $27,000. The building had a front of 120 feet on Bedford Avenue, and had two wings 72 feet in depth. It was three stories in height, with an attic and basement. The grounds attached comprised fourteen lots, and extend from Bedford

avenue to Spencer Street, affording ample space for exercise in fine weather. About 159 feet in the rear was a wooden shed about 30 by 75 feet in extent, which was designed for a playhouse in inclement weather. The main building was divided into apartments for the accommodation of the superintendent and assistants, and conveniences were provided for 350 children. The second, third and fourth floors were used as sleeping apartments. Heat was furnished by means of furnaces, two of which were located in the basement under the north wing and two under the south wing.

About two o'clock on the morning of Sunday, November 9, 1862, the building took fire from some defect in the heating apparatus, and was totally consumed. There were 248 children asleep within its walls when the fire broke out. A snow storm prevailed at the time, and the little orphans were turned into the street in their night-clothes, leaving, unfortunately, three [41] of their number behind, who perished in the flames. The residents of the vicinity kindly opened their doors and sheltered the children from the "pelting of the pitiless storm."

Collections were made and contributions in money poured in from all sects and classes with equal liberality, so that the temporary wants of the orphans were amply supplied. [42]

The *Manual of the Common Council* also does not mention any Franciscan Brothers in charge or in attendance.

An article in *The Independent*, a Brooklyn Congregationalist newspaper, confirms the contributions "from all sects," mentioned in the *Manual*. The Rev. Mr. Henry Ward Beecher, the famous Pastor of the Plymouth

Church of the Pilgrims, and the editor of the paper, begged for money for the poor Catholic orphans in a colorful and graphic article published on Wednesday of that week:

ORPHANS

The burning of the Roman Catholic Orphan Asylum of Brooklyn, by which 250 children were suddenly turned into the streets in the midst of a furious storm, leaving behind them in the flames two of their little mates to perish by a dreadful death, excites intense, sympathy in all circles throughout these neighboring cities.

In the midst of a fire that so quickly spread through the whole building, breaking out before the dawn and while the children and their guardians were yet in their beds, during which, after the day broke and the fire-alarm was sounded, the usual multitude of volunteer assistants at a fire was kept scanty by the driving sleet - how, in the midst of these extraordinary difficulties, so great a number of children could have been caught up from their sleep, hurried out of their rooms and down the stairways amid smoke and threatening flame, till the whole five stories were emptied with a loss of only two of that great household, neither maiming nor wounding any of the rest, is a marvel of praiseworthy exertion, for which public thanks are due to the officers of the asylum, and to the firemen of the city.

The little children, mostly in their night-clothes, barefooted and bareheaded, after their rescue from the fire, stood partly in the open storm, and partly under the shelter of a play-ground shed, until kind neighbors picked them up one by one, wrapped them in blankets and shawls, and ran with them through the rain to their *houses, and warmed them at their hearths. But who could tell how many of the little ones were left ungathered? The books, the papers, the lists of names, all were lost before anyone dared to think of saving anything but the children. The anxiety at one time was fearful. It was believed that twenty or thirty were missing. But at last, one of the roll-books was found, and every child answered to the call except two voices: when, soon after, two little charred bodies were brought out of the ruins, and it was found that **the two voices had given their answer in silence into God's ear.***

In his closing paragraphs, the reader can visualize The Reverend Mr. Beecher in the pulpit of his Church in Brooklyn Heights, commanding his flock to outdo their neighbors in their support of the orphans:

So, just now, this throng of homeless children reach out their hands to all kind hearts, for help. Their appeal is tender and touching. The fire that stripped the clothes from their backs and the shoes from their feet - that destroyed the beds whereon they slept, the board at which they ate, the roof that was their only shelter - left them with nothing but their lives, their orphanage, and their poverty. As it was charity that clothed them at first, so it must be charity that shall clothe them again. . . . We are sure that tender-hearted fathers and mothers, ... looking upon the destitution of these little ones, motherless and fatherless, will not allow the bodily wants of such helpless creatures to go unprovided for, or any needful personal care to be withheld. The local arrangements made for receiving gifts of clothes, bedding, shoes, or money, need not be repeated here. Only, let us say, it ought to be a pleasure to our friends and neighbors on the other side of the East River [Manhattan] to see that, not for a single day, shall one of these Little Ones suffer for that Cup of Cold Water which never fails of its reward.

Brooklyn is the city of Protestant churches: will any one stop his charity, saying, This was a Roman Catholic institution? Such a man, calling himself a Christian, deserves a place neither in the Protestant nor the Catholic Church. . . . But with little children - too young to know the difference between kindness and neglect - is it possible that, in the midst of their sudden and pressing wants, they will receive a whit the less of watch and care by reason of their birth into the Church of their fathers? . . . . Meanwhile we hear a solemn voice saying: **"Inasmuch as ye did it not to one of the least of these, ye did it not to me."** [43]

FORTY YEARS AFTER THE FIRE

The account [44] of Rev. Patrick Creighton (1817-1904), about his role in the terrible fire, gives another version of the tragedy and indicates that at least one Franciscan Brother was present in the Orphan Asylum that night, possibly as sacristan to set up and serve his Mass. As the Pastor of St. Malachy's Church in East New York, Brooklyn, Father Creighton had the duty of saying an early Mass at the Orphanage on all Sundays and Holy Days of Obligation. His small, 22-page pamphlet, written almost forty years after the fire, contains two pages of colorful narration of his heroics in saving the sisters and almost all the boys, especially the little children:

REV. PATRICK CREIGHTON, c. 1900 [45]

When we look back on the fearful scenes of that night, how clearly can we see the protecting hand of Divine Providence, towards the orphans, in obliging the writer to be present on that frightful occasion.

There were two women there who had charge of the dormitory where sixty-two very small children were sleeping, and we regret very much that we have forgotten their names. . . . . To arouse from their slumbers and carry to a place of safety sixty-two helpless little children can be readily seen as not an easy task. But at the first cry of fire those brave women, like skillful generals surveying the field of battle, took in the situation, and seeing with them was action, and by their actions it was easy to perceive that the saving of their own lives was but a secondary consideration, when they saw the lives of the children in danger. The dense smoke, nor the scorching heat deterred them not till the last one of their charge was safely secured, and passing by the writer, with hearts and voices uplifted in thanksgiving to God, informed him that all their children had been saved.

The fire broke out in the southerly wing of the building, and those little ones, with the greater number of the children, were located in that wing, and all were accustomed to go down the back stairway both in going to the bath room and the play ground. But that stairway acted as a flue for the dense smoke rushing upward, and it was certain death to any who would go down them. This the writer saw at a glance, and knowing the habits of the children, placed himself as a sentinel at the head of the stairway, and God alone knows how he acquired strength to keep back the frightened orphans from rushing to certain death. With all his efforts, he was unable to prevent three of the larger boys from plunging down the stairs, but it was only when he saw that his own life would also be lost, that he let go his hold of them.

Seeing that all had left the southerly wing, he thought of himself, and going to the northerly stairway, by which he thought all had made their escape, to his great surprise, he found every soul in the building huddled up on that stairway; for in the confusion of the moment, the matron, who had charge of the place, could find no keys, the door being strong could not be broken open without having proper means for doing so.

In this emergency there was no time for thinking, action was necessary, for the smoke and flame, by a strong wind, was rushing across the building; hence a **Franciscan Brother, who like the writer, <u>happened to be in the place</u>** *was appealed to, and with his consent, was dropped from the window of the stairway into the yard, and into his arms the writer dropped every child in the house, and after them the matron and eight women, all escaping without injury . . . . [After*

*returning with difficulty to his room to rescue the Pyx
and Chalice needed for Mass at St. Malachy's later that
day], Fr. Creighton reached the only place of exit, some
one from the outside had broken open the door, so that
he had not to jump from the window.*

Father Creighton continues his story with a graphic
description of the early blizzard and his heroic efforts to
save the children from the effects of that stormy, fire-filled
night:

*Oh! What a terrible night to look back upon! It
seemed as if the Omnipotent God especially let loose
the natural elements to show to man the divinity of his
power. The wind, which blew a hurricane, was
accompanied by rain, and hail, and snow, in torrents,
and the frost was so terrible that it covered with icicles
the garments of all who were exposed to the storm.*

*After escaping the burning building, another surprise
awaited the writer. Every soul that had been rescued
from the flames was again huddled up under the
wooden shed in the rear of the yard, with nothing to
keep life in the little limbs of the orphans save the
terrific heat from the burning down of their happy
home. Those who should have secured shelter for them
stood like statues of wood terrified with fright and were
unable to render any assistance. Having asked one of
them why he did not seek some shelter for the homeless,
the answer was that the gate could not be opened.
Taking from his hands a stout piece of wood, with one
or two sharp strokes of the same, the lock of the gate
soon gave way, and then shelter was procured for the
half-famished orphans and those who had charge of
them. Be it said to the praise of those neighbors, to*

whatever denomination they belonged, that with one accord had doors open and fires prepared to meet the distressed little orphans as they entered their dwellings. [46]

"LADY" THROWS CHILDREN
BACK INTO BLIZZARD

One exception to Patrick Creighton's memory of "doors open and fires prepared" by the orphans' neighbors, was noted in a newspaper 40 years earlier:

In the hurry and confusion of getting the children out, but few of them had time to get all of their clothing, and none of them, their shoes. Their sufferings, when exposed in that condition to the storm which raged at the time, were very intense. Many of the families in the neighborhood took the little sufferers in and warmed them, and otherwise provided for them. There was, however, we are sorry to say, one exception, at least it is so represented to us. In one house (the names of the occupants of which we shall at present suppress) about twenty-five of the children were placed out of the storm by the firemen, but in a few moments they were all turned out again into the storm by the "lady" of the house. As soon as the firemen heard this, they broke the doors and windows of the house in their anger at the inhumanity of the act. We understand that Coroner Norris is to look into the matter, and if the matter turns out as represented to us, we shall assuredly publish the names of the actors of this most contemptible piece of meanness. [47]

In a letter to the editor, written on the same day, Charles Warner, the owner of the house, seeks to contradict the above story:

Bedford Avenue, East Brooklyn
Nov. 10th, 1862

To the Editor of the Brooklyn Eagle:

I take the liberty of seeking permission, through the medium of your paper, to contradict a current report in this vicinity, that, during the conflagration of the Roman Catholic Orphan Asylum, on Sunday morning, I refused to admit or shelter any of its inmates, and to assert that instead of such being the fact, my house (which is directly opposite) was open to any of the unfortunate sufferers by this sad calamity. As soon as I discovered the institution to be in flames, I immediately started to see if I could be of any service, and found that all the children were sheltered. I then took in with me the matron and seamstress, and did all in my power to relieve their necessities. I refer to them to substantiate these facts.

Yours truly, Charles Warner

P.S. - Since writing the above, several of the Directors have called upon me and are desirous of correcting the report.   *Charles Warner* [48]

Confirming the terrible weather of that November North-Easter, the *Tribune* gives a graphic account of the storm:

The storm, which set in on Thursday last, still continued on Saturday and yesterday, with a still north-east wind, and snow falling most of the time. About 12 o'clock on Saturday night, the weather moderated slightly, when there was a heavy fall of rain, but toward morning the atmosphere became colder, and snow again appeared. At different periods during the day the fall of snow was quite heavy, but it melted almost immediately upon reaching the ground. Walking was anything but agreeable, and so wretched and disagreeable was the weather that but few persons ventured abroad during the day, the churches, as a consequence, being slimly attended.[49]

Except for Father Creighton's story, the failure to mention Franciscan Brothers in what are, otherwise, very thorough news reports, plus the presence of fourteen Sisters of Mercy at the orphan asylum, seems to be clear evidence that brothers were not in charge of the boys orphanage at the time of the fire.[50]

The reader is presented with different versions of the tragic drama which was played out during that terrible night of 9 November 1862. The number of children lost (two or three), the presence of any brothers, the role of Patrick Creighton, are all parts of the mystery of that terrible night. It would seem that one Franciscan brother "happened to be present," perhaps to serve Father Creighton's Mass, but it is unlikely that the Franciscan Brothers were actually in charge of the Orphanage on that terrible night.

As reported in Chapter One, John McMahon, the superior, with four professed brothers, and one novice, went to Santa Barbara, California, to try to join the First Order Franciscans in late May or early June of 1862, after the school year was completed, and five months before the fire. They left the diocese without John Loughlin's permission when he was away from Brooklyn on his first *Ad Limina* visit to Rome from late May to mid-August. Sharp states that: "He was back in Brooklyn in August, for he entertained Bishop Timon at his Jay Street residence on the 27th."[51]

The Bishops of New York and Brooklyn learned well from their Irish colleagues. In their efforts to preserve the Catholic Faith of their people from what they perceived to be the dangers of the American Protestant majority, they imitated what had been successful in nineteenth- century Ireland, and invited Irish and other European religious communities to their dioceses to open and staff the schools and orphanages which became the unique heritage of the American Catholic Church in the last three-quarters of the nineteenth century.

Notes

[1] Elizabeth McKeown and Dorothy M. Brown. "Saving New York's Children," *U.S. Catholic Historian*, Vol 13, #3, Summer, 1995, pp. 77-95.

[2] Maureen Fitzgerald, "Saving the Children: Irish-Catholic Nuns," in *The Irish in America*, edited by Michael Coffey, with text by Terry Golway, Hyperion, 1997, pp. 60-66.

[3] Maureen Fitzgerald, "Irish -Catholic Nuns and the Development of New York City's Welfare System, 1840-1900," Ph. D. Dissertation, University of Wisconsin-Madison, 1992, p. 415.

[4] Stephen O'Connor, *Orphan Trains: the Story of Charles Loring Brace and the Children He Saved and Failed*, Houghton Mifflin, 2001, illustration following p. 170.

[5] Henry R. Stiles, *A History of the City of Brooklyn, including The Old*

Town and Village of Brooklyn, the Town of Bushwick, and the Village and City of Williamsburgh, 3 vols, Brooklyn, N.Y., 1870, Vol. 3, pp. 735-739.

[6] Joseph W. Carroll, "Beginning of the Roman Catholic Orphan Asylum Society," *Brooklyn Catholic Historical Society Records,* 1901, [only issue ever published], pp. 37-48.

[7] *Manual of the Common Council of the City of Brooklyn for 1863,* "Roman Catholic Orphan Asylum," pp. 194-197.

[8] *Carroll,* p. 43.

[9] *Ibid.,* p. 44.

[10] Marie Veronica Tarpey, (Sister Bernard Mary, S.C.H.), "The History of Cornelius Heeney, 1754-1848, and the Brooklyn Benevolent Society," Masters Dissertation, St. John's University, New York, 1959.

[11] *Manual . . .,* p. 196

[12] Sister Rita Agnes, "History of Saint Paul's Parish," 1971, p. 14.

[13] Tarpey, p. 62.

[14] Tarpey, p. 84.

[15] *The Brooklyn Catholic,* 23 April 1870, "The Catholic Orphan Asylum Society, Fortieth Annual Report of the Treasurer," states that $73,841. 44 was raised for the Society from many sources, of which $6,689.94 was donated by the Brooklyn Benevolent Society,

[16] John K. Sharp. *History of the Diocese of Brooklyn, 1853-1953: The Catholic Church on Long Island,* Vol I, p. 215.

[17] *The New York Times,* 19 June 1858 - however, the same paper, on 10 November 1862, in a front-page article after the disastrous fire of 9 November 1862, describes the building as larger, and states that it was five stories high, 150 feet in front and 100 feet in depth. A contemporary illustration of the fire also shows a five-story building.

[18] Sharp, *History ...,* Vol 1, p. 370, note 68.

[19] *Ibid.,* Vol 1, p. 371, note 71.

[20] *The Long Island Star,* June 7, 1858.

[21] *The Brooklyn Evening Star*, October 30, 1858.

[22] Fitzgerald, "Irish-Catholic . . . , pp. 621-622.

[23] *Ibid*, pp. 404-405.

[24] Lawrence J. McCaffrey, *The Irish Catholic Diaspora in America*, Catholic University of America Press, 1984, p. 67.

[25] Marc Linder and Lawrence S. Zacharias, *Of Cabbages and Kings County: Agriculture and the Formation of Modern Brooklyn*, University of Iowa Press, 1999, pp. 90-91.

[26] Joseph Robins, *The Lost Children: a Study of Charity Children in Ireland, 1700-1900*, Institute of Public Administration, Dublin, 1980, p. 144.

[27] Fitzgerald, "Irish-Catholic Nuns . . . ", pp. 408-409.

[28] "Early Catholic History, A Public Meeting of That Church's Historical Society, " *Brooklyn Eagle*, April 26, 1894, reports that Joseph W. Carroll spoke about the "early hardships of the brothers who taught and cared for the boys; of the small means at the command of those who controlled the asylum. . . ".

[29] Carroll, p. 45.

[30] *Ibid*.

[31] *Sadliers Catholic Directory, 1860*, p. 170, reports two professed Brothers, 11 novices, and 30 pupils in residence at 82 East Baltic Street, which was the Monastery and Academy of the Brothers of the Third Order of St. Francis. These data would have been gathered in 1859 for the Sadliers Catholic Directory for 1860.

[32] *The Diamond Jubilee History of the Franciscan Brothers*, 1933, p. 22.

[33] Ibid.

[34] *The New York Times*, 10 November, 1862, p. 1 , *The New York Daily Tribune*, 10 November, p. 3., and *The Brooklyn Daily Eagle*, 10 November 1862, p. 2, all published essentially the same story.

[35] Names of donors who aided the orphans are listed in three articles on pages 2, 4 and 8, of the next day's *New York Times* on Tuesday, 11 November.

[36] Roman Catholic Orphan Asylum Society, "Minutes, Dec. 11, 1859 - Mar. 19, 1894," p. 43, 9 November 1862 (Archives of the Brooklyn

Diocese).

37 *Ibid.*, 10 November 1862, p. 45.

38 *Ibid,* p. 47.

39 Ibid., p. 50.

40 *Manual of the Common Council of the City of Brooklyn for 1863,* "Burning of the Roman Catholic Orphan Asylum, November 9, 1862," p. 194, shows firemen fighting the fire as the building is totally consumed in flames.

41 The number of children who perished is variously given as two or three, but only two are listed by name in *The New York Times* article and Beecher's Appeal (below), mentions "Two Voices Into God's Ear".

42 *Manual of the Common Council of the City of Brooklyn for 1863*, "Roman Catholic Orphan Asylum," pp. 196-197.

43 *The Independent*, (Brooklyn Congregationalist weekly, edited by Henry Ward Beecher), 13 Nov. 1862, p. 4.

44 Patrick Creighton, "A Brief Sketch of the Beginning of St. Malachy's Church and the Church of Our Lady of Victory, by their First Pastor, Rev. Patrick Creighton," P.F. McBreen & Sons, Printers, 47 Ann Street, New York, 1901, pp. 5-7.

45 "A Century of Religious Life, 1870-1970," Anniversary Booklet, St. John the Evangelist Parish, Riverhead, N.Y., 1970

46 Creighton. . . , pp. 5 -6.

47 *The Brooklyn Daily Eagle*, 10 November 1862, p. 2.

48 *The Brooklyn Daily Eagle*, 13 November, 1862, p. 2.

49 *The New York Daily Tribune,* 10 November, 1862, p. 8.

50 The 1860 Federal Census lists: P.W, Cahill, priest, Joseph Gannon, Lawrence O' Beirne, Francis Rooney, Benedict Reilly, and Anthony Gallagher as brothers in the Catholic Orphanage. Only O'Beirne was present in the Monastery in 1862.

51 Sharp, *History...* Vol 2, p. 2.

CHAPTER THREE

BROTHERS' TRADITION AS EDUCATORS IN IRELAND RECOMMENDS THEM TO BISHOPS IN AMERICA

Although the Brothers were first assigned to the new Male Catholic Orphan Asylum when they arrived in 1858, for almost five centuries they were successful Franciscan educators in Ireland. This reputation recommended them to pastors and parents, and they soon took up education in their own St. Francis Academy and in parish schools of the Brooklyn diocese.

Friars of the Irish Third Order Regular were well known for the schools attached to their "monasteries,"[1] from Killeenbrenan in the Archdiocese of Tuam (1426), to the suppression of forty-seven of their houses during the Penal days (1558-1760). In their houses they supported themselves by manual labor and farming the fields around their friaries. Rather than Latin, rhetoric, philosophy and theology which were taught to the sons of the rich and privileged, the free curriculum of the friars' schools "focused on native learning--the grammar, poetry, histories, and sagas of Gaelic Ireland, as well as the genealogies of important families".[2]

In response to the Irish bishops' fear of Protestant proselytism, the Third Order Regular Franciscan Brothers re-emerged as teachers after 1818, first in Milltown and Dalkey in the Archdiocese of Dublin, and later in Mountbellew, Roundstone, Clifden and many other towns in the Archdiocese of Tuam in the West of Ireland. Called "Monks of the West," the Franciscan Brothers also continued working as skilled stone masons, carpenters and farmers to support the brothers who were offering free education in useful trades for working-class young men, and primary education for poor children.[3] This custom of free education is an Irish tradition going back over a millennium to the seventh century, when Bede recounts that many English went to Ireland to study at the monasteries: "And all these the Irish most freely received, and made it their study to provide them with food from day to day without any charge, with books to read and with free teaching."[4]

From the time of the suppression of the monasteries after the Reformation, education of poor children in Ireland was often left to itinerant hedge school masters. The physical conditions of the "schools" where they taught could be a corner of a barn, or under a hedge on a country road. Connolly writes that "[I]n 1824, about 300,000 Catholic children were attending private, elementary day schools of this kind." Although they were called "hedge schools," they were also known as "pay schools," since the master received a small fee from his pupils. [5]

The quality of these hedge schools varied widely. After the "Beginnings of the Troubles in 1641," they gradually replaced the Bardic schools, the ancient professional schools of Ireland, which prepared the Brehan scholars, and the suppressed monastery schools.[6] Although some of these masters, who had often studied for the priesthood, had a classical education, the hedge schools were never at the level of the clerical monastery schools or the secular Bardic schools, but offered primary education with a smattering of Latin for their young scholars. As "Pay Schools," they were a means of a poor livelihood for their teachers, whose patrons had become landless, homeless, or exiles on the continent.[7] In addition to English and Irish, these hedge-masters often had other European languages because of their sojourns in the seminaries of Spain, France and Italy.

One of the students from such a school, which must have been one of the better examples of private "hedge schools," was the great scholar, calligrapher and translator Eugene O'Curry, who was born in 1796 in Carrigaholt, on the Loop-Head Peninsula in County Clare. Although he had no formal education beyond the "hedge school" level, he became a great *shanachai* or storyteller like his father Owen Curry, who may have been a Bardic School scholar. Considered by John O'Donovan, the great historian and translator of the *Annals of the Kingdom of Ireland by the Four Masters*, to be a "natural genius who was able to overcome his lack of formal education," O'Curry had a wide knowledge of Irish language, literature and history, and worked as a cataloger of ancient Irish manuscripts in Trinity College, the Royal Irish Academy in Dublin, and the British Museum in London.

O'Curry was later appointed by John Cardinal Newman as Professor of Irish History and Archaeology in the new Catholic University of Ireland in 1854. Three volumes of his lectures, given between 1857 and 1862, were published posthumously in 1873, as *The Manners and Customs of the Ancient Irish.* [8] At his death he was described as "the one great modern interpreter of the Irish language in its oldest written form". [9] Cardinal Newman, who had the highest regard for him as a scholar, wrote of him: *"Requiescat in Pace, Anima Candida.* May his brilliant soul rest in peace". [10]

In the late eighteenth century, Irish Catholics were beginning to emerge from two centuries of Penal Laws. Enacted first by the English Parliament and then by the Protestant-controlled Irish Parliament in 1695, the Irish Penal Laws forbade Catholics education, ownership of land, and closed entry of Irish Catholics to the professions. These Penal Laws were as so many nails that held them fast in the bondage where half a century of warfare had left them "a hewer of wood and a drawer of water to his conqueror," as Swift aptly said. [11] Frightened by threats to the security of the state, these Penal Laws, relating to Catholic worship, organization and personal rights, had been enacted in England from the time of Elizabeth I. Despite the Protestant victory at Limerick in October 1691, Protestants saw the Catholics in Ireland as a continuing threat. As long as William III was at war with Catholic France, the English law named Catholics as enemies of the State. [12]

During the Restoration of the Catholic Charles II (1660), the Irish Catholic hierarchy was re-established and Catholic bishops received pensions from the King. Following the "Glorious Revolution" and the Protestant victory at the Battle of the Boyne, 12 July 1690, the Treaty of Limerick, "broken ere the ink wherewith 'twas writ could dry,'" prompted many of the Irish Catholic bishops to flee the country. Further, the Banishment Act of 1697 was passed by the Protestant Irish Parliament: "banishing all Papists exercising any ecclesiastical jurisdiction, and all regulars (priests and brothers of religious orders), of the popish clergy out of the kingdom." [13]

Fines were also imposed against persons harboring bishops, priests, or regulars who returned to Ireland, "£20 for the first offense, £40 for the second offense, and forfeiture of all lands, goods, and chattels for the third offense." Justices of the Peace were empowered, and fined £100 if they neglected their duty, to arrest all ecclesiastics remaining in the country, contrary to the statute, and to suppress "all monasteries, friaries, nunneries, or other popish fraternities or societies." The suppression resulted in the completion of the process begun during Elizabeth I's reign: [14]

When the Emperor Leopold of Austria's Ambassador to King William protested that this expulsion of bishops, contrary to the "capitulation of Limerick," would mean that the ordination of priests would be impossible and that, in time, the Catholic religion must die out in Ireland, he was assured that no church dignitaries would be expelled, only the regulars, who were working night and day against the Government, ... and who had no property and lived on alms, and the people were too poor to support them." [15]

In 1798, the "Year of the French," French Republicans, at the invitation of the United Irishmen, invaded Ireland in support of the short-lived Irish Republic. The Society of United Irishmen of Dublin, which was created on 30th December 1791, had as its primary object to make:

> [A]n United Society of the Irish nation; to make all Irishmen – Citizens; all Citizens - Irishmen; nothing appearing to us more natural at all times, and at this crisis of Europe more seasonable, than that those who have common interests, and common enemies, who suffer common wrongs, and lay claim to common rights, should know each other and should act together. In our opinion ignorance has been the demon of discord, which has so long deprived Irishmen, not only of the blessings of well regulated government, but even the common benefits of civil society. For a century past there has been tranquillity, but to most of our dear countrymen it has been the tranquillity of a dungeon; and if the land has lately prospered, it has been owing to the goodness of Providence, and the strong efforts of human nature resisting and overcoming the malignant influence of a miserable administration.
>
> To resist this influence, which rules by discord and embroils by system, it is vain to act as individuals or as

parties, - It becomes necessary by an union of minds,
and a knowledge of each other, to will and to act as a
nation. To know each other is to know ourselves - the
weakness of one and the strength of many. Union,
therefore, is power - it is wisdom - it must prove liberty.

Our design, therefore, in forming this Society, is to
give an example, which, when followed, must collect the
public will, and concentrate the public power into one
solid mass, the effect of which, once put into motion,
must be rapid, momentous, and consequential. [16]

Unfortunately, the "public power" the United Irishmen desired was "rapid, momentous, and consequential" **against** them, because the feared invasion of the British Isles by Napoleon Bonaparte at the turn of the eighteenth and nineteenth centuries made it treasonous to promote connections to France or other European countries controlled by him. The ideals of the United Irishmen, "for a nation united by common interests, resisting the malignant influence of a miserable administration," were not to be achieved. Many United Irishmen were executed or exiled to America and Australia, because of this fear of a European invasion. Catholic Emancipation, was not achieved until 1829, well after the defeat of Bonaparte in 1815. When Catholic Emancipation was finally made law by the Imperial Parliament of Great Britain and Ireland, most Catholics and the Catholic secular clergy felt relief. The Law removed many of the Post-Reformation Penal Laws, which forced Catholics to support the Established Church, prevented the Catholic Church from owning property, or to benefit from wills.

The religious struggles of the sixteenth, and seventeenth centuries had also resulted in a redistribution of land, wealth and political power in Ireland from the

Catholic majority to the Protestant minority. Kevin Whelan notes how this redistribution was unique to Ireland:

> *The net result was the creation of a **dominant minority** of colonists who, for the most part, subscribed to the established Church (Protestant) and a now dispossessed majority population who gave their allegiance to the Catholic Church. It was not exceptional for a ruling group to subscribe to a different denomination from the majority population, especially in colonial circumstances. What was exceptional in Ireland was that these changes led to the wholesale adoption of the existing parish network and its suite of features (church, graveyard, and glebeland) by the **minority religious group**. Backed by political, legal and military power, the colonists were enabled to totally disinherit the majority religious group. These changes, beginning on the mid-sixteenth century and concluding by the late seventeenth century, had the very unusual result of **turning the majority religion into an outcast Church, territorially rootless and without material resources.** [17]*

In his recently revised study on *The Irish Catholic Diaspora* in America McCaffrey writes:

> *In the last decade of the seventeenth and the first two decades of the eighteenth centuries, British and Irish Parliaments, purged of Catholic representatives, enacted laws abolishing the civil rights of papists and outlawing Catholic worship. . . .The Penal Laws . . . . exiled Catholic bishops, forbade the entry of priests into the country, **outlawed religious orders**, and restricted the movements of resident secular clergy. . .*

. In addition to assailing Catholic institutions and curtailing Catholic worship, the Irish Penal Laws also relegated Catholics to **subcitizen** *status. They could not vote, sit in Parliament, hold commissions in the armed forces, serve as government employees,* **establish schools,** *practice law, possess weapons,* **or purchase property.** *If the son of a Catholic landowner became a Protestant he could seize his father's land, reducing his parents to the status of life tenants.* [18]

OPPOSITION TO CATHOLIC EMANCIPATION

Although the political emancipation of Catholics was moving toward a resolution in Parliament, the "reformation movement" held that this emancipation "would lead to the collapse of the established church, the destruction of the Protestant interest in Ireland and the eventual separation of the two islands." [19] Catholic Emancipation became a prime concern of the United Parliament of England and Ireland after William Pitt raised the issue with George III on 31 January 1801. However, the King's intransigence and that of his immediate successor would keep Catholic Emancipation off the statute book for almost thirty years. [20]

With the overwhelming victory of Daniel O'Connell as the MP from County Clare in 1828, the issue of the anti-Catholic Parliamentary Oath, which required the new member to swear: "That the sacrifice of the mass, and the invocation of the blessed Virgin Mary, and the other saints, as now practiced in the church of Rome, are impious and idolatrous," forced Wellington and Pitt into a reassessment of the oath. [21] As an unseated MP from Clare, O'Connell worked for the Roman Catholic Relief Act very effectively. In a letter to E. Dwyer (6 March 1829), organizing opposition to the Franchise Restrictions Bill, he wrote:

My dear Friend,

> *We will plant a laurel tree,*
> *and we will call it liberty.*

Yes, there is much good. The Committee have unanimously decided in my favour. Peel's bill for Emancipation is good, very good; frank, direct, complete; no veto, no control, no payment of the clergy...

The second Bill is to prevent the extension of monastic institutions and to prevent the Catholic Bishops being called lords. I will stake my existence that I will run a coach-and-six three times through his Act...

The third Bill is the freehold wing, somewhat modified, that is, reduced to £10 qualification. 'This must be opposed in every shape and form.'

Although O'Connell staked his existence that he would "run a coach-and-six" through the Second Bill, the King required this restriction on religious orders before he would support the Emancipation of Catholics. Catholic Emancipation (1829), therefore, did not free members of religious orders from the old Penal Laws. Conlan writes that regulars, religious whose major superior resided outside the British Isles, had to register as agents of a foreign power under pain of a fine of £50.00 a month [about $2,000 in current value]. More drastic to the future existence of their communities, regulars were not able to have novitiates or receive novices from their houses on the continent.[22]

This had a very serious effect on the Franciscan First Order Friars Minor. By the 1850's only four friars were still alive in England. In Ireland in 1837, the number of Friars Minor numbered about 55 priests. These friars were living mainly in separate parishes throughout Ireland, dressing as secular priests in black suits. They did not live in regular Franciscan communities with their traditional brown habits.[23] James Doyle, the Bishop of Kildare and Leighlin, tried to prevent Franciscans from living alone as parish priests in his diocese. [24]

Although O'Connell, believed that these parts of the old Penal Laws would never be enforced, the brothers of the Third Order Regular in Mountbellew were directly affected by it. They were then under the obedience of Philip Anthony Lyons, O.F.M., Provincial of the Irish Province of the Friars Minor from 1828 to1831. [25] In order to survive, and at the direction of their patron, Michael Dillon Bellew, the Third Order Regular brothers requested and received permission from the Holy See in 1830 to change their obedience from the First Order Friars Minor to their local ordinary, Archbishop Oliver Kelly of Tuam.[26]

In their letter to Dr. Kelly, the seven brothers of the Mountbellew Monastery:

> *[M]ost earnestly beg leave . . . that you would be graciously pleased to take our infant Community under your Pastoral care and become our immediate superior.*
>
> *The motives which have induced us to wish to transfer our obedience to your Grace and to place ourselves under your immediate jurisdiction are as follows: viz. The relaxation of discipline in this house arising partly from the inability of the Provincial [of the Friars Minor] to attend to our spiritual wants; and on account of his very great age and corporal infirmities; and the remoteness of the place. Moreover on a late occasion we have been treated with a degree of harshness and severity which we consider unmerited and uncalled for, solely because we refused to admit*

*into our community a new member contrary to a
statute enacted last year by the Imperial Parliament of
Great Britain and Ireland; on which occasion his
Visitator and secretary the Rev. Mr. Feely menaced in
the name of the Provincial to cut us off from the Order
and that he would insert in the Public papers our
degradation.*

*From the unbounded influence which your Grace
possesses over our lay Patron Michael Dillon Bellew of
Mountbellew, we confidently anticipate that by having
your Grace as our Superior, you obtain for us a
permanent and secure tenure of our House and lands
attached to it, which tenure the aforesaid Mr. Bellew
has already refused to grant us on any other conditions.
We are also convinced that we could more effectually
and speedily extend other religious Branch Houses from
our own to different parishes in this Diocese, through
the influence of your Grace, and Parochial Clergy
among the affluent and respectable portion of their
different flocks who may be easily induced to follow the
good example of Mr. Bellew by a gratuitous grant of
land to build on.* [27]

The petition of the Mountbellew Brothers was granted
by Pope Pius VIII on 19th September, 1830. [28]

PRIMARY EDUCATION IN
NINETEENTH-CENTURY IRELAND

The "Society for Promoting the Education of the Poor
in Ireland," known as the Kildare Place Society because of
the location of its office on Kildare Place in Dublin, was
created in 1811 by a group of Dublin professional men
who believed that, "in the wake of the rebellion of 1798, the

education of the lower classes could alone correct their turbulence, and turn their minds to industry and respect for the laws". [29] The Society believed that some of the spirit underlying the attempt to create an Irish Republic in 1798 could be traced to chapbooks used in the hedge schools and to the oral traditions of the peripatetic school masters who were seen as a potential threat to the integration of English colonists and Irish subjects, because . . . . "to his little store of learning, he [the school master] generally adds some traditionary [sic] tales of his country, of a character to keep alive discontent." [30]

One of the books used by these school masters was "A Sketch of Irish History by Way of Questions and Answers for the Use of the Schools," a copy of which was found by the Commissioners of the Board of Education in a school of the Irish Christian Brothers.[31] The study of history, especially Irish history, which might promote "democracy" and a "foolish hankering after undefined liberty," was discouraged in the Kildare Place schools, as were:

> *The Greek and Roman histories* [which were seen]
> *to inculcate democracy and a foolish hankering after*
> *undefined liberty, not necessary in Ireland.* [32]

The Kildare Place Society also insisted on the reading of Protestant Scriptures, even though without note or comment; was seen as proselytism by Roman Catholics. In 1821, the "Irish National Society for Promoting the Education of the Poor" was established by Catholics as an alternative educational system, but was unable to secure state funding.[33] However, the Protestant "Dublin Auxiliary to the London Hibernian Society for Establishing Schools and Circulating the Holy Scriptures in Ireland," **was** able to receive large sums of money from the Lord Lieutenant's Fund voted annually for school buildings.[34] The purpose of the Hibernian Society is clearly stated on the title page of one of its pamphlets in the Haliday Collection of the Royal Irish Academy:

> *Their chief object is to give them* (their Catholic pupils) *Scriptural Instruction. They are required not only to read the Scriptures in the Schools, but to commit considerable parts of them to memory; for which purpose it becomes necessary that they should take the books to their respective houses.* Commissioners Report to Parliament, May, 1830.[35]

The 1830 "Report of the Dublin Auxiliary of the Society" quotes a Rev. Mr. Charles Gayer of Florence-Court, near Dublin:

> *I am gratified to state, that several Roman Catholic children, who had been removed some time ago from the School by order of their priest, have returned again, and it was a Roman Catholic to whom I gave the last premium. . . . We may indeed on other systems educate children, and make good scholars; but I assert, that without a Bible education we are only bringing them up to be proud of their knowledge, and worshippers of reason, which is, alas! the great stumbling block of this generation.* [36]

"The Irish Society for Promoting the Education of the Native Irish Through the Medium of Their Own Language," was another Protestant proselytizing society.

Created in 1827, it had as its avowed purpose the proselytism of Catholic children through the creation and funding of schools which would use Irish-language Protestant Bibles. As reported in a meeting of the society on 17 March 1830:

> [W]e hear with much pleasure, that the number of Female Scholars has increased in some of the Schools of the Society, and as their instruction in reading their native language, with the view of bringing them to the perusal of the Sacred Scriptures, has been hitherto lamentably neglected; we recommend it to the serious attention, and the zealous patronage of the Ladies who are favorable to the promotion of our object. [37]

The practice of reading the Protestant Bible in the Kildare Place schools eventually led to the withholding of the government grants which kept the Society's schools alive. In addition, the introduction of a whole range of basic readers into their schools, books which ignored Irish history and culture and promoted the ethics and values of the English Protestant minority, led many bishops, at the prompting of Propaganda Fide in Rome, to warn Catholics not to send their children to the Society's schools. Moreover, the Irish Christian Brothers withdrew their schools from the supervision of the National Commissioners because:

> "The class books of the National Board, considered in relation to Catholic teaching, do not supply to Catholic youth references to religion or moral subjects in conformity with Catholic doctrine."

By the 1840s, the Irish Christian Brothers began to publish their own texts from their North Monastery in Cork. Brother T.J. Wiseman, the principal compiler of these books has been described as "a militant nationalist," who led a group of Christian Brothers, "who reflected and exemplified a new mood of confident Catholicism, assertive Irishness and anti-English sentiment."[38]

In July of 1831, Daniel O'Connell, Member of Parliament from Clare, addressed the House of Commons with a Petition from the St. Patrick's Society of Kingstown which urged that the Kildare Place Society be replaced and that the "Public Monies be divided proportionately to the wants and numbers of the People, amongst the Guardians of each class respectively, who will thus be enabled to educate them agreeably to their conscience and religion."[39]

Persuaded by O'Connell, the Parliament established the National System of Education in Ireland which replaced the Kildare Place schools and brought about a "dramatic increase in the educational resources of the Irish Catholic Church, by creating a network of schools funded by the state but under the direct control of its clergy".[40] The founders of the National School System, who thought they had created a system in which pupils of all religions, by keeping the two scrupulously apart, would receive a **common secular education, but a separate religious education.** [author's emphasis]

The

𝕱𝖔𝖑𝖑𝖔𝖜𝖎𝖓𝖌 𝕻𝖊𝖙𝖎𝖙𝖎𝖔𝖓,

WAS PRESENTED BY

Mr. O'CONNELL,

TO THE

HOUSE OF COMMONS,

JULY, 1831.

From St. Patrick's Society, Kingstown,

AND ORDERED TO BE PRINTED:

*To the Honorable and Honorable the Knights, Citizens, and Burgesses of the
United Kingdom of Great Britain and Ireland, in Parliament assembled.*

The Petition of the undersigned, Guardians of SAINT PATRICK'S Free
Schools, KINGSTOWN.

Humbly Sheweth,

THAT it is the interest of a wise and just Legislature, to support a System of
Education, founded upon the pure dictates of conscience, and best calculated to secure the peace and happiness of the people:

That the System of Education supported by the *Legislature* in Ireland,
being Sectarian in its nature, and opposed to the wants, wishes, and religion
of seven-eights of the Irish people, has been the fruitful source of divisions,
and never can make them happy or contented.

That the subject of Education, for which memorialists contend, is one no
less in accordance with the rights of conscience, than with those principles of
civil and religious liberty, for which not only their own Prelates have so often contended, in Petitions to your Honorable House, but which so many
Members of the Legislature have zealously supported.

That Petitioners therefore beg, that your Honorable House will no longer
allow the Public Money to be misapplied, but to divide such grants, as may
be deemed right to bestow on Public Education in Ireland, proportionately
to the wants and numbers of the People, amongst the Guardians of each
class respectively, who will thus be enabled to educate them agreeably to
their conscience and religion.

That Petitioners then, implore your Honorable House, to adopt a mode of
allocating the Public Funds, towards general Education in Ireland, which instead of giving £25,000 exclusively to Kildare-place Society, a Society in
which the great mass of the People have no confidence, would allow at least
a few Thousands to the Committee of the Book Society, at 5, Essex-Bridge,
Dublin, a Society founded and patronised by the Catholic Prelates, to supply
School requisites to their flocks, and to bestow in the same manner, other
sums on other Societies, calculated to instruct those of their communion.

That whilst Petitioners thus unite with their Countrymen, in their general
request, they earnestly and respectfully solicit the attention of your Honorable
House, to the *Poor Schools of Kingstown*, now sought to be erected for the
Education of about 500 Children, under the patronage of the Catholic Clergy;
and pray, that a place which his late Majesty honored by his gracious presence, will not be dishonored by ignorance and vice; but that means will be
advanced to erect there, a Monument of Morality and Instruction, more per-
ment than that which now commemorates the Royal Visit.

And your Petitioners will pray.

DANIEL O'CONNELL'S ADDRESS TO PARLIAMENT[41]

However, the National System also introduced lesson books for use in their schools which held to the view "that knowledge and virtue were synonymous," and that such books were intended to inculcate a "preferred set of moral principles, those being either implied, or enunciated at the end of each lesson".[42] In its naïveté the Board believed these books would support a secular education. In reality, the National School System taught a Protestant-dominated secularity, which would eventually turn some bishops against the National System, chief among them was John MacHale, the Archbishop of Tuam in the West of Ireland. The efforts of Protestant evangelicals to use education as a means of proselytizing Catholic children, especially in the West of Ireland, became a concern of Irish bishops and the Holy See. In 1819, Propaganda Fide issued a warning in the form of a letter from Cardinal Fontana, the Prefect of the Propaganda, to the bishops of Ireland:

> . . . [I]nformation has reached the ears of the Sacred Congregation that Bible schools, supported by the funds of the Catholics, have been established in almost every part of Ireland, in which, under the pretext of charity, the inexperienced of both sexes, but particularly peasants and the poor, are allured by the blandishments, and even gifts of the masters, and infected with the fatal poison of depraved doctrine. It is further stated, that the directors of the schools are generally speaking, Methodists, who introduce Bibles, translated into English by the Bible Society, and propt up by errors, with the sole view of seducing the young . . . . Every possible exertion must be made, therefore, to keep the youth away from these destructive schools . . . . But for the purpose of escaping the snares of adversaries, **no plan seems more appropriate than the establishing**

of schools, wherein salutary instructions may be imparted to the poor and illiterate country persons. [43]

This letter was still being quoted almost a century later in an Irish edition of the 1918 *Code of Canon Law*. Who supplied the information to the "ears of the Sacred Congregation" is not known - but some suggest that it was John MacHale when he was teaching in Maynooth. [44]

**ARCHBISHOP JOHN MacHALE
"LION OF THE WEST" AND
PATRON OF THE BROTHERS**

Called the "Lion of the West," MacHale was a fervent Irish patriot as well as the Metropolitan of the Province of Tuam. He was the first Irish bishop since the introduction of the Penal Code to have been educated solely in Ireland.[45] Feared because of his fiery Irish nationalism, the British government tried unsuccessfully to prevent his appointment to Tuam after the death of Archbishop Oliver

Kelly in 1834. As an independent and powerful speaker and prolific writer, MacHale was one of the most important prelates in Ireland in the nineteenth century, and was very influential in the development of Catholic education for Irish emigrants in the Americas.

His fiery reputation followed him into literature when James Joyce, in his short story "Grace" in the *Dubliners*, has him shout his famous "Credo" at Vatican Council I, when, despite his opposition, the doctrine of Papal Infallibility was pronounced. Joyce also has one of his characters, "Kernan" describe MacHale: "From his sick bed Kernan remembers MacHale: 'I never saw such an eye in a man's head. It was as much to say: I have you properly taped, my lad. He had an eye like a hawk.'" [46]

Except for a few brothers in the dioceses of Meath and Elphin, MacHale was the ecclesiastical superior of most of the Franciscan Brothers of Ireland during his almost half-century in the See of Tuam (July, 1834 to November, 1881). But it was as an Irish patriot, opposed to the National School System, that MacHale may have had the greatest influence on the Franciscan Brothers and other religious communities in the West of Ireland during his 47 years as the Metropolitan of the Province of Connacht.

Born in Tubbernavine, County Mayo on 6 March 1791,[47] MacHale's native language was Irish. He was first educated in the local hedge school in Laherdane, and later at the preparatory school under the direction of Patrick Stanton in Castlelebar, County Mayo. In 1807, with a scholarship, he completed his education in St. Patrick's Seminary in Maynooth, where he excelled in theology and languages and lectured in theology while still a subdeacon. Ordained in 1814, he taught at Maynooth, first as an assistant, and later as a professor, from 1814 to 1825. The Republican uprising of 1798, and the execution of Andrew

Conroy, the priest who had baptized him, fired young MacHale's patriotism. His life-long opposition to British imperialism in Ireland, and his deep distrust of the proselytizing activities of the Protestant evangelicals in the West of Ireland were evident all his life. [48] His opposition to Paul Cullen, the Archbishop of Dublin, symbol of British "Castle" rule and ultramontane Roman interference in the Irish church, was best seen in MacHale's protection of Patrick Levelle, Fenian priest who delivered an oration, in direct defiance of Cullen's ban, at the funeral of Terence Bellew McManus in November 1861. [49]

MacHale was particularly opposed to the attempts of the evangelicals to organize schools in the West of Ireland under the aegis of the "Hibernian Bible Society" and the "Irish Church Mission," led by the Rev. Edward Nangle. In many letters to the press, under the pseudonym "Hierophilus," MacHale exhibited an ardent belief in the cause he was defending and a disdain of his opponent's point of view. His virility, erudition, and the elegance of his style of writing combined to make more effective the disconcerting savagery of his denunciations, which made him one of the best-hated and best-loved figures of his day. [50]

In 1826, he joined with James Doyle, the famous patriotic Bishop of Kildare and Leighlin (who wrote under the pseudonym "J.K.L." - "James, Kildare Leighlin"), in denouncing this proselytizing society whose schools were funded, after 1822, by the Protestant Established Church of Ireland, who were determined to save the children "from Popery". [51] When these schools were replaced by the National School System, MacHale at first permitted the National Schools, which already existed in his Archdiocese, to continue to seek funding from Dublin; but by 1839, he notified the Board that he would not permit

Protestant inspectors in the Catholic schools of the Province of Tuam. By the Autumn of that year, " he ordered the National School System to remove from the Diocese"[52]

By the mid-nineteenth century, most of the bishops of Ireland had grudgingly accepted National Schools in their dioceses. In 1859, the bishops met in Dublin and gave the National School System their support. The lone dissenting voice was again John MacHale, [53] who remained implacably opposed to National Schools until his death in 1881. "He saw the National Schools not only as dangerous to the Catholic religion but as destructive of the national culture. One rhyme, often quoted to support this view, was in a National School text for Irish schools:

> *I thank the goodness and the grace,*
> *Which on my birth has smiled,*
> *And made me in these Christian days*
> *A happy English child."* [54]

The extent of his opposition can be seen in the content, and especially the tone of a letter, he wrote to his clergy and people in the spring of 1840:

> *When we raised our warning voice against the hateful*
> *and pestilential novelty of the National Board, and*
> *when you, impressed with the force of our reasons,*
> *withdrew the children under your care from the*
> *contagion of the deadly errors solemnly circulated by*
> *that very Board, it was natural to expect that we should*
> *be assailed by unsparing vituperation. Accordingly, we*
> *were not only denounced as the foes of education,*
> *because we would not surrender its direction to the*

enemies of our creed, but we were also accused of letting in worse errors . . . . It could scarcely have been imagined that persons with any pretensions to veracity should rely for the support of their cause on the notoriously lying reports of the "Hibernian Bible Society". Yet the advocates of the National Board have appealed to such testimony; and, mortified at the exclusion of their own pernicious system, have represented the province of Tuam as teeming with the pupils of the Hibernian Society's schools.

Having now traversed every district of this extensive diocese, we have it in our power unequivocally to state, and we owe it to your zeal and piety to manifest the truth, that never, . . . has been uttered a fouler calumny. In the greater number of the parishes of this diocese such a thing as an Hibernian school is not to be found. And where, as in the case of the few wretched National Schools, fraud and menace were resorted to, to bring over the Catholic children, their efforts have been completely abortive. [55]

MacHale's solution to the National Schools was his strong support for religious teaching communities in his Province, especially the Franciscan Brothers, newly committed to him in obedience:

"In Westport, on the suppression of the National Schools, some of the old bigots of that town thought to seduce a few children to some obscure schools of the Biblicals. But, thanks to the zeal of the clergy and people, these attempts completely failed. At their joint request, we sent some of **the monks of St. Francis,** *whose pious labors had been already crowned with such success in Mount Bellew, Brooklodge, Tuam,*

Roundstone, and Clifden. No sooner had they arrived than they were hailed as a blessing by the people of Westport. The second day after the opening of the school, it was crowded with two hundred scholars. And, instead of languishing under either of the congenial systems of the Board or the Bible Society, the schools are flourishing in the freedom of a pure Catholic education."

*"Dr. McHale ceased not to exert himself in the same divine cause, till the monasteries and monastic schools already mentioned of Roundstone, Clifden, Brooklodge, and Errew, founded by himself, and to that of Mount Bellew, founded by Archbishop Kelly, he had added those of Partry, Kilkerrin, Annadown, Cummer, Achill, and Kiltullagh. All these were under the **Monks of the Third Order of St. Francis.**"* [56]

As MacHale's men, Franciscan Brothers were also opposed to National Schools wherever they had monasteries. The problem of who should control the education of Catholic children became the most significant issue for Church-State relations in Ireland for the rest of the century. MacHale's objections to the National School System secured an increasing number of supporters from among the bishops of Ireland when the National Education Board secured the exclusion of Catholic priests from schools under Protestant management. In the West of Ireland, the Protestant missionary activities, especially the "Irish Church Mission" on Achill Island, were sufficiently successful among the poverty-stricken Killala peasants in Mayo to make MacHale suspicious of all Protestant-dominated organizations. [57]

By 1850, three-fifths of the island of Achill was owned by the "Irish Church Mission" with the anti-Catholic Rev.

Edward Nangle as its chief agent. Nangle was the first Protestant in the six hundred year history of the Nangle family, who were the Catholic Barons of Navan until the eighteenth century. He had a consuming hatred of the Roman Church and his exaggerated reports of "many conversions from Popery," published in his *Achill Herald,* drew increasing financial support from Evangelical Fundamentalists in England and Ireland. Despite Nangle, MacHale was finally able, through the McLoughlins, a Catholic family of Achill Island, to buy land in Bunacurry for a monastery, school and chapel.

BUNACURRY MONASTERY IN ACHILL ISLAND, c.1900 [58]

Of all the Monastery schools of the West of Ireland, none had a more adventurous story in its creation than the Franciscan Brothers' Monastery on Achill Island, County Mayo. First settled in 1852, with Brother Michael O'Neill from Roundstone as Superior, the brothers finally established their Monastery and school at Bunacurry in 1855, and with the help of their American confreres in Brooklyn, continued to assist their very poor people. [59] In building their Monastery the brothers met with great opposition from the proselytizers. Nangle reacted by calling on the Orange Order in Belfast to come to his aid. The building stones the brothers used for their Monastery in Bunacurry, were frequently torn down at night by Nangle's men. This went on until a crowd of young men who were quarrying these stones with the brothers in Currane, came across Achill Sound and put the fear of God into the "Mission" disturbers. [60]

Strongly recommended by Rome, the "establishing of schools" became the duty of the Catholic bishops of Ireland, and they came to realize that parish schools, taught by new religious orders of men and women created for this purpose, would be a solution to their problem. This period saw the rise of the Presentation Sisters founded by Nano Nagle, who began work in Cork in 1777, and who had 28 schools in different parts of Ireland by 1830; the Presentation Brothers, founded by Blessed Edmund Rice in 1802 in Waterford and later the Irish Christian Brothers; the Franciscan Brothers founded in Dublin and Mountbellew, Galway, by Brothers Michael Dillon and Bonaventure Lee in 1818; and the Sisters of Mercy, founded by Blessed Catherine McAuley in Dublin in 1831. By the middle of the century, MacHale was able to boast that there were 13,500 Catholic children in his archdiocese receiving a Catholic education under the tutelage of these orders.

In 1850, at the Synod of Thurles, the bishops disapproved, without directly condemning, all National Schools, and demanded that all books used in them containing anything contrary to Catholic teaching should be set aside, and that books used in Catholic schools should be approved by the bishops. In 1869, Cardinal Cullen, presided over a meeting of archbishops and bishops which formally condemned the whole system of mixed-religion education, both primary and secondary. This condemnation was ratified in the same year by Pope Pius IX. This was considered by many to be "the greatest triumph of Dr. MacHale's life." [61] When MacHale died on 7 November 1881, the Brothers suffered for their loyalty to him because John MacEvilly, waiting down in Galway, who was coadjutor with right of succession to a reluctant MacHale, supported the National School System and allowed pastors to establish National Schools in towns where the Brothers already had schools.

BROTHERS AS TEACHERS IN BROOKLYN

Although it was separate from that of New York City, the system of education the Brothers found in the City of Brooklyn in 1858, combined private, church and "Common Schools". In 1805, in New York City, a private Free School Society was created to educate the many children who were not enrolled in schools attached to churches, or those conducted by masters and ladies in private homes for children who could pay for their services. Created by a dozen wealthy men, primarily Quakers who were from the highest levels of the New York gentry, the Society's purpose was to "establish a Free School in the City of New York, for the education of such poor children as do not belong to, or are not provided for, by any religious society." [62] Diane Ravitch tells us that the Society's Quaker influence made their schools strictly nonsectarian. In seeking State funding for their schools, this policy was both the Society's greatest strength and its fatal flaw. As a nonsectarian school system, the Society eventually became the public school system of the City of New York. Its nonsectarianism was in reality nonsectarian Protestantism, which repelled Catholic parents and the Catholic clergy.

Conscious of a growing Catholic immigrant population, and convinced that the Roman Catholic Church was subversive of true Americanism, Protestants caused many states to become hotbeds of Nativism. Seeing these Common Schools as reflecting the dominant Protestant ethos which permeated American culture, newly arrived Catholics could not accept sending their children to schools conducted mainly by Protestant teachers, with a Protestant viewpoint, and with religious instruction and religious exercises of a decidedly Protestant character.

American bishops, many of whom were born in Ireland, familiar with this same problem in Ireland, were very aware of the value of religious teaching communities as a solution to the similar problem in Irish education. They sought the help of their Irish colleagues when they began to create Catholic schools to protect their children from the influence of the Common Schools. Ravitch describes the Catholic response to these schools:

> *The Catholic clergy understood that they were in a Protestant society, surrounded by hostility. Their people were poor, and the Church could offer them little more than spiritual comfort . . . . All they could do was to guard their flock's faith and ward off inducements to assimilate, which they saw as Protestant attempts to destroy the Church. The clergy found that the only significant way they could protect their people from Protestant propaganda was to discourage their followers from using the schools of the Public School Society. Of about 12,000 Catholic children in the city in the late 1830s, only a few hundred were enrolled in the public schools.* [63]

ARCHBISHOP JOHN HUGHES 64

John Hughes (1794-1864) was known as "Dagger John," not only for the cross he placed before his name as a bishop, but also because of his aggressive leadership. He emerged in 1829-1830, as a defender of the Catholic Faith when, under the pseudonym, "Cranmer," he sent fake news reports on the "Catholic invasion of Pennsylvania" to *The Protestant*, a virulently anti-Catholic newspaper. In a subsequent article in a Catholic newspaper, on 3 July 1830, Hughes revealed his identity as "Cranmer," proving that he had hoodwinked the anti-Catholic Nativists. 65Hughes became the passionate and articulate defender of the Catholic position on the unacceptability of the "Protestant" Common Schools.66 By 1840, Catholics were seeking state support for "Catholic public schools" as a solution to their opposition to the Public School Society's text books and curriculum. Reflecting the views of Bishop Hughes, the editor of the newly created *Freeman's Journal* wrote:

. . . [A] state where only one religion was practiced had no problem with religion in its schools. But in a state were religious liberty prevailed, some religious group must find their principles endangered in the schools, since it was impossible for schools to teach hostile creeds simultaneously or one creed only. Yet, the elimination of all religious instruction from the schools was also unacceptable to Catholics, "for, with a Catholic, Religion forms a vital part of education" [67]

In that same year, the American bishops met in Baltimore and directly attacked the Protestantism of the Common Schools:

Since it is evident that the nature of public education...serves heresy, as well as the minds of Catholic children are little by little imbued with the false principles of the sects, we admonish pastors that they must see to the Christian and Catholic education of Catholic children with all the zeal they have, and diligently watch that no Protestant version of the Bible be used, nor hymns of the sects be sung, nor prayers be recited . . . . These efforts of the sects are to be resisted everywhere, constantly and moderately, imploring the help of those who have authority to use a fitting remedy.[68]

Most of the bishops of the United States took the recommendation seriously and sought help from religious communities in Europe. Each of the Irish communities mentioned above sent members to the United States. The Sisters of Mercy were the first, sending sisters to Pittsburgh in 1843 . The Sisters of the Presentation went to San Francisco in 1854, and the Franciscan Brothers first sent members to Louisville, Kentucky in 1846, to St. John's,

Newfoundland in 1846, to Loretto, Pennsylvania in 1847, and to Brooklyn in 1858. Three Presentation Brothers went from Cork in Ireland to Pittsburgh in 1845, but tragedy struck the young community when, according to one story, two were killed by lightning and the third returned to Ireland; or, in another version of their history, one was killed by lightening, the second was drowned, and the third, "losing heart," either became an Augustinian or returned to Ireland. [69]

The Congregation of Christian Brothers (Irish Christian Brothers), arrived later in the United States in the last century, when they sent brothers to New York City in 1906. Many other communities sent religious to America from all over Europe - with 44 different congregations of women arriving between 1829 and 1884. From 1841 to 1884, eleven communities of brothers arrived in the United States. [70]

Bishop Hughes had succeeded in obtaining a number of religious communities to teach in the Diocese of New York. The Jesuits took charge of St. John's College, later to be Fordham University, and the Sisters of Charity had charge of teaching in a few elementary schools.

His efforts to have brothers to teach the boys, however, was not immediately successful because he seemed not to be willing to pay them a suitable wage. In a letter to Father Sorin, the President of Notre Dame, he writes: "Nothing can be more reasonable than that the priest requiring a Brother, should pay his traveling expenses, and I will not say forty dollars, which I think too little, but fifty dollars a year for clothing." [71] However, Bishop Hughes' fifty dollars a year was not considered "a sufficient salary" by the De La Salle Christian Brothers who recalled two Brothers who had been sent to New York in 1847 by Brother Philippe, the Superior General [72].

The Franciscan Brothers opened St. Francis Academy in 1859 at 300 Baltic Street in the Red Hook section of Brooklyn. It was a three-story building which had been a Protestant church and a public school. The brothers converted it into a private academy and lived in its basement until April of 1862, when they were able to purchase a house at 41 Butler Street. St. Francis College later evolved from this academy and became an educational institution which was granted the ability to award the Bachelor of Arts degree by the University of the State of New York in 1884. [73]

Notes

[1] Patrick Quinn, T.O.R., "The Third Order Regular of St. Francis in Ireland," *ANALECTA TOR*: XXIV/153   (1993), pp. 247-263. (Franciscan friaries were known as "monasteries" throughout the West of Ireland).

[2] *Ibid.*, p. 253.

[3] Michael J. Higgins, T.O.R., "History of the Province of the Most Sacred Heart of Jesus, U.S.A.," *ANALECTA, TOR*: XXV/155, (1994), pp. 325-354, on p. 327..

[4] Robin Flower, *The Irish Tradition*, Lilliput Press, Dublin, 1994, pp. 11-12.

[5] S.J. Connolly, *Priests and People in Pre-Famine Ireland, 1780-1845*, St. Martin's Press, New York, 1982, p. 82.

[6] Daniel Corkery. *The Hidden Ireland: A Study of Gaelic Munster in the Eighteenth Century*, Gill and Macmillan, Dublin, 1934, chapter on the "Bardic Schools," pp. 68-94.

[7] P. J. Dowling, *The Hedge Schools of Ireland*, Mercier Press, Dublin, 1968, p. 7.

[8] Eugene O'Curry, M.R.I.A., *On the Manners and Customs of the Ancient Irish, a Series of Lectures*, 3 volumes, Williams and Norgate, London;

W.B. Kelly, Dublin; and Scribner, New York, 1873.

9 *Freeman's Journal and Catholic Register,* 23 August, 1862.

10 J.B. Nolan, "Eugene O'Curry - *Anima Candida"*, *Clare Champion Newspaper,* January, 1991.

11 Corkery., p. 39.

12 Charles Ivar McGrath. "Securing the Protestant interest: the origins and purpose of the penal laws of 1695," *Irish Historical Studies,* Vol. 30, no. 117 (May 1996), pp. 25-46.

13 *All popish archbishops, bishops, vicars general, deans, Jesuits, monks, friars and all other regular popish clergy and all Papists exercising ecclesiastical jurisdiction, shall depart out of this kingdom before the 1st of May, 1698. If any of the said ecclesiastical persons shall be at any time after the said 1st of May, 1698, within the kingdom, they and every one of them shall suffer imprisonment, until he or they shall be transported beyond the seas; and if any person so transported shall return again into this kingdom, they and every of them shall be guilty of high treason, and suffer and forfeit as in cases of high treason (i.e. death and forfeiture of goods).* Maureen Wall, *The Penal Laws, 1691-1769,* Dublin Historical Society, 1976, pp. 11-12.

14 *[B]y the end of 1698, 383 members of religious orders were in Paris or its environs who had been banished from Ireland: 118 Dominicans, 214 Franciscans, 26 Augustinians, 12 Capuchins, 5 Jesuits, 5 Canons Regular, and 3 Carmelites.* Wall, *The Penal Laws,* pp. 1-12.

15 *Ibid.,* p. 13.

16 "Society of United Irishmen of Dublin, "Circular Letter adopted at a Meeting of the Society reported by the Committee of Correspondence, Friday, 30th December, 1791, Royal Irish Academy, Haliday Pamphlet Collection, 1791, pp 276-277. [The Haliday Pamphlet Collection in the Royal Irish Academy is a remarkable treasure of about 30,000 18th and 19th century pamphlets collected by Charles Haliday and donated by his widow in 1855. Organized and bound by the year of publication, these remarkable sources of contemporary history are accessed by a comprehensive index].

17 Kevin Whelan, "The Catholic Parish, the Catholic Chapel, and Village Development in Ireland," *Irish Geography,* Vol. 16, 1983, pp. 1-2.

18 Lawrence J. McCaffrey, *The Irish Catholic Diaspora in America*, Catholic University of America Press, 1997, pp. 24-25

19 Irene Whelan, "Evangelical Religion and the Polarization of Protestant-Catholic Relations in Ireland, 1780-1840," Doctoral dissertation, University of Wisconsin-Madison, 1994, p. 423.

20 *Irish Historical Documents Since 1800*, edited by Alan O'Day and John Stevenson, Gill and Macmillan, 1992, p. 10

21 *Ibid.*, pp. 32-33

22 Patrick Conlan, O.F.M., *Franciscan Ireland*, Lilliput Press, Mullingar, Ireland, 1988, pp. 56- 63.

23 *Ibid.*, pp. 56-57.

24 Thomas McGrath, *Religious Renewal and Reform in the Pastoral Ministry of Bishop James Doyle, of Kildare and Leighlin, 1786 - 1834*, Four Courts Press, Dublin, 1999, pp. 100-102.

25 *Ibid.*, p. 156.

26 PFA, *Lettere e Decreti* . . . , 1830, Vol. 311, Fol. 863v.

27 Letter of Franciscan Brothers to Archbishop Oliver Kelly, 5 June 1830, FBA, Mountbellew, Ireland.

28 *The Rule of the Regular Third Order of Our Holy Father Saint Francis . . . .* Dublin. 1877. P. 10.

29 Eileen T. Whelan, "Primary School Readers in the Nineteenth Century," *Oideas*, Vol. 19, (1977), pp. 39-50, p. 40.

30 Whelan, p. 39.

31 Dowling, p. 68.

32 *Ibid.*

33 McGrath, Thomas G. "Archbishop Slattery and the Episcopal Controversy on Irish National Education, 1838-1841," *Archivum Hibernicam*, Vol. 39, pp. 13-31, 1984, p. 14.

34 Dowling, p. 31.

35 "The Third Annual Report of the Dublin Auxiliary to the London Hibernian Society for Establishing Schools, and Circulating the Holy Scriptures in Ireland", Dublin, M. Goodwin, 29, Denmark-Street,

1830, title page.

36 "Third Annual . . . . " , 1830, p. 16.

37 "Twelfth Report of the Irish Society, for Promoting The Education of the Native Irish Through the Medium of Their Native Language, For the Year Ending 17th March, 1830, with an Appendix," Dublin, M. Goodwin, 29, Denmark-Street, 1830, p. 4, [Haliday Pamphlet Collection, Royal Irish Academy, 1830].

38 Lorcan Walsh, "The Social, Political, and Economic Content of Nineteenth Century Schoolbooks," *Oideas*, Vol. 33, (1988), p. 40.

39 *Ibid.*

40 Connolly, p. 86

41 "The Following Petition. . . .", [Address of Daniel O'Connell to the House of Commons, July, 1831, Haliday Pamphlet Collection (HDC), Royal Irish Academy, 1831].

42 Whelan, p. 44.

43 *Ibid.*

44 Desmond J. Keenan., *The Catholic Church in Nineteenth-Century Ireland: a Sociological Study,* Gill and Macmillan, 1983, p. 175.

45 Hilary Andrews, *The Lion of the West, a Biography of John MacHale,* Veritas, Dublin, 2001, p. 7

46 James Joyce, *Dubliners,* Viking edition, 1961, pp. 169-170.

47 Early information about MacHale's life comes mostly from Bernard O'Reilly, *The Life and Times of John MacHale,* (1890) and Ulick Bourke, *The Life and Times of the Most Reverend John MacHale,* (1883). O'Reilly gives the date of 1791 for MacHale's birth, but Bourke, who was a family friend, gives 1789. (Andrews, p. 19).

48 Andrews, p. 14.

49 Liam Bane, " Bishop John MacEvilly and the Catholic Church in Late Nineteenth Century Galway," in *Galway: History and Society, Interdisciplinary Essays on the History of an Irish County,* Gerard Moran, Ed., Geography Publications, Dublin, 1996, p. 432.

50 Nuala Costello, *John MacHale, Archbishop of Tuam,* Phoenix Pub. Co., Dublin, 1938, pp. 22-23

51 McGrath, ...*Bishop James Doyle*, pp. 140-147.

52 Bernard Mac Uaid, O.S.F., "The Brothers of the Third Order Regular in the Diocese of Tuam," *ANALECTA, TOR*, XVI/ 137, (1983), pp. 334-409, p. 344.

53 Liam Bane, *The Bishop in Politics - Loyal Friend, Bitter Foe - Life and Career of John MacEvilly*, Westport Historical Society, 1993, p. 84.

54 Andrews, p. 79.

55 Bernard O'Reilly. *John McHale, Archbishop of Tuam: His Life, Times, and Correspondence*, New York, 1890, pp. 470-473.

56 O'Reilly, pp. 472-473.

57 *New Catholic Encyclopedia*, Vol VII, p. 623.

58 Brian M. Walker, Art O'Broin, Sean McMahon, *Faces of Ireland, 1875-1925*, Amaryllis Press, 1984, (Connacht, Book Two), p. 17.

59 Loans were made to the Achill Monastery by St. Francis Monastery. "Monastery and Fund Accounts Book, 1872-1894," reveal that from 1875 to 1880, $1,800 was loaned to the Achill Monastery in Bunacurry, which was repaid on 18 August 1880.

60 Bernardine Cowan, O.S.F. " The Story of the Irish Franciscan Brothers," Manuscript, Mountbellew Monastery, 1955, pp. 23-24.

61 Costello, *John MacHale*, pp. 74-75.

62 Diane Ravitch. *The Great School Wars: New York City, 1805-1973: A History of the Public Schools as Battlefields of Social Change*, Basic Books, 1994, pp. 8-9.

63 *Ibid.*, pp. 31-32.

64 Thomas J. Shelley, *The History of the Archdiocese of New York*, Editions du Signe, Strasbourg, 1999, p. 66.

65 Richard Shaw, *Dagger John, The Unquiet Life and Times of Archbishop John Hughes of New York*, Paulist Press, New York, 1977, pp. 63-70.

66 *Ibid.*, pp. 139-175.

67 Ravitch, p. 45.

68 *Ibid.*

[69] John Finbarr Prior, C.F.C., "Presentation Brothers, Pittsburgh, First American Experience 1845-1848," *Christian Brothers' Educational Record,* 1987, pp. 193-211.

[70] Harold A. Buetow. *Of Singular Benefit: The Story of Catholic Education in the United States.* Macmillan, London, 1970, p. 115.

[71] Hughes to Sorin, 21 April 1844, Archives of the Archdiocese of New York.

[72] An 1840 letter of Bishop Bouvier of Le Mans, France to Pope Gregory XVI, stating that the Christian Brothers require $120 annually for each Brother before they will accept a school, in Angelus Gabriel, F.S.C., *The Christian Brothers in the United States, 1848-1948,* Declan X. McMullen, New York, 1948, p. 56.

[73] Roger Nagle, O.S.F., "Historical Growth and Development of the Franciscan Brothers of Brooklyn," M.A. Thesis, St. John's University, 1943, p. 70.

CHAPTER FOUR

SAINT FRANCIS ACADEMY AND COLLEGE

The creation of St. Francis Academy and College in the nineteenth century and the evolution of their separate legal and physical developments in the twentieth century, is a complex story involving Franciscan Brothers, five bishops, and "The St. Francis Monastery of the City of Brooklyn," the legal corporation of the Community. When John McMahon, Vincent Hayes and the eight other young men emigrated to Brooklyn in 1858, they found that the Orphan Asylum to which they had been assigned was unsuitable as a monastery and novitiate .

In a Minute Book of the Congregation, John McMahon, who was the first Superior and had been a Novice Master in Ireland, found that:

> the training of postulants and novices for the new foundation was impossible in the Orphan Asylum, [and] secured permission from the Right Reverend Bishop of Brooklyn to purchase a building at 300 Baltic Street between Smith and Court Streets as early as 1859. This building was used as a residence and St. Francis Academy. Owing to the increase of novices and resident students, another building was purchased in 1860 [1862], on Butler Street, opposite and adjoining the Baltic Street property. From this small beginning grew the present flourishing Institute known as the Franciscan Brothers of the Diocese of Brooklyn. [1]

It was actually John Loughlin who bought the three-story building at 300 Baltic Street in St. Paul's Parish on 1 September 1859, which had served as a Protestant church and public school. He assigned it to the brothers for use as a school and residence, and later in that same month, "with the aid of Martin St. Leger, a gentleman of scholarly attainment," St. Francis Academy, with two brothers and three lay men, was opened as the first Catholic private academy in the Diocese of Brooklyn. [2] Shortly after the brothers arrived from Ireland, Bishop John Loughlin appointed his friend, Martin St. Leger, to attend to their need for housing. An astute businessman and "college-trained gentleman, " it was actually St. Leger who secured the building at 300 Baltic Street in the name of the Bishop. Impressed by the vigor and virtue of the pioneer brothers, he shared their academic goals and joined the young community in 1859. Somewhere between 47 and 54 years of age, St. Leger was received on 15 August 1860, and professed on 6 January 1862, taking the name Brother Paul. He began his postulancy in the Orphan Asylum, but moved to the Academy on Baltic Street in 1860, as a novice. Brother Paul taught Latin and was known as the "smartest man in the faculty" according to Dr. John Greene, a former student. Paul St. Leger, known as "little Paul," to distinguish him from Brother Paul Hill, "big Paul," served the congregation in many capacities. He was principal of St. Michael's School in Flushing which opened in 1864, and later was Dean and President of St. Francis College. He served as Treasurer General, General Consultor, and Assistant Superior General of the Congregation. From 1863 to 1866 and from 1875 to 1876, he was the Superior General of the Community. A pioneer in Catholic education, Paul St. Leger helped organize the curriculum for St. Francis Academy, which was the first private Catholic secondary school in Brooklyn. As a teacher of the Classics, he prepared many men for the priesthood. He died after a short illness on 29 September 1882.

A graphic "Deed Transferral Map" [3] showing the plots of land on Baltic and Butler Streets and dates of transferrals, recorded in the Brooklyn Hall of Records, was drawn up when the last piece of Butler Street property was bought by St. Francis Monastery in 1937. This map corrects the above dates and shows that John Loughlin actually purchased the Baltic Street building for the young community, through the agency of a Peter Kean, on 11 September 1859. The same document shows that the first building the brothers themselves bought, at 41 Butler Street, was to be the address of St. Francis Monastery and College for over a century.

While the brothers converted the "damp cellar" of their Baltic Street building into a residence, the floors above were used as the academy for primary and secondary level students.[4] The brothers lived in the basement of the Academy from 1859 to 1862, until a house was purchased by John McMahon from J. W. Dearing, on Butler Street on 8 March 1862.[5] This private house at 41 Butler Street, which was directly behind their Baltic Street academy, would be the first of five buildings to eventually house "The St. Francis Monastery of the City of Brooklyn, New York". This title was used by the Franciscan Brothers for their incorporation by the New York State Legislature on 2 June 1868 as a "membership corporation" under Chapter 851 of the Laws of 1868. When this State Charter was granted to the Brothers, giving them legal incorporation, John Loughlin deeded the Baltic Street property to the Community on 27 October 1868. [6]

ST. FRANCIS MONASTERY AND COLLEGE BUILDINGS (1880)

SAINT FRANCIS MONASTERY [7]

In a little over a quarter-century, the small community had increased from six to seventy brothers with most of them emigrating from the West of Ireland. In an article in *The Brooklyn Citizen* newspaper in 1886, St. Francis College's origins as St. Francis Academy are recounted: [8]

> *When the Franciscans first came to Brooklyn they had charge of the old Male Orphan Asylum, which was burned down in 1862, but in October, 1859, they established the college in Baltic Street, beginning with thirty scholars and six Brothers. Now there are 406 students, of which 100 are boarders, and a community of 70 Brothers. It was first called Saint Francis Academy, and as such was incorporated in 1868; in 1884, however, it was chartered as a regular college, authorized to confer degrees. . . . The college is one of the largest institutions of its class in the city, and is*

well located, with spacious surroundings. It contains sixteen classrooms, two study halls, a museum, music rooms, gymnasium, and all the appliances of a modern school. It has always received a large patronage from Brooklynites, and a number of our well-known citizens were graduated from its walls. It has this year sent a large representation of candidates for the priesthood to the Seminary at Emmitsburg, Maryland. [9]

Two years after the Bishop deeded the school to the community, a school retreat for the students is reported at length in *The Brooklyn Catholic:*

Religious Exercises at St. Francis Academy, Baltic Street

The union of religion with secular education is a grand characteristic of our Catholic schools. We have always insisted on the necessity of this and endeavored to impress our people with its importance. . . . Our youth must always be educated, not alone socially, but religiously as well, if we want them to be not alone good members of the community, but good Christians besides. . . .

We are really glad to place before our people a notice of religious services [a school retreat] *which took place last week at the above institution. They commenced on Tuesday, the 7th inst., and terminated on the following Friday. They were directed by the very estimable and zealous missionary, Rev. Anacletus Roccagorga, O.S.F., of Sullivan St., New York.* [St. Anthony's Church directed by First Order Friar Minor Franciscans]. *The priest preached twice each day to the pupils. His discourses were eloquent and soul stirring, still suited to the youthful capacities of his hearers.*

The Brooklyn Catholic reporter continues his article, describing what may have been the First Communions of fifty of the boys of the Academy:

> *One of the floors of the Academy served as a temporary chapel in which an altar was tastefully put up for the occasion. The lights were pleasantly arranged; and a profusion of flowers made their temporary abode of the Holy of Holies smile like an Eden. Two hundred boys approached the holy Table - fifty of them held candles in their hands; a ceremony usually observed by those who for the first time are going to receive their Lord.*
>
> *The concluding sermon was on heaven. The good Father reminded the children that they were then truly the heirs of heaven - in fact, that they had a heaven on earth. He exhorted them to continue to be true to the good resolutions they had made. And we have no doubt that the impression made on their young minds will long continue; and in years to come their memory will flutter back with pleasure to them as the happiest event of their lives.* [10]

About five years later, another newspaper records a graduation exercise held by the College at the old Academy of Music on Montaque Street:

> *Bishop Loughlin conferred the degrees and diplomas, and the "Saint Francis College Grand March" was played by the college orchestra. Five Bachelor of Arts and five Master of Arts degrees were awarded, while twelve students received commercial diplomas. Awards in excellence were presented in each academic area and the old Academy was crowded with standees in the aisles, exuding "enthusiasm warmer than the weather."* [11]

From 1885 to 1897 about 130 students were graduated from St. Francis College. Eighty-six of these were from Brooklyn, others were from New York, New Jersey, Rhode Island, New Hampshire, Connecticut, Maine, Los Angeles, and even students from Latin America, Italy and Ireland. Of this number, about one-third became priests and others entered various religious communities. In 1898, eight students were awarded the Bachelor of Arts degree, and three received a Master of Arts degree. [12]

The four-year course of instruction at the College included twenty-six hours per week in each year, with a recommendation that students study five hours a day outside of class time. The tuition in 1897 was $15.00 per quarter for day students and $250.00 annual board and tuition for resident students. Rules for resident students were somewhat monastic:

Students are obliged to accompany prefects on school days and other days appointed to Prospect Park or some other suburban resort.

Students are not allowed to leave the premises without permission.

Parents or guardians are permitted to visit the first Sunday of each month from 2 to 5.

The use of tobacco is strictly forbidden as injurious to the health of youth.

All letters written by students must be submitted for inspection.

Every communication addressed to them shall be opened before they receive it.

Resident students, whose families must have had some means, were asked to bring "necessary supplies," which were as follows:

6 dress shirts, 6 undershirts, 6 pr stockings, 6 pr. drawers, 3 suits of clothes, 3 pr. shoes, 6 towels, 6 napkins, knife, fork, spoon, goblet, with the name on each --hair brush, tooth brush, shoe polish, and soap. [13]

Milo F. McDonald, a New York City high school principal, remembered his days at the old St. Francis Academy:

My mind is filled with pleasant recollections of the years I spent with the Franciscan Brothers. At "Old St. Francis" I entered the primary class. I can vividly recall the teacher of this class, Brother Matthew [Flynn], who was one of the most gentle men I have ever met. His patience, as I view it through the long vista of years, was remarkable. He was an ideal teacher of children and did much to help all the boys in the class in achieving a firm grasp upon the fundamentals of a good education.

I have seen many teachers in my experience, but I have never met one superior in his appreciation of the needs of adolescent boys than was Brother Cosmas [Burns]. He was a man, every inch of him. I loved him then and I love him now. Combined with my hope of the hereafter is the thought that I may have the opportunity of meeting him face to face and of talking over the pleasant times we enjoyed together at "Old St. Francis".[14]

**BROTHER DAVID McPARTLAND AND
THE 1901 ST FRANCIS ACADEMY VIOLIN ORCHESTRA**

In addition to graduation exercises at the Old Academy of Music, public exhibitions took place annually to show off the talents and academic abilities of the St. Francis Academy boys, who were in those days considered the best public speakers in the city. [15] At the end of each school year, these public examinations were advertised in the newspapers and attracted large audiences of parents, relatives and friends who cheered their boys when they successfully answered the difficult questions posed by members of the audience. Brothers from other Franciscan Brothers' schools marched their pupils to these exhibitions to help cheer on the St. Francis boys. A vivid interest in theatricals was also found in the students at St. Francis because they were able to present their plays at the Old Academy of Music which could accommodate a larger audience than was possible within the school. [16]

BROTHER LOUIS AND THE RESIDENT STUDENTS

St. Francis Academy and College also served about one hundred resident students who lived at the school on Baltic Street. These young men and boys were supervised by brothers assigned to their care who saw that they were well fed in their own Student Dining Room with food from the Monastery kitchen. Evidence from the Franciscan Brothers' Archives suggests that Brother Louis Johnson was one of the brothers assigned to this task. From the Brothers' Necrology we read the brief account of his religious life:

> *Brother Louis Johnson, a native of Ireland, entered St. Francis Monastery on July 18, 1892, and was admitted to the Habit on September 8th that year. After his profession, October 4, 1893, Brother Louis filled many domestic assignments in the Monastery. His death occurred on November 19, 1910.* [17]

In recent years, however, more has been learned about Brother Louis. A relative of Brother Louis informed the community that Bro. Louis was born George Johnston [not Johnson, as he spelled his name], the son of George Johnston and Anne McManus Johnston, both of County Fermanagh in Ireland. He remembers that it was a family legend that Bro. Louis was so loved by the boys he cared for, and that they cried "on his coffin".[18] Research in the account books of the Monastery amplifies the brief obituary note in the Brothers' Necrology, that he "filled many domestic assignments in the Monastery," and suggests that Brother Louis may have been a cook who made apple pies for the boys he cared for. [19]

To escape the heat of the Summer the brothers rented a summer cottage in Rockaway Beach in 1887.[20] In 1888, the Chalmer's Estate, on the North shore of Centerport Harbor in Huntington, was purchased by the Community. The hotel on the property, directly on the cool shores of Centerport Harbor, suited their need to offer the brothers a pleasant place to spend the Summer away from the hot city. A number of the boarding students at the Academy and College, who lived a distance from Brooklyn, first went to Centerport in 1889. Young men from Havana, Cuba, the Yucatan, Mexico, and parts of the United States, distant from Brooklyn, did not return to their homes during the Summer, but went with the brothers to Centerport. [21]

The estate of Mrs. Susan Martin was purchased in 1901 to increase the property of the brothers. Named Alvernia, after the rural retreat of St. Francis above Assisi, this twenty-four acre property is still located on the North Shore of Long Island on Centerport Harbor.[22] As the oldest Catholic camp in the United States, Camp Alvernia has served the youth of Brooklyn, Long Island and New York City for the last one hundred and twenty years. As a Summer boarding camp for boys from the brothers' schools in the city, Alvernia was created when cottages were built to replace the tents first used for the academy and college boarders.

BROTHERS' MONASTERY--CENTERPORT, LONG ISLAND

"OUR MODESTY DESERVES CENSURE FOR NOT MAKING OUR NEEDS KNOWN LONG AGO" 1923 FUND RAISING DRIVE FOR A NEW MONASTERY AND COLLEGE

Because of the surge of new students after "the Great War"(World War I), when the enrollment increased from 500 to 900 students, it became evident that the building used by St. Francis Academy and College on Baltic Street, and St. Francis Monastery at 41 Butler Street, had long since served their purpose. A "Great Drive" was begun by the Brothers in 1923 to raise between $750,000 and $1,000,000 dollars to replace these aged buildings.

Brother David McPartland's address to the Drive Committee, as it began its work to raise this money for new buildings, emphasized that "the old buildings are crowded to the doors". As Superior General of the Community and President of the College, he thanked the St. Francis College Drive Committee at its first meeting and succinctly stated the reasons for the campaign.

> It is the oldest Catholic institution for higher education on Long Island. Its good work, among the youth of the City of Brooklyn, commenced three years before Abraham Lincoln was elected President of the United States. And during all the years that have intervened since the days of Lincoln, St. Francis College has made no special appeal for money to the people of Brooklyn.
>
> It will not be denied that we have been very modest, but I think our modesty deserves censure for not making our needs known long ago. The antiquated buildings on Butler and Baltic streets, are so old that some people claim they were built before Washington fought the Battle of Long Island.

These buildings have, long ago, served their purpose. They are together inadequate for the educational needs of the present time. . . . Now we are forced to tell the people that the old buildings are crowded to the doors, and in addition to that, about 150 high school boys are crowded into the Brothers' study halls in the Monastery Building.

With compliments to Thomas E. Molloy, [23] the young, newly appointed Bishop of the Brooklyn Diocese, who had been a student of the College, Brother David closed his remarks:

The moment the Brothers revealed this condition to our Rt. Rev. Bishop, plans were commenced to remedy it. The love for higher education, together with the youth and energy of our Rt. Rev. Bishop give life and energy to the movement which brings us together today.

I again thank, from my heart, all who are determined to listen to the call which is sixty-five years in coming and at last will reach the people of Long Island. These buildings have, long ago, served their purpose. They are altogether inadequate for the educational needs of the present time. . . . Now we are forced to tell the people that the old buildings are crowded to the doors, and in addition to that, about 150 high school boys are crowded into the Brothers' study halls in the Monastery Building. [24]

Two beautiful buildings for the Monastery and College, planned by the architect, J. Sarsfield Kennedy, would have cost between $750,000 and $1,000,000 dollars. Many alumni and friends of the brothers were very generous in support of the "Great Drive," but the goal of $1,000,000 was not achieved.

The Board requested a financial report from the St. Francis College Building Fund and learned that as of 20 October 1923, only $92,296.30 had been raised, and that $23,259.65 was still outstanding in pledges. [25] The St. Francis Monastery Board considered Kennedy's plan to be excessive and decided to use another architect. The alarm of the brothers is revealed when the consultors of the Community considered the expenses of the "Headquarters of the Great Drive" to be too high, [26] and the Board engaged the architect, Philip McGovern, to submit tentative plans for a new College building. [27] That decision, however, would cost the Monastery a total of $11,213.54 for Kennedy's plans and specifications. [28]

J. SARSFIELD KENNEDY'S DESIGN
OF THE PROPOSED
SAINT FRANCIS COLLEGE AND MONASTERY--1923[29]

The final amount raised came to almost $650,000, which the Community used to complete a much smaller St. Francis College building at 35 Butler Street in 1926, down the street near the old St. Francis Monastery at 41 Butler Street. The new college building ,based on architect Philip McGovern's plan for a grammar school, had nine classrooms, a small library, limited laboratory classrooms and an all-purpose gymnasium, so small that one wall served as the boundary line of the basketball court. [30]

THE NEW SAINT FRANCIS COLLEGE
35 BUTLER STREET - 1926

The Brothers' "modesty" still continued, because a new Monastery, which many friends and alumni felt was more needed than the College, was never built. Brothers were often reminded by donors that a new residence for the Brothers had been part of their donations for the campaign. Bishop Molloy also mentioned the need for "proper housing for the Brothers" in his distinctive and fulsome letter to Brother David McPartland, when he approved and blessed the "Great Drive."

MOST REVEREND THOMAS E. MOLLOY
THE YOUTHFUL BISHOP OF BROOKLYN - 1922

BISHOP'S HOUSE
367 CLERMONT AVENUE
BROOKLYN, N.Y.

October 1st, 1923 [31]

V. Rev. Brother David, O.S.F.
President, St. Francis College,
Brooklyn, New York

Very Reverend dear Brother David:

The announcement of your coming campaign for funds to provide suitable and adequate facilities for the more efficient and effective fulfillment of your noble work of Christian education merits indeed the considerable attention of the Catholic clergy and laity of the diocese of Brooklyn.

For more than sixty years the Brothers of St. Francis have given unstintingly and unselfishly their time, talents, energies, yea even their very lives, for the mental and moral training of boys and young men. It is impossible to estimate the vast amount of good your pious, zealous, capable religious confreres have accomplished during such a long period for the betterment of the individual, for the welfare of society and for the advancement of the Kingdom of God here in our midst.

*We all readily recognize the fact that you, your associates and predecessors have achieved these notable and beneficent results even while hindered and hampered by many severe limitations. **I refer particularly to the lack of proper housing accommodations for the Brothers and to the inadequate equipment for the performance of their religious and professional duties.***

The remarkable growth, moreover, in the size of the student body, especially in recent years, has rendered your labors very trying and burdensome since you have not been able to provide the required classroom and laboratory space for this increased enrollment.

In a spirit of patient self-denial, however, you have submitted to these conditions until this moment when you undoubtedly feel that the quality of your work will suffer and the high standards of your respected institution of learning will not be maintained unless you extend your present building and improve your educational equipment.

To relieve your pressing needs in this regard, you are about to open your campaign for financial assistance. I wish to assure you that in recognition of the splendid services of the Brothers of St. Francis as religious teachers and professional educators I shall heartily recommend your appeal to the priests and people of the diocese and I shall express the hope that your efforts in this worthy undertaking will realize the fullest measure of success so that dear old St. Francis College may long continue its useful, fruitful, blessed career as an agency of intellectual culture and moral righteousness.

Faithfully yours in Christ,
+THOMAS E. MOLLOY
Bishop of Brooklyn

During the next thirty years "plans were formulated and programs initiated to provide for further expansion of the College, as requirements for Middle States accreditation and increased enrollment outgrew the boundaries of the Butler Street building." As early as 1935, the Board of Trustees of the college was made aware of these needs. Among the recommendations was the addition of a fourth floor to the new building at 35 Butler Street in order to create expanded library space, lecture and science demonstration rooms.

However, growth was not to be in the buildings on Baltic and Butlers Streets.[32] In the late 1950s, classes were held in rented space at 16 Court Street, while the sciences still remained at Butler Street. In 1963, St. Francis College finally left 35 Butler Street and relocated in two renovated Brooklyn Union Gas buildings at 180 Remsen Street. With the completion of a Science Building on Remsen Street, an Olympic-size swimming pool and Gymnasium and a Faculty Residence on Joralemon Street for over forty brothers, five new buildings now housed St. Francis College in Brooklyn Heights.

When the new Faculty Residence was completed in 1966, the Brothers of St. Francis College, after more than a century (1858-1966), finally had "proper housing accommodations," which Bishop Molloy had recommended over forty years earlier in 1923. "The St. Francis Monastery" ceded the property to the College, which was able to sell the Butler/Baltic Street property to New York City, returning it to its original identity as a Public School. [33]

ST. FRANCIS PREPARATORY SCHOOL
MOVES FROM BALTIC STREET

Bernard Costa, OSF, who became the principal of St. Francis Prep in 1944, decided to remove the noisome outhouse facility located in a shed in the school yard near Baltic Street and install a brand new bathroom with sinks and showers near the back of the main building. This was to be located to the left of the entrance behind the Arbor, in the oldest part of the school dating from about 1840, when it was a Presbyterian church and public school. This part of the school had been the "damp cellar" the brothers lived in from 1859 to 1862, before they purchased a residence at 41 Butler Street in March of 1862. When the plumbers were working on the installation in 1949, they pulled the wooden paneling off the walls and discovered the building to be without a foundation. Experts were brought in and the decision was made to underpin the building and tie the outside walls which were buckling. The opening of school was delayed for two weeks while the necessary work was done. The dangerous condition of the building required that the Prep be moved to another location, and in 1952, after the new Prep Friary was completed, St. Francis Prep relocated to St. Vincent de Paul's school in North Sixth Street in Williamsburgh. [34]

**PROPOSED NEW MONASTERY AT
41 BUTLER STREET**[35]

ST. FRANCIS PREP MOVES TO FRESH MEADOWS

The Diocese of Brooklyn built five new diocesan high schools in the 1960s. One of these was Bishop Reilly Memorial High School at 6100 Francis Lewis Boulevard, Fresh Meadows, which was a co-institutional high school with almost 3,000 young men and women educated in separate wings who shared the library, the auditorium, the gymnasium and the cafeteria, the common rooms of the school. The Henry Hald Association, the educational corporation of the Brooklyn Diocese, administered these five new schools as well as the three diocesan high schools already in existence.

ST. FRANCIS PREP IN FRESH MEADOWS

When the finances of these diocesan high schools became a pressing burden on the diocese in 1971, Francis J. Mugavero, the Ordinary of the Brooklyn diocese, called on some of the experts in the diocese to assist him in solving the problem of central administration of these schools. A pressing concern of the diocesan administrators was the unionization of the increasing number of lay teachers caused by the declining numbers of religious teachers. One of the solutions suggested to the bishop was to offer the schools to the religious communities to own and administer in hopes that they might be able to assign more religious teachers if the schools were their own. The Franciscan Brothers, after discussion among themselves about which school to take, decided to request Bishop Reilly Memorial High School. St. Francis Preparatory School moved to Fresh Meadows and assumed the responsibility of this now co-educational institution in 1974, which was the first time the brothers taught young ladies.

In 1983-4, the first year the United States Department of Education surveyed private schools across the nation, St. Francis Preparatory School was selected as an outstanding school worthy of national recognition. From St. Francis Academy with two brothers, three lay men and about 100 students in 1859, the Prep' enrollment in 2000, was 2,739 students. In that same year, St. Francis Prep students were winners of over $16 million in academic scholarships and over 98% of them pursued higher education in college.

Notes

1 "Council Minutes and General Chapters, Aug 2, 1894 to Nov. 19, 1906", p. 1, Archives of the Franciscan Brothers of Brooklyn.

2 "Souvenir of the Diamond Jubilee of the Franciscan Brothers, Brooklyn, N.Y., 1858 - 1933," p. 24.

3 "Deed Transferral Document, 1937," Property transfer map of the Baltic - Butler Street property of St. Francis Monastery, drawn in

1937, when the last piece of "The St. Francis Monastery" - Butler Street property was purchased, Archives of the Franciscan Brother of Brooklyn.

4 "Souvenir......," p.24

5 "Deed Transferral Document, 1937"

6 "Deed Transferral Document, 1937"

7 *The Brooklyn Eagle,* December 1, 1906, *The Brooklyn Eagle* Picture Collection, Brooklyn Public Library.

8 The name "St. Francis College" was used for the academy and collegiate levels of the school.

9 "Brooklyn's Friary, Medieval Monks in Modern Days: How the Sons of St. Francis Live and Teach," *The Brooklyn Citizen,* October 24, 1886.

10 *The Brooklyn Catholic,* 18 June 1870, "Religious Exercises at St. Francis Academy, Baltic Street"

11 *The Brooklyn Citizen,* June 26, 1875.

12 The College awarded Bachelor's of Arts and Science degrees "in kind," and "honorary" Master of Art's and Doctor of Philosophy degrees from 1885 until 1906, when the Board of Trustees reassessed its "Honorary Degree" granting program. Chapter Nine treats this in more detail.

13 "Souvenir of the Diamond Jubilee of the Franciscan Brothers, 1858-1933, " p. 74.

14 *Ibid.*

15 *Ibid.,* p. 42.

16 *Ibid..,* p. 54.

17 Franciscan Brothers of Brooklyn, "Necrology" , November 19, 1910.

18 Letter of Kevin F. Wolfe to Brother Thomas Grady, 4 June 1995, Franciscan Brothers Archives.

19 "Account Book," monies to Bro. Lewis: January 1, 1895, $2.00 for "household expenses," March 19, 1897, $2.25 for "apples, " and on December 15, 1897, $2.00 for "pans", Franciscan Brothers Archives.

20 Rockaway House for the brothers first discussed (June 1, 1883) and

McMahon's Cottage was rented for $400 for the Summer, (29 May, 1887), Council Minutes, FBA.

[21] St. Francis Academy and College, "Student Account Books, " Four volumes from 1896 to 1930.

[22] "Acts of The St. Francis Monastery . . . , 1881 - 1957," (A complete surveyor's description of the Alvernia property is found in these pages with the purchase price of $4,750, and $1,250 for the needed repairs, all coming   from a $6,000 mortgage on the property approved at the meeting of 31 October 1901), pp. 54-59.

[23] "Student Account Books," 1903-1904, p. 232, Thomas Edmond Molloy, 10 E. Park Street, Nashua, N.H., is listed as a boarder in the Senior Class of St. Francis Academy (College), who received his handwritten Diploma ($10) on 23 June 1904. His total bill came to $273.75, including a $10 Doctor's bill for five visits incurred during the year.

[24] "Great Drive" Brochure in the "Brooklyn Eagle Picture Collection," Brooklyn Public Library, c. 1923.

[25] "Acts of the St. Francis Monastery . . . ., 1881 - 1957,", 20 October 1923, pp. 73-74.

[26] " Minutes of the Community and Consultors , 15 December 1922 to 2 August 1942,"   11 November 1923, p. 5. , FBA.

[27] "Acts . . . ., 1 May 1925, p. 80.

[28] "Acts of the St. Francis Monastery, 1881 - 1957," 1 May 1925, p. 79.

[29] *Brooklyn Eagle,* Brooklyn Public Library, *Brooklyn Eagle* Picture Collection, October, 1923.

[30] Conversation with Brother Edmund Holmes, O.S.F., May 10, 1999.

[31] *Souvenir of the Diamond Jubilee of the Franciscan Brothers, Brooklyn, N.Y.: 1858-1933,* p. 59.

[32] Lillian Ross, "One Saturday in Brooklyn," *The New Yorker Magazine,* Dec. 18, 1965, [a review in the form of a short play, of William Alfred's play "Hogan's Goat," in "The Talk of the Town" column. Alfred speaks with affection of St. Francis Prep on Baltic Street: "I went to St. Francis Prep on Baltic Street . . . . It was run by Franciscan Brothers, and we had such good times. I fell in love with that school

from the start. It was next to St. Francis College and St. Francis Monastery which had a garden and a beautiful fountain, and you'd see the old brothers sitting around the fountain on sunny days. It was so tranquil."].

33 "Acts of The St. Francis Monastery," 27 October 1964.

34 Bernard Costa, O.S.F., Interviewed by Gerard O'Brien, O.S.F. , 8th March 1971, three page MS, Franciscan Brothers Archives.

35 A "Franciscan Brothers Monastery Fund" Drive was conducted in 1950 to raise $750,000 for a much needed new Monastery at 41 Butler Street. The monies raised by this Drive were used to build the new Friary at North Sixth Street for the 40 brothers teaching across the Street in St. Francis Prep.

CHAPTER FIVE

BROTHERS' ACADEMIES AND SCHOOLS IN THE NINETEENTH AND TWENTIETH CENTURIES

Shortly after the Brothers established St. Francis Academy on Baltic Street in 1859 as the first independent secondary school in Brooklyn, they began teaching in parish elementary schools of the Brooklyn Diocese. St. Joseph's on Dean Street was their first parish school in 1859, followed by St. Paul's on Court and Congress Streets and Our Lady of Mercy on DeBevoise Place in 1861. Subjects taught in these elementary schools included many now found in the first year of high school, with higher level Mathematics especially remembered by their students.

In the middle of the twentieth century the Franciscan Brothers expanded their ministries to teach in elementary schools in other parts of the Brooklyn Diocese which then comprised all four counties of Long Island. With the growth of vocations following the Second World War, the Community was able to respond to the many requests of pastors for brothers to teach in the boys departments of schools in Queens, Nassau, Suffolk counties on Long Island, and, in the last 20 years, in the states of Florida, North Carolina, Missouri, and Connecticut.

Some of the "parish schools" which the Brothers conducted were actually secondary schools as we know them today. The course of instruction included classical, scientific and commercial subjects which were distinct and separate from the courses in the elementary branches. The first of these parish academies was St. Bonaventure's in St. Michael's Parish in Flushing (1864-1871) where the brothers continued teaching in the parish school until they withdrew in 1876. Other parish academies were St. Peter's on Hicks Street in 1870, to be followed by St. Patrick's, Kent Avenue in 1871, St. Vincent de Paul's, North Sixth in 1886, and Sacred Heart, Adelphi Street in 1888. The Brothers opened their own St. Leonard's Academy in 1880 on South Fourth Street in Williamsburg. The only other "academy" in the Diocese at that time was St. James' on Tillery Street, under the care of the De La Salle Christian Brothers.

St. Peter's Parish was founded at Hicks and Warren Streets in 1859 under the direction of Father Joseph Fransioli, a Swiss-born educator. He began the school at the same time as he built the church. Through his financial skills, the finest school building in Brooklyn was completed in 1866, with a frescoed hall, and a great gymnasium supplied with the best athletic equipment from Europe, at an estimated cost of $100,000.

Charles Webber, of the class of 1877, shared his memories of the brothers, who served at **St. Peter's Academy** from 1870 to 1933: [1]

> *The curriculum, besides the usual courses, included geometry, plane and solid, trigonometry, and in the last year even calculus - differential and integral, surveying and field work. Physics with laboratory experiments, and debates with other schools, were also very popular. Dramatics won us fame then and brought is into the "Leonardis," the most renowned Catholic amateur dramatic society of that heyday of amateurs. . . . In addition, military training with the redoubtable Major Hines of the Papal Zuaves was included.*

ST. PETER'S LYCIUM, KNOWN AS "THE ROOMS"
LOCATION OF THE ACADEMY c. 1886

In comparing the level of education at St. Peter's Academy, which had over 600 boys, Webber states that:

> *There were no high schools in those pioneer days - public or parochial. When the first public high school was opened on Court Street, one of our boys sought to enter, but was told that he was beyond their courses! Yet, it was hard to convince our own people that our schools were so excellent. One method we tried at St. Peter's was public examinations held in our big hall at night with the public invited to come and quiz. There on the stage stood our first class, at the end of each year, ready for examination by anyone in the audience. . . . We were prepared. For several weeks before, the Brothers from St. Francis College- "Little Old Paul"*

*and "Young Paul," Jerome, and Leo, as well as jovial
"Little Bruno," had come to our classrooms in the
afternoon and grilled us for battle. We welcomed them,
always glad to demonstrate what we had learned.*

*When the great night came, visiting Brothers were
there with many other teachers from among the
Brothers. We were ready! A crowded hall and proud
parents applauded as we proved our efficiency, each
striving to be first with his answer. It was a real test -
a trying one, but we enjoyed it, and showed the public
what the Hicks Street Boys could do in those days. No
public school of the day could have offered such an
exhibition. We did it to convince our reluctant public
that **it was not all catechism.** We had need to do it in
those days. Now examinations, open to the public, are
unnecessary. The Regents stamp our efficiency.* [2]

Another parochial school the brothers opened was in
the basement of **St. Paul's** Church on Court and Congress
Streets (1860 to 1878), three blocks from St. Francis
Monastery at 41 Butler Street. One of the students of that
school, William T. Vlymen, became the Principal of Eastern
District High School. His memories of the Brother who
taught him Algebra in the Church basement go back
before 1888, when the "new" St. Paul's was opened on
Warren Street. His recollections were still vivid in 1933,
five years after the brothers left the school:

*The fundamentals of all I ever knew of Algebra I got
there. The method used I afterwards adopted in P.S. No.
5 when I was its principal. The Brother in charge gave
us a large number of examples, short and simple. Well
within our powers of execution. The constant repetition
of easy problems fastened in our minds the fundamental*

principles so that they lingered while many other subjects, not so separated, are gone.

We used slates for the work. The Brother would read the problems and immediately the sound of scratching slate pencils would begin. As soon as a pupil had the answer he would rush, slate in hand, to the Brother and flourish it in his face. As many of the pupils finished about the same time, the Brother would be surrounded by a crowd of boys eager to be the first to get his attention. The first boy would get at the top of his slate a straight line, perpendicular, drawn in chalk. At the end of the period the Brother would call for the boy or boys having the largest number of chalk marks to stand. Every boy was eager to get as many of these chalk marks as possible, so that at times the Brother would find it hard to select the first one completing the example, so many boys rushing at him at practically the same moment, all eager to get the coveted chalk on the slate.

I imagine that I was not so pushing as some, as I recall that at times the Brother would make us all withdraw and then select some one boy who would get the mark. I was sometimes the one selected in this way, the Brother calling me from the rear in his kindness. This action on his part still renews my gratitude as he was keen enough to see that, though I might have finished first, I was too shy to thrust myself upon his attention.

The atmosphere was one of eagerness to do the work and to do it promptly. Many easy questions made it possible for even the dull boys to succeed and at the end of the lesson, as I remember it, every boy had more or less marks on his slate. These marks were carefully counted and any boy who would surreptitiously use a piece of chalk to increase the number would receive short shrift at the hands of his critical comrades. [3]

St. Patrick's parish was established in 1843, on Kent Avenue in the section known as East Brooklyn as the sixth Catholic parish in the City of Brooklyn. In 1872, Thomas Taaffe began his long term as pastor until his death in 1920. In 1872 the Franciscan Brothers began teaching in the separate boys academy, which had been an old Methodist school building. Mathematics was also a strong subject at **St. Patrick's Academy** - Matthew J. McKenna of the Class of 1876 recalls that:

> *A feature of the Brothers' teaching was the attention they gave to Mathematics; they succeeded in developing so many accomplished students in this study that public exhibitions were given of their proficiency, . . . and to these exhibitions were invited teachers from the public schools to examine our scholars. These public tests created considerable interest and the results were pronounced creditable to the students and their teachers.*
>
> *Another activity of the Brothers was the presentation of one or two Dramatic Shows during the year - generally plays or dramas, with an occasional try at Shakespeare. They didn't shy even at the operetta for they produced "Pinafore" a whole week. In the original production of this musical comedy the female parts were taken by the boys. Joe Campbell, who afterwards taught music in the public schools, sang the part of Josephine, and Michael Hayes the role of Little Buttercup or Cousin Hebe. P.E. Callahan was the Admiral and Tommy Fitzpatrick, Ralph Rackstraw.*
>
> *They were the good old days - happy days, sunshiny days, care-free days, yet days of work and preparation for the life ahead. The Brothers had been teaching at the Academy many years previous to the time I am writing*

about and have been in charge ever since. [The Brothers began at St. Patrick's only five years earlier in 1872, and left almost a century later in 1967]. *What their pupils are today and such success as they have met within their various line of endeavor are due to their teachers' advice, to their solicitude, to their example of holiness, and to the training of heart and mind for which these sons of the great St. Francis are justly famous. I cannot speak too highly of the work of these great educators . . . so kind and lovable men as Brothers Aloysius, Fidelis, Sebastian and Jerome.*[4]

BROTHER JEROME MAGNER

It was under the leadership of Thomas Taaffe and Jerome Magner that St. Patrick's Academy grew so rapidly that it could no longer accommodate all the boys of the parish. In 1876, when Jerome Magner was again elected Superior General, Leo Wall was appointed principal, and two classrooms were built on the second floor which had formerly been an auditorium. [5]

Brother Jerome, a native of Tipperary, Ireland, entered the Franciscan Brothers Monastery at Roundstone on 21 March 1857, and received the Habit on 11 November 1858. He was professed one year later and transferred to the Brooklyn Congregation in March 1862. He was first elected Superior of the Brothers in 1866, a position he was re-elected to for a total of twenty-seven years. Considered the second founder of the Brooklyn Community, Jerome was the Superior when the Congregation was incorporated in 1868, and also when St. Francis College was empowered to confer academic degrees in 1884. He frequently went to Ireland seeking vocations to the Brooklyn Community.[6] To this pioneer member of the Community the Franciscan Brothers are indebted for the firm establishment of the Congregation in the Diocese of Brooklyn. He died after a short illness on 12 December 1912.[7]

St. Mary Star of the Sea Parish in South Brooklyn began in 1851 and the church was completed in 1855 at a cost of fifty thousand dollars. The parishioners were primarily from the Irish laboring class, with many of the men away at sea for long periods of time. Their connection with the sea can be seen in the stone for St. Mary's church which was carried from Europe as ballast in their ships arriving in the Brooklyn piers of Red Hook.

Catholic education began in St. Mary's Parish in what was known as Mrs. Daly's School, located in a small house on Nelson Street, which was later moved to Smith Street. The first parish school was opened in 1856 under the direction of the Sisters of Charity of New York, who maintained the direction of the girls' department after the brothers arrived in 1869. Brothers were invited by the pastor, Eugene Cassidy to take charge of the boys department in the new school completed that year. The average attendance was over 500 boys in the 1870's.

Although **St. Mary's** was not an "academy," it was also famous for its Mathematics program. The curriculum covered the elements of simple and quadratic equations, plane and solid geometry, and trigonometry. On Sundays the boys were encouraged to attend both Mass and Vespers. After Vespers they were permitted to borrow books from the parish library for their outside reading. The course of reading prescribed by the brothers was unique; there is no evidence of a similar course of reading in the early public schools until 1887, when the Brooklyn public schools began to encourage general outside reading for their pupils. Early principals of St. Mary's were Francis Butler, later one of the founders of St. Bonaventure's College in Olean, New York, and Eugene Shanahan, Anthony Helion and Ignatius Culhane. [8]

St. Charles Borromeo Parish was founded on Sydney Place in Brooklyn Heights in 1849 by Charles Constantine Pise, who was the first Catholic Chaplain of the United States Senate. The Brothers served this parish school from 1870 until 1923. Dramatics, music, religion and bible history were subjects the brothers were known for at St. Charles. Examinations in these subjects were held publicly in the auditorium and lasted for three days. A gold watch was awarded to the boy who received the highest rating in catechism and bible history in these examinations. [9]

At **St. Mary's** parish church in Roundout, New York, "The Brothers' School," as it was popularly known, was housed in the residence of the brothers. It became so respected by people of all faiths that the taxpayers voted to finance their salaries. However, after an inquiry by the Community Council about over-spending, and because the brothers' salaries were no longer paid by taxes, the school was closed in 1895. After 20 years in Roundout (1875-1895), the brothers returned to Brooklyn.

FINANCES OF THE BRANCH HOUSES

After the depression of 1893, the finances of the three branch houses became a concern of the community. After the election of 2 August 1894, many items of business were decided at the first meeting of the new Council.

Among the many appointments of brothers to positions in the College and the Monastery, one excerpt from the Minutes reveals a concern about the finances of the branch houses:

> *It was moved and seconded that the appointment of Brother Superiors of Branch Houses be deferred until after the financial conditions of these houses be determined. . . . Brothers Dominic and Raphael are appointed a "Committee of Scrutiny" by the Consultors to examine into the financial conditions of the Branch Houses at Williamsburgh (St. Leonard's Academy), Roundout (St. Mary's), and Jersey City (St. Brigid's) and to make a report at an early date to the consultors.*
>
> *Moved and seconded that the reports of St. Mary's, Roundout and St. Leonard's, Williamsburgh be read. Brother Dominic reads as instructed.*
>
> *It is moved and seconded that the Committee of Scrutiny find the financial condition of these houses for one year.* [10]

St. Leonard's Academy seems to have satisfied the financial concerns of the Council because at their meeting of 22 August 1894, they voted to elect Brother Fidelis the Superior and Brother Basil the Treasurer and Bookkeeper of that house. But they were still concerned about Roundout and voted:

A resolution was adopted to the effect that the books in the Branch Houses be kept according to the method adopted in the Mother House, subject, however, to the supervision of the Branch House.

It was also required that Bro. Ambrose make an itemized report of the Branch House in Roundout by one week from this date.

On September 1st, 1894, the Council met and examined the report of the Roundout House and also appointed a superior for that house:

The statement was accepted as read, embracing, as it does, a correct statement of the monies received and expended. Report is given to Treasurer.

However, after seeing the income and expenses of St. Mary's, Roundout, it was:

"Resolved that we consider the expenses for the year ending, Aug. 1, 1894, exorbitant in the Roundout House."

The Council then elected Brother Joseph Caffrey as Superior of the Roundout House for three years and Brother Ambrose was elected the Treasurer of the house. Although these two brothers were elected for a term of three years, because the brothers' salaries were no longer being paid by town taxes, the school was closed a year later in 1895. [11]

The two financial depressions of the last quarter of the nineteenth century (1873 and 1893), forced the brothers to leave some of their schools because the pastors were unable to pay their salaries. In subtle language, "not favorable" and "not giving the encouragement necessary," the earliest Minutes of the Community, [12] give details of two such difficulties:

> In February 1864 a house [St. Michael's] was opened in Flushing, Rev. James O'Beirne, pastor. It was continued during this pastor's time in the parish, but being succeeded by Rev. Henry O'Loughlin, who was not favorable to the Brothers, it was decided to discontinue the school, and the Brothers were withdrawn in July 1876.

Again, another pastor does not "encourage" the brothers:

> In January 1866, a mission was commenced in Williamsburgh, at St. Mary's (Immaculate Conception). This continued until August 1871. . . . The pastor not giving the encouragement necessary, it was deemed better to discontinue proceedings in that district. The pastor was Rev. John R. McDonald.

In addition to financial difficulties, the relocation of Catholic populations from parts of Brooklyn to outlying sections of Long Island and even Jersey City, meant that brothers would be moved from schools no longer able to support them, to other schools desiring their services. The brothers' salary of $300 per year was agreed to by most pastors, but sometimes the brothers had to wait years for this salary to be paid. Council Minutes in 1892 reveal one such partially successful effort to obtain these needed salaries:

A meeting was called for the purpose of considering the propriety of taking off from the debt due the Community by St. Anne's parish under the pastorship of Rev. James Durick, the total $6,464 due from Father McMul's [sic] time. [James McMeel - died 9/16/1888]. The reduction demanded is $1,464. He promises to pay the balance due as soon as he can. He has already paid $2,000 out of the total amount as above. It was decided to take off half - $732.

It was proposed to present a statement of our whole affairs to the new Bishop [Charles McDonnell], and to request him to aid us in getting our salaries, and for a yearly donation to the support of our novitiate. [13]

ST. LEONARD'S ACADEMY

In response to the needs of the Catholics of Williamsburgh and Greenpoint, the second academy owned by the Franciscan Brothers was **St. Leonard's Academy,** opened in 1880 at 180 South Fourth Street in the Eastern District of Brooklyn. Under the direction of Fidelis O'Connor, the founding principal, this two-year school offered classical and scientific courses and was especially noted for its thorough curriculum in business and secretarial training. The rapid increase of students required expansion and the Community purchased property at138-140 South Fourth Street (near Bedford Avenue) at a cost of $12,500. In 1926 the school moved to 26 Brevoort Place, near Atlantic Avenue in Brooklyn, and continued its two-year curriculum in business subjects. After the two-year academy became a four-year high school in 1958, it expanded into a building on Cypress Avenue in Ridgewood. After an heroic, but unsuccessful effort to provide the necessary full range of educational accommodations required by the New York State Education Department for a four-year high school, "The St. Francis Monastery" corporation, which had to approve all legal and financial actions of schools owned by the Community, determined that funds needed to bring it into compliance with the State Education Department's secondary school requirements for physical education and a sufficient library were not approved. St. Leonard's High School closed in 1965.

Through the rest of the nineteenth century, the Brothers taught the upper grades in Our Lady of Mercy, DeBevoise Place in 1861; St. Michael's, Flushing in 1864; Immaculate Conception, Maujer Street in 1866; St. Mary, Star of the Sea, Court Street in 1869; St. John the Evangelist, 21st Street in 1870; St. Charles, Sydney Place in 1870; St. Anne's, Front Street in 1873; St. Mary's in Roundout, New York in 1875; Assumption, York Street in 1882; St. Antony's, Greenpoint, in 1886; the new St. Paul's, Warren Street in 1888; St. Bridget's, Jersey City, in 1890; The Visitation School, Red Hook in 1890; Our Lady Of Lourdes, 1892; Our Lady of Good Counsel, Putnam Avenue in 1894; and St. Joachim's, Matteawan, New York, in 1896.

From 1859, most of the brothers who staffed parish schools lived in St. Francis Monastery at 41 Butler Street, and traveled each morning to their assignments. Very often, because of the scarcity of funds, they would walk back and forth many miles to their schools. Hardships were endured in the cold, snowy, and wet weather, when they often had to tend to the heat in the schools before the students arrived. At lunch time, they looked forward to the horse-drawn "Dinner Wagon" which brought them their hot, mid-day dinner from the Monastery, or from Mrs. Skelly on Oakland Street for the brothers in St. Antony's in Greenpoint. Boys vied with each other to assist in carrying the dishes back to Mrs. Skelly in hopes of sharing some sweet left-overs. [14]

From their first years in Brooklyn, some of the brothers would see "greener grass" in other parts of America and Australia and leave the shores of the East River in Brooklyn, New York. John McMahon and five other brothers departed for Santa Barbara, California in early summer 1862, trying to join the First Order Franciscans. A few others would follow their example through the rest of the century.

BROTHERS JOIN
SAINT BONAVENTURE'S UNIVERSITY

In 1874, five brothers who had served as principals and teachers in the schools left Brooklyn for Allegany County in upstate New York to assist the Order of Friars Minor to establish **Saint Bonaventure's University.** Each of these men joined the First Order Friars Minor and were ordained to the priesthood. Francis Butler, who entered the Franciscan Brothers in 1863, was the first principal of St. Mary Star of the Sea, principal of St. Mary, Maujer Street, and a teacher in St. Paul's on Congress Street in Brooklyn. He would eventually become the President of Saint Bonaventure University and Rector of the seminary. Angelus O'Connor, who entered the Irish Franciscan Brothers in 1859, transferred to Brooklyn that same year. He was the first principal of St. Charles Borromeo, and would also serve as principal of St. Joseph's, Dean Street, and St. Mary's, Maujer Street. Joachim Molloy, a native of Galway, entered the Brooklyn Congregation and pronounced his vows in 1861. He taught at St. Francis Academy on Baltic Street and served as principal of Our Lady of Mercy, Debevoise Place, until joining the friars in 1874. He would serve as Vice-President of Saint Bonaventure University for three years and as a teacher for ten years.

Bernardine McCabe was professed in the Brooklyn Community in 1862 and taught in St. Francis Academy, Baltic Street. As a Friar he spent most of his priestly years in St. Anthony's, Sullivan Street in New York City. Anthony Ennis, a native of England, joined the Irish Franciscan Brothers and transferred to Brooklyn in 1867. He was the first principal of St. Peter's School, Hicks Street. He also spent most of his priestly life in St. Anthony's Parish on Sullivan Street.[15]

Three of these men, under their legal names, John Molloy, Michael A. O'Connor, and William Butler, would appear on the Charter granted on 1 March 1875, by the Regents of the State of New York empowering St. Bonaventure's College to "confer the Academic and Honorary Degrees usually conferred by Universities." [16]

BROTHERS TO THE WILDS OF AUSTRALIA

A letter to Celestine McGarry from Bernardine Cowan tells the sad story of three brothers who went to Australia from Ireland and America in February of 1892. [17] "Assured by the Friars Minor, to whom they were going in Australia, that things would be all right," Antony Donlan, the superior of Mountbellew, Alexander O'Rourke, from Brooklyn, and Francis Wangler, the superior in Loretto, all went to St. Charles Parish, Waverley, New South Wales, Australia, without seeking the necessary permissions from their bishops in Tuam, Brooklyn and Loretto. Conditions in Australia were very bad - the friars made no provision for a residence for the brothers, and within two years they were seeking to return to their communities.

Antony Donlan was twice refused permission by the Archbishop of Tuam and eventually joined the Augustinians in England and died in that community. Alexander O'Rourke was refused permission by Bishop Charles McDonnell to return to the Brooklyn community, but was eventually accepted by the Third Order Regular community in Spalding and died there after making his Solemn Vows on 8 April 1908. Francis Wangler, who was the superior in Loretto when he left, tried to return to Loretto but was refused by the Bishop. He went to Mountbellew in Ireland in 1895, seeking to enter that community but became violently ill the same night he arrived. He was attended by the priest and doctor, and was nursed back to health by Bernardine Cowan.[18] Francis Wangler was eventually accepted back to his Loretto Community by Father Kittell, the Vicar of the Bishop of Pittsburgh. However, since another brother had taken the name Francis in his absence, he was given the name Leonard. Eventually ordained in the Third Order Regular community, Leonard Wangler died at Loretto on 2 March 1934.[19]

In the next half-century the Franciscan Brothers had to give up many of their schools because of the decline in their numbers. From a high number of 101 professed brothers, eight novices and six postulants in 1907, the Community was reduced to 66 professed brothers, two novices and two postulants in 1908. The Community's unsuccessful attempt to unite with the Third Order Regular in Rome was prevented by Bishop Charles McDonnell. However, 27 brothers did request dispensations from the Brooklyn Community and left to join the Third Order Regular Community in Spaulding in July of 1907.[20]

Only a decade after the Brothers opened the Male School at St. Joseph's on Dean Street, what sounds like a very successful "Exhibition of the Pupils of St. Joseph's," was held on Thursday, 2nd June 1870 at 7:30 PM. The reporter enjoyed the music provided by the St. Francis Academy Band, "trained and led by Prof. Ebbets of Flushing," commended the "Introductory Address" spoken "with great feeling and clearness of utterance" by Master Lenihan; but commented on the discomfort of the school hall where 1,000 persons crowded into the auditorium meant for 700. He recommended that "the Brothers hire a hall in future capable of accommodating the large crowds that are in the habit of attending their exhibitions." [21]

In 1905, the brothers began to live in **St. Antony's** Friary in Greenpoint to be close to the school which was a distance from St. Francis Monastery. From 1886, the brothers traveled from Butler Street to Greenpoint via the crosstown trolley. Delays at the Wallabout Market and the little bridge that crossed the Wallabout Basin often caused the brothers to be late for school. In 1905, a house was rented on Milton Street, opposite the church. When this house proved inadequate, the pastor purchased a house on Leonard Street which served the local community as its friary until the Franciscan Brothers left St. Antony's in 1965. Many vocations to the Community came from this parish.

In September of 1914, at the invitation of Rev. David J. Hickey, the brothers took charge of the boys' department of **St. Francis Xavier,** Park Slope, the new school he built on President Street. Brother Eugene Dunne was the founding principal and remained for 38 years until 1952. From the initial 114 boys in 1914, the enrollment increased to more than 500 students by 1927, when a new addition of eight classrooms was built. The brothers traveled from St. Francis Monastery to Park Slope until a new friary was built in 1952. When the number of brothers declined, the Sisters of St. Joseph assumed control of the entire school in 1975.

The brothers had served in **Our Lady of Lourdes** parish from 1892 to 1896, when it was Saint Francis de Sales Parish. When the Fathers of Mercy took over this parish its name was changed to Our Lady of Lourdes and Columba Reilly and Bonaventure Dunne undertook Sunday School work in 1919. The old school building was replaced in 1920 with a modern school in the style of architecture of the Church. The brothers taught Sunday School until 1923, when they were invited to take over the boys' department and live in a private house remodeled as a friary, at 11 Aberdeen Street. Brother Egidius Mason was the founding principal and superior. When the brothers could no longer staff the school, they left Our Lady of Lourdes in 1967.

**LARGE NOVITIATE CLASS OF SPRING 1962,
OYSTER BAY**

**BROTHER COLUMBA REILLY SCHOLASTICATE
82 PIERREPONT STREET, BROOKLYN HEIGHTS**

After the Second World War, vocations to the Community began to increase so that by the mid-nineteen-fifties, classes of 20 or more young men were being accepted to the novitiate. The size of these large classes prompted the community to move the novitiate from Smithtown to Deer Park in Wyandanch, Long Island and to open the Brother Columba Reilly Scholasticate at 82 Pierrepont Street for young brothers attending Saint Francis College in Brooklyn Heights.

POST-VATICAN TWO DECLINE IN VOCATIONS

As the photograph of the Novitiate Class of 1962 suggests, the brothers received many applications to the Community in the post-World War II years. However, by the 1970s, more young men were leaving religious life than were entering. The increasing numbers who chose to teach in St. Francis Prep and St. Anthony's High School, which are owned or administered by the Franciscan Brothers, completed the decline in the numbers of brothers who served in elementary schools during the last half century, and will be discussed below and in Chapter Nine.

Lawrence H. Bracken invited the Brothers to begin teaching at **St. Brigid's** in 1951, where they taught first in the old school for four years, in the Ridgewood Times Building for a year and a half, and then in the new wing of the school in 1957. During their 25 years in Ridgewood, the Brothers lived in their Friary at Greene Avenue. Brother Bertrand Ryan was the founding principal and superior. The brothers left St. Brigid's in 1976.

Daniel A. Dwyer, a graduate of Saint Francis College, invited the Brothers to staff the boys' department of **Saint Bartholomew's** grammar school in 1954. Brother Dominic Allen served as the founding principal and superior of the friary on Elmhurst Avenue. The Brothers first taught in the original school building on Whitney Avenue, and in 1957, moved into the newly constructed boys' school on Judge Street. The brothers left the school in 1977.

In 1954, Peter L. Nolan, who was taught by the brothers at Sacred Heart Institute on Adelphi Street, and who worked with the brothers at Saint Francis Xavier's for 25 years, invited the Brothers to staff **St. Joseph's School** in Babylon. Brother Bernardine Voute, who had served with Msgr. Nolan for sixteen years at St. Francis Xaviers' in Brooklyn, was the founding principal and superior. In 1976, when the community could no longer assign a principal, St. Joseph's was administered by the Sisters. Two brothers still taught in the school until 1981.

In 1957, Alfred A. Loewe, an alumnus of Saint Francis College, and a long-time friend of the brothers at Camp Alvernia, built a new boys' school and friary at **St. Aidan's**, Williston Park. When the Community could no longer staff the school, the Brothers left in 1976.

In 1957, the brothers opened the newly built Boys' Department in **Notre Dame** Parish, New Hyde Park. They lived in a Friary converted from a family dwelling, Again, when the Community did not have brothers to assign to the school, they left in 1969.

In 1958, the centenary year of the Franciscan Brothers arrival in Brooklyn, Bishop Edmund J. Reilly invited the brothers to staff the new boys' school in **Our Lady of Angels** in Bay Ridge. While the school was being completed on 74th Street, the brothers lived in two unused classrooms, before their friary was completed at 330 73rd Street. Because of the decline in numbers of students, the brothers left Our Lady of Angels School in 1991.

In 2002, the Franciscan Brothers completed the renovation of the former Convent of the Parish into a new Friary at 344 73rd Street. It will be able to house 16 Brothers and offices of the Congregation. The Archives and the offices of the Vocation Director and Development Director are located in this building.

In 1977, the Brothers accepted the administration and staffing of **Tampa Catholic High School** and some Brothers also taught in the **Academy of the Holy Names** and administered **St. Lawrence Elementary School** and worked in parish ministry at **Christ the King Parish** in Tampa, Florida. The Tampa local Friary also served as a Winter vacation home for Brothers each year. After a number of years, the Brothers accepted **St. Joseph's Academy** and also served in parish ministry in a local soup kitchen in St. Augustine, Florida.

From 1980 until 1997, the brothers administered and staffed the school of **Our Lady of Hope Parish** in Middle Village.

In 1985, the brothers accepted the administration and staffing of **St. Peter's Parish School** in Greenville, North Carolina. It became a very successful institution, attracting the children of many professors in the Greenville university community, and was the first elementary school in North Carolina to receive accreditation from the Southern States Association of Schools and Colleges. After 14 years in Greenville, the brothers left St. Peter's in 1999.

From 1982 to 1997, the Brothers administered, staffed and taught in a number of schools in Connecticut: **St. Augustine's** School in Bridgeport: **St. Mary's High School** in Greenwich; **Trinity Catholic High School** in Stamford; **St. Joseph's High School** in Trumbull; and **St. Gabriel's School** in Milford.

St. John's International School in Waterloo, Belgium was served by two brothers from 1978 to 1987. In 1994, the Community accepted the administration and staffing **of Cardinal Gibbons High School** in Raleigh, North Carolina. In 1997, ground was broken for a larger building which was needed because of increasing enrollment which was occupied in 2000.

Brothers have served as administrators or teachers in a number of schools and colleges on Long Island, in New York City, New Mexico, and Cape Girardeau in Missouri. Pastoral ministries are also served by brothers who work for the dioceses of Brooklyn, Paterson, Bridgeport, Rockville Centre and the archdiocese of Newark.

Notes

[1] "Souvenir of the Diamond Jubilee of the Franciscan Brothers', 1858-1933," pp. 34-36.

[2] *Ibid.*

[3] "Souvenir of the Diamond Jubilee of the Franciscan Brothers, 1858-1933, p. 58.

[4] *Ibid.*, pp. 42-46.

[5] "The First Twenty-five Years, 1858-1883," Franciscan Brothers' Newsletter, January, 1983, p 13.

[6] As will be seen in Chapter Eight, Brother Jerome was criticized in *The Brooklyn Daily Eagle* (21 August 1891), for seeking vocations in Ireland, instead of America.

[7] "Necrology of the Franciscan Brothers".

[8] "The First Twenty-five years, 1858-1883," Franciscan Brothers Newsletter, January, 1983, p. 11.

[9] *Ibid.*, p. 12.

[10] Minutes of The St. Francis Monastery, Aug. 2, 1894, p. 17.

[11] Minute Book of St. Francis Monastery, September 1, 1894, p. 23.

[12] "Oldest Minute Book of Saint Francis Monastery," 1878, p. 6. [There is no evidence that Community records were systematically kept prior to the appointment of Brother Paul Hill as Secretary in 1878. The fact that Brother Paul began this book with an introductory summary of the early history of the Congregation in Brooklyn would seem to indicate that no earlier written document was extant - Bro. Celestine McGarry, Secretary General, c. 1944].

[13] "Oldest Minute Book of Saint Francis Monastery," February 28, 1892, p. 23.

[14] "The Second Twenty-five Years," Franciscan Brothers Newsletter, February, 1983, p. 11.

[15] " The First 25 Years," Newsletter of the Franciscan Brothers, January, 1983, p. 9.

[16] Walter Hammon, O.F.M., *The First Bonaventure Men: The Early History of St. Bonaventure University and the Allegany Franciscans*, St. Bonaventure University, 1958, pp 168-169.

[17] Letter from Bernardine Cowan, O.S.F. to Celestine McGarry, O.S.F., 11 December 1952, Franciscan Brothers' Archives.

[18] Bernardine Cowan, O.S.F. was a young man from England, newly received in Mount Bellew in 1895, who would eventually become the Superior General of the Irish Community as well as the historian of his Congregation.

[19] Copy of a Letter of Bonaventure Keily, T.O.R., Archivist of the Sacred Heart Province of the Third Order Regular, to Bernardine Cowan, O.S.F., 24 September 1958, FBA..

[20] This painful experience will be examined in Chapter Seven.

[21] *The Brooklyn Catholic*, 18 June, 1870.

CHAPTER SIX

CHANGING CONSTITUTIONS: THE EVOLUTION OF A FRANCISCAN CHARISM IN THE CHURCH

In many exhortations to religious communities since Vatican Council II, the Holy See has frequently urged that religious return to the "charism of your founders," or to respect their "particular characteristics and work" and "their founders' spirit and special aims". In an interesting study on the nature of "religious charism," Margaret Susan Thompson writes that the term "charism" does not appear at all in the Vatican II Council Document, *Perfectae Caritatis,* but is mentioned ten times in the Sacred Congregation for Religious and Secular Institutes' 1983 Document, "Essential Elements in the Church's Teaching on Religious Life as Applied to Institutes Dedicated to Works of the Apostolate," and is found eighty-six times in John Paul II's Apostolic Letter, *Vita Consecrata.* Thompson argues that "religious charism," especially in the United States, is a combination of that particular spiritual gift of a first founder with the historically specific work given by American bishops to religious congregations in the nineteenth and twentieth centuries. This "instrumental motivation" was the "religious charism" the American bishops gave to each community to prevent "leakage" from the Catholic faith: by educating children, by preserving the ethnic heritage and language of the numerous immigrant groups of that time, by serving the needs of Catholic orphans, and by providing healthcare and relief for indigent immigrants. [1]

The evolution of the "charism" of the Brothers of the Franciscan Third Order Regular, who emigrated in 1858, from Roundstone, County Galway, Ireland, to the Diocese of Brooklyn, involved a radical change from their **inclusive** Irish monastic-style of life, when they were able to teach the poor without charge, to that of a community of teachers **exclusively,** modeled after the Irish Christian Brothers. The gradual return of the Franciscan Brothers community to an **inclusive style of life,** involving many ministries in the Church, is a result of the influence of Vatican Council II and the *Rule and Life* approved in 1982.

As these Rules and Constitutions [2] changed over the centuries, the efforts of the brothers to discover and state their own charism and identity will be constantly influenced by the hierarchy, at the Papal and diocesan levels, and by the brothers' ties to the Franciscan First Order Friars Minor and the Third Order Regular in Rome. In tracing the evolution of the Congregation's charism, fourteen different Writings, Rules and Constitutions will be compared, and brevity, hopefully, served, by examining only the paragraphs on the nature of each community, the qualities required in the admission of new members, and the description of an ideal novice master.

"LETTER TO ALL THE FAITHFUL"

St. Francis of Assisi's "Letter to All the Faithful" is generally thought to be the document in which Francis outlined the rules to be followed by the penitents of the Third Order Secular.[3]

The Omnibus describes the "Letter to All the Faithful" as:

> *an earnest appeal to all the faithful to sanctify themselves by prayer, by the use of the sacraments, by mortification, and by the practice of justice, charity, and humility; to establish peace by the forgiveness of enemies and by love for them; to observe the commandments and precepts of Christ; to show respect for the Blessed Eucharist; and to live the Catholic life in all its fullness. It is especially noteworthy for its graphic description of the last moments of an impenitent possessor of ill-gotten goods.* [4]

> *The "Letter to All the Faithful" has been called the most beautiful and most vivid of all Francis' writings. It is replete with quotations from Holy Scripture, particularly those passages that seem to have been particularly dear to Francis. The more than ordinary elegance of its style suggest that it has been touched up.*[5]

Chapter Ten of Raffaele Pazzelli's *St. Francis and the Third Order*, "Francis' Directives For His Penitents," is a complete study of the "*Recensio prior*" and the "Letter to All the Faithful". He summarizes five elements of doing penance from the "*Recensio prior*" as:

1. *Love God;*
2. *Love one's neighbor;*
3. *Resist the sinful tendencies of our fallen nature;*
4. *Participate in the sacramental life, especially the Eucharist; and*
5. *Act in conformity with the conversion that the person accepted.* [6]

Pazzelli describes the "Letter to All the Faithful" not as an organic or systematic development of the *"Recensio prior"* as it might have done by an academician, but rather as:

> *...the work of a person in love with God, who freely reveals his inner soul, touching again and again those five themes, adding new ones, developing them, and passing from one to the other with no concern than that of being able to give abundant spiritual nourishment to his followers. Thus we find in it the original ideas of the spirituality of Francis.* [7]

The last three pages of Pazzelli's study [8] is an excellent synthesis of the first century (c1207-1289) of the early history of the Franciscan Third Order of Penance. He believes that:

> *During the lifetime of St. Francis hermits and recluses entered the Order of Penance and were recognized by the ecclesiastical order of that day as religious. Some of these were inducted by the saint himself, such as Blessed Verdiana of Castel Fiorantino, the noblewoman Praxides of Rome, and Gherardo of Villamagna near Florence. There is also evidence of a community of penitents, that of Bartholomew Baro, was instituted directly by St. Francis.*
>
> *From this we can see that, even during Francis' lifetime, the beginnings of a "regular religious life", both eremitical and communal forms, were to be found.*

The Rule approved by Nicholas IV formalized the life of the Penitents of the Third Order Secular in 1289. When Leo X approved the *Rule of the Religious of the Third Order of Saint Francis* for the regulars in 1521, Pazzelli believes that men and women had been living a recognized religious life with the three vows of poverty, chastity and obedience for almost three hundred years.

T H E
RVLE OF THE
RELIGIOVS,
OF THE THIRDE
ORDER OF SAINT
FRANÇIS,

For both fexes, making the three
vovves, and luuing together
in Communitie and Cloyffer.
VVith certaine other things
vvhich the leaf follovving
doth shevve.

IHS.

AT BRVXELLES,
By Ihon Pepermans, at the
golden bible, 1624.

BRUSSELS *RVLE* OF 1624

A copy of the earliest English language Brussels *Rvle* [9] is in Trinity College Library in Dublin. It was printed for a recusant [10] English Catholic Third Order Regular community of sisters, which was in exile on the Continent in Brussels because of the anti-Catholic Penal Laws of post-

Elizabethan England. This *Rvle*, with many words spelled quite differently from current orthography, was found in the library of the Third Order Franciscan Sisters when they joined with the Poor Clares in Arundel, England in 1972. For ease of reading, this Rvle will be translated into contemporary English. Chapter I of the *Rule*, "Of the entrance of Novices," begins by naming the qualities required of those seeking entrance:

> *The Brothers, or sisters to this third Order to be received ought to be faithful Catholics, not tied in marriage, free of debts, sound in body, prompt in mind, not taxed with any vulgar infamy, reconciled with their neighbors. And of all these things, before they be received, of him who hath faculties to receive them, they are diligently to be examined.* [11]

In Chapter II, although the duties of a novice master are not mentioned expressly, the year of novitiate is described succinctly:

> *The Brothers, and Sisters, after they have for a whole year borne the habit of probation (which ought to be of course cloth according to the judgement of the visitor) if their conversation shall be thought laudable in the convent wherein they have borne the habit of probation, by the counsel of the discretes of the said Convent, let them be received to the profession of the said order. In which profession let them promise to keep the commandments of God, and to make satisfaction for the transgressions which they shall commit against this third Rule, when of their prelates they shall be required, living in obedience, without property, and in chastity.[12]*

Describing the life they had left and the things to be avoided by those who join the Third Order, Chapter VI of this Rule, *"Of the manner of Conversing within and without,"* admonishes the religious:

> *Whereas the brothers and sisters of this fraternity are called of penance, it behoveth them to abstain from all curiosity, as well in vesture, as other things whatsoever. And according to the wholesome counsel of the prince of the Apostles Saint Peter, other vain ornaments of this world laid aside, they ought to carry no corporal ornament, but only an humble, and necessary tegumet [garment] of their body. They ought also to avoid by all means access to the courts of Princes, lords, or ladies where the delicacies of this world are had; as our savior doth witness; Nor ever at any time to be present at dances, plays, sports, and other vanities of players.*[13]

Chapter VIII *"Of the visitation which the Prelates ought to make of the Brothers and Sisters"* indicates that Provincials of the Friars Minor were to conduct visitations of the Third Order Regular, a practice which was still in effect for the Brothers in Ireland until 1830:

> *The Provincial minister of the Friars Minors, or the visitor of the same order, to whom he shall commit it, shall visit every year, once only in every house, with presence of the elders,* [14] . . . .

Following the Rule of Leo X, this document contains a Bull of the same Pope affirming the status of members of the Order as true religious:

The Brothers and Sisters of the aforesaid third Order, bearing the habit thereof and leading collegially virginal, and vidual [widowhood], or continent life by express vow, ought to enjoy all the privileges of the Friars Minor, [15] . . . .

The purpose of this Bull, which is found in subsequent Third Order Rules and many Constitutions, required that all prelates and rectors of parishes recognize that brothers and sisters of the Third Order:

. . . may have freely, and lawfully, oratories with a low steeple and bell, and in the same oratories the Sacrament of the Eucharist, in a comely and decent place, and also holy oils for their own use only, and hollowed burial in which the bodies of the Sisters deceased by their confessor may be buried, and in the same oratories holy water be solemnly made, and masses . . solemnly to be sung and celebrated. [16]

IRISH *RULES AND CONSTITUTIONS*

The four different Rules and Constitutions of the Brothers in Ireland reflect their relationship to the Friars Minor from 1818 to 1830, and eventually their 100 years of diocesan status from 1830 to 1930. [17]

In 1818, men dedicated to the education of boys and young men in parishes of the Friars Minor in Dublin and Killiney, Ireland, received permission to take the three vows of poverty, chastity and obedience, with the fourth vow of "teaching catechism," and to live in Community as religious of the Third Order of Saint Francis. Benignus Millet, O.F.M., the Archivist of the Irish Province of the

Friars Minor, believes they were members of the Friars' Archconfraternity of the Cord at Adam and Eve's on Merchants Quay, in Dublin. [18] In the West of Ireland, Christopher Dillon Bellew invited these Brothers to establish a monastery [19] and school on his estate in Mountbellew, County Galway and assisted them in their work by becoming their patron.

Independent of the First Order Friars, the brothers observed a "Rule" similar to the Brussels English Rule of Pope Leo X. This *Rule* was sent to Rome in 1830 with their request for diocesan status. Although the Archives in Mountbellew does not have a separate, printed copy of this 1830 *Rule*, the Propaganda Fide Archives indicate that it was sent to Rome at this time. [20] It was reported missing by Propaganda Fide Archives in 1897, when Charles McDonnell of Brooklyn wrote to Rome asking if the 1866 Rule and Constitutions of the Brooklyn Brothers and the 1877 Irish Brothers Rule and Constitution had ever been approved by the Holy See. [21] The 1830 document was also reported missing by Propaganda Fide, when the Irish Brothers wrote to Rome in 1897, requesting union of their three Irish communities with the Third Order Regular in Rome. The Archives of Mountbellew, however, does have a copy of an early *Rules* of the Irish Brothers approved by Archbishop John MacHale on 4 November, 1837, which appeared in the *Irish Catholic Directory* that year. These *Rules*, which are actually Constitutions in their nature, may very well be the same as the lost *Rules* which were sent to Rome only seven years earlier.

RULES

OF

THE THIRD ORDER

OF

Saint Francis.

WITH THE

CEREMONIES

OF

RECEPTION AND PROFESSION.

———

DUBLIN:

PRINTED BY WILLIAM POWELL,
M, THOMAS-STREET.
1842.

RULES OF THE RELIGIOUS PENITENTS OF THE THIRD ORDER OF SAINT FRANCIS

The ten chapters of this 1837 *Rules*,[22] follow the ten chapters of the *Rule of Leo X*. Chapter One is concerned with the nature of the community and states:

They shall promise Poverty, Chastity, and Obedience:
these being the Three essential vows which constitute a

*Religious State, making a Fourth Vow of teaching and catechising youth, with the permission of the Bishop in whose Diocess they reside: that is to say, there shall be one, two, or more, if circumstances shall permit or require, who will devote themselves in a particular manner to the instruction of the poor male children. **The Mechanics and every other individual, to be employed in their different pursuits of industry for the support of the Monastery:** where every thing is to be in common, and nothing to belong to any of the Brethern in particular: the word ours, and not mine, or thine to be used in speaking.* [23]

This chapter, with its emphasis on both teachers and mechanics, reveals the "monastic" nature and purpose of the Irish community. It reveals how the "pursuits of industry" of the "Mechanics" in each monastery supported the work of the teaching brothers in the community.

Chapter Two states the conditions for admission of novices and tells how the community is to be protected from unsuitable candidates:

When any person presents himself to be admitted into this Order, the Superior shall take special care concerning his life, conduct, and vocation, also his abilities for teaching, catechising, mechanism, &c. If the qualities of the person presented excite hopes of his subsequent good conduct, he may be admitted as a Postulant, by the consent of the brethern. But if after six months probation, he is found to be of a turbulent spirit, or of an uneasy disposition or temper, and not spiritually inclined to a Religious State, he is to be excluded, for the greater preservation of the order, peace, and integrity of the Community .

If, after six months the Superior, together with the senior Brethern, find that the Postulant is a fit and proper person to be received into a Noviciate, the Superior will present him to the Ordinary of the Diocess, who will examine his vocation, and if approved of, will receive his Vow of teaching and catechising: after which the Reverend Father Director will receive him to the habit. [24]

The "order, peace, and integrity of the Community" were still being preserved into the 20th century by the decision of all the life professed brothers who still voted for the admission of novices to profession until the 1940s.

SELECTION OF AN IDEAL MASTER OF NOVICES

Chapter Three, on the Profession of the Brothers, describes the spirit to be instilled into the Novices and the qualities to be found in selecting a Master of Novices:

Let the Novices have good religious principles early instilled into them: such impressions as are suitable to their vocation and the spirit of penance: true and sound notions of Poverty, Obedience and Chastity; Modesty, Humility, and Simplicity. And there should be appointed or elected a Master of Novices; a man rich in virtue, cunning in knowledge, and taught in discipline; free from partiality, patient, affable, pious, devout and quick sighted who would know how to dive into the bottom of their inclinations, to find out their weak side, and manage them with discretion, always giving to every one a station suited to his capacity, likewise prescribing remedies to each for conquering his passions and overcoming his temptations: being particularly cautious to admit no man to Profession unfit for religion, and to reject no man of merit or expectation. This Master of Novices should spend a year in each Monastery, to the that all might live according to one Rule and one Spirit; afterwards visiting them as he shall think expedient. [25]

This last sentence suggests that when John MacHale approved this Rule in 1837, there were numbers of postulants in different monasteries in the Archdiocese of Tuam who needed to complete a year of Novitiate before they could be professed and would seem to describe an itinerant Novice Master, traveling through the West of Ireland, who provided a year of Novitiate for each monastery which had postulants needing his year of spiritual guidance.

In the last paragraph of Chapter Three below, we see that only one year of novitiate was required before profession. This was the common practice in the Brothers' communities until Brooklyn's Charles McDonnell, in anticipation of the 1918 Code of Canon Law, changed the Brooklyn Constitutions at the end of the nineteenth century to a three year temporary profession before life profession. [26]

The year of probation being ended let the Novices be professed by the Reverend Father Director, who will consult with the Superior, and the Master of Novices, regarding the future residence of the newly received Brethern; in no case upon any account, pretext, or colour whatever, shall it be lawful for them to go out of this Order. ---According to the words of our Redeemer: He that puts his hand to the plough, and then looks back, is not fit for the kingdom of Heaven -- Luke IX, 62. It is also strictly prohibited, that any members should aspire to the Priesthood. [27]

According to an oral tradition still alive in the Irish community, during the twelve years the Brothers were under the obedience of the Provincial of the Friars Minor (1818-1830), the brightest of their postulants and novices were sometimes "poached" by the Friars for the First Order. [28] It was hoped that this last sentence in the paragraph above would prohibit brothers from "aspiring to the Priesthood".

A handwritten "Rule and General Rules" of the Loretto Brothers, [29] found in the Archives of Mountbellew, seems to date from about 1850, when that Community was settled under the obedience of the Archbishop of Pittsburgh. The "Rule" is the same as the Leo X *Rule* above. However, the "General Rules" or Constitutions, which are similar in many respects to the 1837 Tuam *Rules*, are also unique in many of their parts. A brief excerpt will illustrate the point:

> *The object proposed to themselves by the Members of this institute, besides their own sanctification, which is the primary objective of all Religious Institutions, is to labour for the instruction of Youth, and to devote themselves to such other works as are characteristically calculated to promote the honour of God and the welfare of Souls, and not incompatable with the essential characteristics of the institute* [30] . . . .

In the name of our Lord beginneth the rule of the third order of St. Francis, called the order of penance.

To our beloved Children the Brethern and Sisters of the third order of St. Francis living in Congregation under the three essential laws.

Leo the tenth: Pope.

Beloved sons and daughters, health and apostolical benediction. Among other things committed to our charge's government, these chiefly do make us solicitous, by which the concupiscence of the world and flesh being bridled the quiet state of innocence and first peace given us from above is known to be reduced to its original state and perfection.

Being, since truly for this cause and respect, Pope Nicholas the fourth, our predecessor, confirmed and approved the third order of St. Francis, which he termed of penance, by which the holy confessor of Christ, full of the spirit of God laboured to further the salvation of all faithful Christians; but for as much as by lapse of time, through the inspiration of the Holy Ghost, not only married persons, and such as dwell in the world, for whom the foresaid third rule was made by St. Francis, but also Choirs of innumerable Virgins taking upon them those three essential laws, and some also that of inclosure by our Authority; and having builded by many monastries, not without manifold fruit and edification of the militant Church submitted their necks under the Yoke of the foresaid third order. And because in the said third rule some things to married persons accommodated are inserted, which to single and virginal estate, under this third rule serving our Lord are two ways convenient, for which the pure effects of chaste minds are now and then averted from entering into the said order, we, according to the will of our Lord, separating the precious from the vile, do confirm anew, and approve the same third Rule: distinguished in manner as followeth. and is such; —

LORETTO "RULE AND GENERAL RULES" c. 1850

SPIRIT OF THE THIRD ORDER

Unique to this document, and found in later Third Order Constitutions, including the 1866 Brooklyn Constitutions, is the beautiful description of the spirit of the Third Order:

It is characteristic of the Third Order of St. Francis that the brothers endeavour to unite great simplicity of character with fervent piety and zeal, and seek their perfection rather in the perfect manner of performing ordinary actions, than in things extraordinary in their own nature. [31]

FRANCISCAN HABIT WORN AT LORETTO

The description of the Franciscan Habit is also instructive, especially in its mention of the Loretto Community and its warning, reflective of Nativist, anti-Catholic "Know Nothing" bigotry, about not wearing the Habit in "public places":

The Franciscan Habit is the dress of the brothers, and should be always worn by the professed and novices, when it can be without danger of insult or injury to Religion. The Capuce may be worn in the Chapel, in public places, and in Solemn occasions. In ordinary cases, at work and School, it should be laid aside. The Franciscan Habit does not admit of a Cap, but merely a Collete and when the head requires to be covered and the Capuce cannot, with propriety be used, this should be used. The Habit may generally be worn at Loretto, even beyond the house and premises of the Community. In other places it should not be worn, in the street or public places. After profession, the brethern should wear one uniform dress; a modest frock coat and dark trousers, excluding whatever is superfluous in clothing and other necessaries of nature: for, according to the Holy Father, St. Francis, an affectation in a Religious Man to curious and superfluous things, is a sign, that the Soul is dead; having food and raiment let us be content, and our Redeemer says, Seek first the Kingdom of God and his justice, and all things shall be given you besides. Math.6.33. [32]

This requirement of a "Franciscan Habit" differs from the descriptions of the "uniform dress" of the professed brother found in Chapter IV of the Irish 1837 *Rules*, and in Chapter II of the Irish 1877 *Rules*, which make no mention of a Franciscan Habit:

After Profession the Brethern should wear one uniform dress -- a course blue frock coat, black waistcoat, dark corduroy small-clothes, grey stockings, and white cravats. The Teachers to wear **black soutans** *in School, excluding whatever is superfluous in clothing, and other necessaries of nature.* [33]

A nineteenth-century photograph of three Franciscan Brothers in front of their Bannacurry Monastery and school on Achill Island (shown above in Chapter Three), shows two men in frock coats and the third in a Franciscan Habit with Capuce and Cord. Two are wearing the customary top hat and the brother in the habit also has on a top hat.

1877 RULE AND CONSTITUTIONS

Although the 1877 *Irish Rule and Constitutions* [34] came after the Brooklyn 1866 *Rule and Constitutions*, they are the first separately printed Rule and Constitution we have for the Irish Brothers. They contain much that is found in the

Mountbellew (1837) and Loretto (1850s) documents and combine the Rule with the Constitutions in one text, with the Constitutions square-bracketed below each chapter of the Rule. Chapter I, "On the Entrance of Novices" is essentially the same as the 1837 document:

> [*When any person presents himself to be admitted into this Order, the Superior shall take special care concerning his life, conduct, and vocation; as also his abilities for teaching, catechising, mechanism, etc. ...If, after six months, the Superior together with the senior brethern, find that the postulant is a fit and proper person to be received into a Noviciate, the Superior will present him to the Ordinary of the diocese, who will examine his vocation, and if approved of, will receive his vow of teaching Catechism; after which he will receive him to the habit. . . .].* [35]*

A number of words and phrases in this chapter are worthy of interest. in examining potential postulants, the superior is first to look at a person's life, conduct and vocation, secondly his abilities for teaching, catechising, and "mechanism," etc. This continues the earlier custom of the Irish communities of receiving men who might not wish to teach, but who would have other talents, such as "mechanism". Evidence of the variety of "mechanics" among the brothers included stone masons and carpenters,[36] as well as farmers. This readiness to accept young men who might have had other talents useful to the Monastery, in addition to teaching, was unique to the Franciscan Brothers and was not found in other communities of teaching brothers founded in Ireland in the nineteenth century. Examination of the Brooklyn 1866 Constitutions will show how this unique, **inclusive,** monastic-character of the membership of the Irish

Franciscan communities was done away with in the mid-nineteenth-century City of Brooklyn.

The description of the qualities of the itinerant Master of Novices is similar in this Irish Constitution and indicates that life profession was granted after only one year of novitiate:

> *There should be appointed or elected a Master of Novices, a man rich in virtue, cunning in knowledge, and taught in discipline . . . . This Master of Novices should spend a year in each monastery, in order that all might live according to one rule and one spirit, afterwards visiting them as he shall think expedient.*[37]

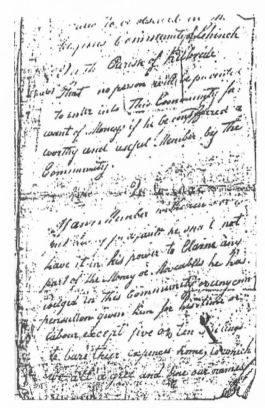

CLARA *"RULES"*

The fourth Irish Rule is a handwritten, six-page document unrelated to all of the above. It is called the "Rules of "The Christian Brethern" [38] and was written for the Clara Monastery in "Lehinch, Parish of Kilbride" in County Offaly in 1821. Created by pious laymen responding to the need of their parish for catechists and their desire to be part of a religious community, these simple "Rules" were eventually replaced when these brothers came under the supervision of the Friars Minor in 1825. The Clara Monastery would eventually be saved by two of the Mountbellew Brothers when the founders became too old to continue their work. [39]

"Rules to be observed
In the Religious Community of Lehinch
In the Parish of Kilbride"

Rule 1
That no person will be prevented to enter this Community for want of Money if he be considered a worthy Member by the Community.

Rule 2
If any Member withdraws, or is put away for a fault, he shall not have it in his power to claim any part of the Money or Moveables he has lodged in this Community or any compensation given him for his time or labour except five or ten shillings to bare their expenses home, to which we all agree and sign our names.

Rule 3
That no person be admitted as a Member of this Community without having first obtained the consent of his Parish Priest and approbation of his confessor.

Rule 4

That every Member, after admission to this Community, shall serve at least a novitiate of one whole year at the expiration of which, if he be considered worthy, he is at liberty to make his solemn profession.

Rule 5

All the Members must rise every Morning throughout the year at about 5 o'clock. Immediately after rising they are to continue about 10 minutes in Meditation, then attend the Community Morning prayer after which they work until about nine and then 10 minutes Meditation after that Breakfast and after-- (a page is missing from the text at this point).

All the Members of this establishment after their Novitiate, if considered worthy, are at liberty to make perpetual vows of Poverty, Chastity and Obedience and to teach the Catechism according to time and Circumstance or the appointment of the Superior.

For Poverty having no Personal Property but what the Superior may think proper to give them which he is at liberty to take from them any time he thinks proper Pleases.

For Chastity to live continent during their whole lives.

For Obedience to obey the Pope, Bishop of the Diocese we live in, the Clergyman or Superior appointed by the Pope or Bishop.

And we take for [the] name of our Rule and Order that of the Christian Brethern. —

We the undernamed do assent and agree to the abovementioned Contract, and Rules,

[signatures of 24 men]

Although twenty-four men signed this "Contract and Rule," Brother Declan Fox tells us that only three brothers made their Profession on 21 November 1822, and that eight received the Franciscan Habit from the Provincial of the Friars Minor on 13 June 1825. [40]

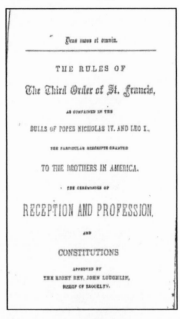

TITLE PAGE 1866 BROOKLYN
RULE AND CONSTITUTIONS

The 1866 Brooklyn *Rule and Constitutions,* [41] approved by John Loughlin, is significantly different from the other nineteenth century Irish documents mentioned above. Although the *Rule* is that of Pope Leo X for the Third Order Regular, most of the *Constitution* is taken directly from the Irish 1832 *Rules and Constitutions of the Society of Religious Brothers,* [42]later known as the Religious Brothers of the Christian Schools, founded by Blessed Edmund Ignatius Rice at the beginning of the nineteenth century and approved by the Holy See in 1820. A few excerpts from both documents will support this conclusion.

Brothers of the Christian Schools
Rules and Constitutions
Chapter I.
Of the End of this Institute

1. -- The end of this Institute is, that all its members labour, in the first place, for their own perfection; and in the second, for that of their neighbour, by a serious application to the instruction of male children, especially the poor, in the principles of religion and christian piety.

The next paragraph requires the Brothers to teach the catechism daily, with an interesting and educationally sound admonition to avoid abstruse or difficult language in explaining it to the children:

2. -- It is a duty incumbent on the Brethern each day of school, to have the children taught the catechism; and also, on those days, to explain it to them, each in his turn, according to the order observed. They are, in the explanation of the Christian doctrine, to speak in a simple and familiar manner, adapting their language to the age and capacity of their hearers, avoiding every thing abstruse or difficult, which might embarrass themselves or the children. [43]

Franciscan Brothers
Constitutions
Article I.
The End of the Third Order

The end of this Order is that the members not only apply themselves to the work of their own salvation, but likewise devote themselves in a particular manner to the religious and literary education of poor male children.

Hence they shall endeavour by prayer, instruction, vigilance, and good example to conduct the children under their charge in the way of salvation, by bringing them up in piety, and instilling into their tender minds true Christian principles. [44]

CHANGE IN COMMUNITY IDENTITY

The second paragraph of this Article I reflects mid-nineteenth-century sociology on the reasons for the existence of the urban Brooklyn Franciscan community, which could have been written by a Catholic Charles Dickens:

ARTICLE I, SECOND PARAGRAPH

It is well known that the laboring class and the poor are commonly without education; and as they are almost unceasingly occupied endeavoring to support themselves and families, they are utterly unable to give their children the necessary instruction. Now the cause of nearly all the disorders among men, but especially among the poor, might be attributed to their having been abandoned when young to their own will and badly brought up, a neglect which is most difficult to repair in a more advanced age, as every one knows how hard it is to eradicate bad habits, no matter what care is taken, either by frequent instructions, or the use of the Sacraments.

"PIOUS AND ZEALOUS FOUNDERS"?

The third paragraph of Article I suggests a significant change in the nature of the Franciscan Brothers' communal life. It seems to preclude membership for the "mechanics," those who by their labors as farmers and carpenter -

builders, supported the teaching brothers instruction of poor children in their Irish Franciscan Monasteries, but whose "avocation... is foreign to the end of our Institute," in the City of Brooklyn.

> *It was chiefly to remedy this evil that this branch of our Order has been instituted, hence it follows that every other avocation, which is not calculated to sustain and promote this most necessary and important object, is foreign to the end of our Institute, and contrary to the benevolent intentions of our pious and zealous founders.* [45]

Ironically, this change in the charism of the Brooklyn Franciscan Brothers' community life was achieved by **"our pious and zealous founders," who imposed the spirit and purpose of the Constitutions of the Brothers of the Christian Schools onto the Constitutions of the Franciscan Brothers** (author's emphasis). The identity of these "pious and zealous founders" is not known, but the tone of the paragraph hints that a legal mind was at work. In marked contrast, the Franciscan Brothers' Community in Loretto, Pennsylvania, would continue the Irish monastic-style of life, as evidenced by their 1850, 1860 and 1870 Federal Decennial Censuses, which listed more brothers as farmers, carpenters and mechanics than teachers. [46]

Brothers of the Christian Schools
Constitutions
Chapter II.

Of the Spirit of this Institute, which is to be the animating principle with all its Members.

1. - That which is of the utmost consequence in a Religious Society, and to which, in every community, the greatest regard should be had, is, that all who compose the body be animated by its peculiar spirit; that the novices labour to acquire it, and that those who have made their vows, make it their first care and chief concern to preserve and augment it in themselves; for it is this spirit that should give life to all their actions, and regulate their whole conduct. Those who possess it not are to be considered, and should consider themselves, as dead members, since they are deprived of the life and spirit of their state; and all should be convinced that without it, it will be extremely difficult to preserve the grace of God.

2. - The spirit of this Institute is that spirit of faith, which inspires its members to view nothing but with the eyes of faith, to do nothing but with a view to God, and to ascribe all to God; at all times entering into the sentiments of holy Job: "The Lord gave" to me, "the Lord hath taken away" from me: "as it hath pleased of the Lord, so it is done: blessed be the name of the Lord!" and also, into other like sentiments, so often expressed in the sacred writings, and by the mouths of the ancient Patriarchs. Thus they will preserve the spirit of holy disengagement. [47]

Franciscan Brothers
Constitutions
Article II.
Of the Community Spirit

One of the most important things in a Community, and to which the greatest attention should be paid is, that all who compose is should be indued with its true spirit.

All the novices should therefore apply themselves to acquire it, and all the professed brothers should be most careful to preserve and augment it, because it is this spirit which should animate all their actions and give motion to all their conduct; and those who have it not, or have lost it, should be regarded and regard themselves as dead members, since they are deprived of the life and grace of their state. They should also be persuaded that without it they will have great difficulty to maintain themselves in the grace of God.

The spirit of this Order is a spirit of faith, which should engage all the members to regard every thing with the eyes of faith --to have God in view in all their undertakings, and to accept all that happens to them, sin excepted, as coming from His hands, ever saying with Job, "The Lord gave, and the Lord hath taken away, as it hath pleased the Lord," &c. They should animate all their actions with sentiments of faith, and have only in view the will of God in the performance of them. [48]

The Irish Brothers' "Monastic-style" Constitution, which the brothers brought with them, welcomed mechanics and farmers, as well as teachers, into their Franciscan community. The brothers in Loretto used this Constitution until they were accepted into the Third Order Regular on 22 May 1908. [49] However, the Brooklyn Brothers' Irish Constitution was changed a half century earlier in 1866, to conform to the Irish Christian Brothers' Constitution, allowing only postulants who would be teachers into the Brooklyn Franciscan Brothers' community. This significant change in the charism of the Franciscan Brothers may be one reason for the exodus to California of John McMahon, the Superior, and half the small community within four years of their arrival.

BROTHERS TRAVEL TO CALIFORNIA

It is evident that the Brooklyn Brothers had a ready population of students needing their services, so why did they plan to go to California in little over a year after they emigrated? Evidence reveals that John McMahon wrote to the First Order Franciscans in Santa Barbara, California in late 1859 or early 1860, seeking their assistance to establish a monastery and college in California. A copy of an 1860 letter from Jose Gonzalez Rubio [1804-1875], the President of the Franciscan Apostolic College of Our Lady of Sorrows in Santa Barbara, to the Superior of the Third Order of St. Francis at Brooklyn, explains the reasons why the brothers were advised **not** to travel to California at that time:

1860 (dated by Maynard Geiger, O.F.M.)

Very Beloved and Respected Brother,

While the Rev. Father Caro[50] was here, he assured me that Bishop [Thaddeus] *Amat* [Bishop of Monterey and Los Angeles], *would expel us from his Diocese or resign his Episcopacy. Up until today, he has not obtained the first, nor do we know if he has made a formal resignation from his Diocese; but it is believed that he will do nothing in our favor and he will even take as many opportunities as present themselves to confound and destroy us.*

From what has been already said you will see the reasons why Bishop Amat does not consent to your founding a house of your Order connected to this College; and even if he might consent to it, it is not prudent that you expose yourself to participate in the disaster or troubles that this College can bring upon you through the public antipathy of this Bishop.

Therefore, since I wish your well-being I will never personally consent (neither will this poor College), to what may be an obstacle for your establishment and progress, or a cause of distaste and troubles; and so it seems very rational that you negotiate under the influence and governance of the Most Rev. Father Pamfilio [Minister General of the First Order] *(as Bishop Amat has suggested), who will certify you in this Diocese and in all the Archdiocese* [of San Francisco], *for the establishment of some houses of the Third Order of our Holy Father Saint Francis. The influence, talents and good qualities of Most Rev. Father Pamfilio will be for you a recommendation and guarantee that I cannot give you, not even with Bishop* [Joseph Sadoc] *Alemany* [Archbishop of San Francisco], *who honors me so much with his friendship.*

Accept then, if it agrees with you, the offers of Bishop Amat and those Bishop Alemany might make, keeping your houses subject to the Custody of Buffalo [Franciscan First Order], *and never to this College, which through its misfortune can hinder the progress and well being that I so wish for you.*

Your most loving servant, etc.

(In the handwriting of Maynard Geiger, O.F.M., the Archivist of the Santa Barbara Mission): *This letter must have been directed to the Superior (or one of the Brothers) of the Third Order of St. Francis at Brooklyn.* [51]

CONTROVERSY BETWEEN
BISHOP AMAT AND THE FRANCISCANS

Archbishop Alemany tried unsuccessfully to mediate between Bishop Amat and Father Gonzalez Rubio.[52] Father Caro, who was also interviewed by Alemany in San Francisco, was of little help in mediating the dispute. When Amat and Gonzalez Rubio returned with Caro to Santa Barbara, as reported in the *Santa Barbara Gazette* on 26 August 1858, the difficulties between Amat and the Franciscans only got worse. Caro's public support of his fellow Franciscans and his public antipathy toward Amat made him a poor Apostolic Visitor. Secular leaders, however, were entirely supportive of the Franciscans. Pablo de la Guerra, a California state senator and president of the Santa Barbara City Council, gave a lengthy testimonial about the controversy between Bishop Amat and the Franciscans. He stated that:

> *The friars have carried out their apostolic mission in such a manner among the pagans and Catholics and their personal conduct has been so pure and conformable to their sacred ministry that they have won for themselves permanently the esteem and religious veneration of the entire old population of California.*[53]

In describing his attempt to mediate between the Bishop and the Friars, de la Guerra writes of the Franciscans' behavior:

> *I never heard from one of them a single word which in any way would becloud or injure the high respect due to the bishop nor against his person nor against the respect due to the secular clergy; but on the contrary they always tried to free the bishop and the secular clergy from blame, attributing the existing difficulties*

only to the adverse reports made by a few persons. Their
charitable self-denial in the matter of their own defense
has always been for me a source of edification and a
corroboration of the ideal I always held of them. [54]

Despite the good conduct of the Friars, it would seem
that Cajetan Sorrentini, a secular priest of the diocese,
would not forget a bad experience he had with Franciscans
in Palestine. He claimed that he had "been appointed by
Pope Pius IX to investigate alleged bad conduct on the part
of Franciscans in Palestine, ...after he discovered possible
links between the Franciscans and Masons there, ... the
Palestinian Franciscans tried to kill him." [55]

After Caro completed his investigation on 10
September 1858, Amat wrote to Propaganda Fide on 24
September, to state "that Caro had allowed himself to be
swayed by anonymous letters attacking both himself and
Father Sorrentini," that Caro had "promised to keep the
investigation out of the public arena, but instead had made
it a public spectacle, and that he had coerced many of the
townspeople of Santa Barbara into testifying in favor of the
friars." Amat concluded, "the religious in question [the
Franciscans], should depart from this diocese, and unless
this takes place immediately I shall depart from it in order
to resign my office of bishop at the feet of His Holiness."[56]

Bishop Amat did decide to go to Rome to plead his
cause in person, but before leaving he revoked the
diocesan faculties "from the entire Franciscan community
in Santa Barbara".[57] This volatile Amat-Franciscan
controversy was perhaps best summed up by Francis
Weber who states, "in later years Sorrentini displayed an
openly hostile attitude toward anything Franciscan and
may well have been the driving force behind the whole
Amat-Franciscan controversy." [58]

This 1860 letter of Jose Gonzalez Rubio is clear evidence that John McMahon and half of the Brooklyn brothers were not intending to stay long in Brooklyn. Within a year of their arrival (late 1859 or early 1860), they were planning to move to California. Whether John McMahon was aware of the controversy between Amat and the Franciscans before he wrote to California, Gonzalez Rubio's letter of response made it abundantly clear that the times were dangerous for Franciscans in Santa Barbara in Bishop Amat's Diocese of Monterey- Los Angeles. Despite Gonzalez Rubio's letter, John McMahon did depart for California with five other brothers in mid-June 1862. They eventually settled in Santa Ines in the hills above Santa Barbara and formed a community and college in the Santa Ines Mission which lasted until 1877.

CONSTITUTIONS OF THE BROTHERS IN CALIFORNIA
"Our clothing is simple, and our table plain."

Although they had plenty of work in Brooklyn, [59] John McMahon, who was the Superior of the Brothers when they arrived from Roundstone, Ireland in 1858, requested entrance into the Friars Minor Apostolic College in Santa Barbara in late 1859 or early 1860. As reported above, the Guardian and President of the College, Jose Gonzalez Rubio, O.F.M., discouraged the Brooklyn Brothers from traveling to California because of a volatile controversy between the Franciscans and Bishop Thaddeus Amat, C.M.

Despite this 1860 letter of discouragement, five professed Brothers: John McMahon, John Cullinan, Paschal Doran, Peter Nolan, Anthony Gallagher, and a novice, Pacificus Wade, left Brooklyn in mid-June of 1862, and arrived in San Francisco about a month later, where they paid their respects to the Archbishop, Joseph Sadoc Alemany, O.P., and stayed for about a week before taking the boat for Santa Barbara. Although they requested entrance to the Franciscan College at Santa Barbara, Gonzalez Rubio could did not give them the First Order Habit until he could determine their status. He wrote to John Loughlin in November or early December, 1862, asking if these five men were free to receive the "*Sanctum Abitum*" and to be professed "*in prima Ordine S.P.S.F.*" [60] After a second letter to Brooklyn a year later, Bishop Loughlin responded to Gonzalez Rubio in a caustic letter, dated 8 December 1863, in which he revealed that these six Brothers had left Brooklyn without his permission, and, except for the novice, Pacificus Wade, were not able to get his "Letter of Freedom" to join the Friars Minor. [61] Wade was eventually ordained in the First Order Friars Minor, and Anthony Gallagher was received into the First Order in the mid 1860s, and lived a very holy life as a lay-brother until he died in the 1890s.

John McMahon, who knew that Loughlin's permission to join the First Order would not be given, did not remain in Santa Barbara, but moved about one hundred miles inland to the Santa Ines Mission in the hills above Santa Barbara to try to set up a college in the ruins of the first seminary of the Church in California. The "*Canada de los Pinos*," popularly known as the College Ranch, embraced 35,499 acres, and was intended to support the Santa Ines mission and seminary, which was established on 4 May 1844, as the *Colegio Seminario de Maria Santisima de Guadalupe de Santa Ines de California.* [62]

In receiving the income from the College Ranch, the Spanish Franciscans "agreed to admit as many poor students as its resources would permit. Preference was to be given to orphans and sons of poor, but respectable,

families. The sons of wealthier families were asked to pay
150 *pesos* per year for tuition, room, and board. Indian boys
were explicitly allowed and encouraged, by means of
financial aid, to attend the seminary. . . . In December of
1845, Jose Joaquin Jimeno, the rector, reported to the
Bishop that the student body had grown to thirty-five
students. However, only a few of these were studying for
the priesthood." [63]

FRANCISCAN MISSIONS SUPPORTED BY "THE PIOUS FUND OF THE CALIFORNIAS"

The ranch and Mission at Santa Ines had been
supported by "The Pious Fund of The Californias" since
1804.[64] However, with the fall of Anastasio Bustamente,
the Mexican president, in 1842, the new Mexican Congress
appropriated the capital which endowed this fund. The
secularization of the missions began in earnest that year
and the confiscation of the Pious Fund left the California
Church with only meager resources. When Manuel
Micheltorena arrived in California as the new governor, he
issued a decree on 29 March 1843, "neutralizing much of
the secularization process by returning twelve of the
missions to the Franciscans with the stipulation that one-
eight of the mission income be paid as a tax for the support
of the military." [65] However, the needs of the military soon
took precedence, and by 24 August 1844, the governor and
the departmental assembly resumed the secularization of
the missions with income from the sales of mission lands
being used to fund the military. After the War with Mexico
concluded with the Treaty of Guadelupe-Hidalgo on 2
February 1848, the United States government eventually
agreed to return to the Church the lands which had been
appropriated before and after the war.

In December of 1855, the general claims of Archbishop Alemany to buildings and land at each of the twenty-one missions of California, in the name of the Catholic Church, had been upheld by the United States Board of Land Commissioners. But the individual declarations of land decisions in regard to specific missions came at various times after this initial verdict. The formal deed granting the Santa Barbara Mission and about 280 acres of land at the mission to the Catholic Church was signed by President Abraham Lincoln on March 18, 1865. [66]

COLLEGE OF SANTA INES

Because the ranch and mission of Santa Ines was administered by the Archdiocese of San Francisco, John McMahon addressed his plan to organize a College in a lengthy and informative letter to James Croke, the Vicar General.[67] On 15 March 1863, in response to two letters Father Croke sent to him, he thanked him for sending $200 and told him how he was repairing the College which had been founded in 1804, after the death of Junipero Serra: [68]

We have a carpenter at work at the college and have got some windows at the Mission which I expect will do for the present, and we have nearly half of our provision, so that I think we will have no necessity to give you much trouble till after Easter. As to books and stationary, we have not much demand for them, and I believe we have enough till we require other necessaries.

In the same letter he continues to answer some of Father Croke's questions about the Third Order, their ownership of property, and how they would support themselves:

I send you enclosed a copy of all the Rules we have regarding your enquiries about the 3rd Order. The Rule I suppose you have, it is contained in a Bull of Leo X dated Jan. 21st, 1521. It is also given in substance in a Prayer Book published by Dunigan, N.Y. called the "Seraphic Manual". **By it you can see we are not prohibited to possess property in common. The object of our vocation is to teach poor male children gratuitously, we can establish wherever we are needed or required, if we get the use of a house and a salary sufficient to find us in food and clothing. In dioceses when Brothers are needed they get in addition to this, aid in the way of lands, colleges, pay schools, etc. to form and educate young teachers. This accounts, in a great measure for whatever property the Brothers possess.**

In response to what seems to be a question regarding their reasons for leaving Brooklyn, John McMahon continues with a number of oblique references to difficulties he may have had with John Loughlin:

We cannot conscientiously leave the Order of our own accord, unless the principle that the Church does not prohibit her children in any state, aspiring to a more perfect one. Some few have acted on this principle, but they are so few that they can neither aid nor injure much. The Ordinary has the same authority over us, that he has over the Brothers of the Christian Schools. They or we desire to have no claim to the schools we conduct more than secular teachers, hence not only can the Ordinary discharge us, but even the manager or patron of the school. On the other hand, we cannot refuse to go wherever we are needed, provided we can live conformably to our Rule, a condition which limits the authority of all superiors. Every Bishop knows well from experience, that unless religious are governed by their own superiors, and the authority of each, even the lowest, sustained and respected, no community could hold, it would therefore be expected that when the Ordinary would need to have a Brother changed he would have it done through the Superior, and should he meet with non-compliance he has the same remedy as with his sexton or servant.

The Superior is sometimes obliged to change the Brothers, should he find a Brother holding an illicit correspondence, and deem his removal the most effectual mode of correcting the dreaded evil, he would change him, and of course, send another in his place.

By the 5th and 8th Chapters of our Rule you can see our connection with the First Order. In some places when the Provincials could not attend to the wants of the Brothers they have obtained a dispensation pro-tem.

Brother John continues to outline the needs of his brothers if they are to establish a school:

*In the E. States the salary of the Brothers is $300 the first year, $100 of which is for the furnishings of the house (see Constitution 2), and $200 for each succeeding year, but as this is not sufficient they are allowed to keep a pay school, to have Exhibitions, etc. This money comes from the parochial Church funds. As to us, we will be satisfied with whatever salary his Grace or you consider sufficient for support. You can form a very practical decision in this head, **our clothing is simple, and our table plain.** If the Brothers are appreciated and required to extend they would expect the encouragement I have above alluded to.*

The salary suggested by Brother John ($300 the first year and $200 yearly thereafter) is in sharp contrast to the $50-60 dollars annual salary suggested for the De La Salle Christian Brothers by Bishop John Hughes in New York, but found not sufficient by them in 1847. [69] It is also better than the $144 annual salary paid to the brothers in the Boys' Orphanage by the Brooklyn Catholic Orphan Asylum Committee in 1858.

Of particular interest to this Chapter, John McMahon concludes his letter to James Croke with "Constitutions," six paragraphs which are more a contract than "constitutions" and suggest a great deal about the negative living and teaching conditions the brothers may have experienced in Brooklyn, and what they wished to avoid in establishing a new community in California:

"Constitutions"

1. The Brothers are forbidden to establish in any place when they cannot live conformably to their Rule & Constitutions and when they cannot have an annual salary sufficient for their support.

2. *The dwelling house and furniture, as well as the school house and school furniture to be provided by the Managers or Patrons of the schools.*

3. *The dwelling house to be sufficiently spacious to accommodate the required no. of Brothers. The classrooms to be contiguous, and separated by glazed partitions.*

4. *A Brother in the Senior class not to be obliged to teach more than 60 pupils, or in the junior class more than 100.*

5. *The Brother Principal to be free to receive pupils, or send them away should their conduct merit such punishment.*

6. *The Superior Provincial to be free to change the Brothers whenever he may judge it useful or necessary.* [70]

Although John McMahon was not able to continue the College in Santa Ines which he planned with Father Croke, John Cullinan, Paschal Doran, and Peter Nolan did begin a college at Santa Ines, which lasted until about 1877. John McMahon opened a school for boys in the basement of St. Mary's Cathedral in San Francisco in the Fall of 1863 and was teaching there until about 1871.[71]

ANOTHER CALIFORNIA "CONSTITUTIONS"

After a year of teaching in the Apostolic College in Santa Barbara, waiting unsuccessfully for Bishop Loughlin's freedom to join the First Order, John Cullinan, Paschal Doran, and Peter Nolan left Santa Barbara and tried to form a community at the College of Santa Ines, which John McMahon had planned with James Croke. After six years of teaching at Santa Ines, they were able to persuade their Ordinary, Thaddeus Amat, C.M., to request a Rescript from the Pope which would have placed them under his obedience. Submitted by Amat, on 29 December 1869, to accompany his request for the Rescript, these three pages of "Constitutions" were primarily designed to document how the brothers would rule each other, with conditions for their employment similar to John McMahon's "Constitutions" above. These "Constitutions" were judged inadequate by Rome in 1871. Propaganda Fide took three years to judge that what they had been sent were not "Constitututions," but a document stating how they would govern each other.

This interesting, curious, handwritten "Constitutions" written by the three Santa Ines brothers, was found in the Archives of Propaganda Fide in Rome. [72] The first six of the 20 rules of these "Constitutions" are very revealing because they document a suspicious hesitation among the **three** brothers in allocating power to one of their own small number as Superior. Rules four, five and six would seem to be an attempt to avoid a repetition of what may have been a difficult parting of the three brothers with John McMahon in 1863, when he left them to go to San Francisco to become the principal of St. Mary's Cathedral Boys School.

Santa Ines "Constitutions"

First --- The Brothers of the Third Order of St. Francis in this diocese shall be under the jurisdiction of the Bishop after he has received the necessary faculties from the Pope.

Second --- The Order shall be governed by a Superior who may be called the Brother Provincial, and a Council, the members of which shall be professed Brothers of the Order.

Third --- The Brothers shall not recognize any ecclesiastical Superior, in this diocese, or province of the Order, except the Bishop who will appoint a Brother Provincial to govern the Order for the term of one year, and he will continue to appoint one every year, till there are five professed Brothers to elect a Br. Provincial for three years.

Fourth --- The Br. Provincial can not carry out any movement in the Order in opposition to the Majority of the votes of the Council, but when the votes are equal for or against the proposed movement, the Br. Provincial shall have the casting vote, which will decide.

Fifth --- Should the Br. Provincial carry out any movement or project in opposition to the Council, he shall be deposed by the Bishop, who will appoint another till the term of office be expired.

Sixth --- No Superior in the diocese can carry out any movement, such as the establishment of schools, &c, in opposition to the Br. Provincial and the Council.

Seventh --- No school can be established without the approbation of the Bishop, and every school duly established by the Order, shall be under the entire control of the Brothers.

Rule Seven may be an attempt to prevent the repetition of a negative experience in St. John's, Newfoundland. Four Irish Franciscan Brothers arrived on 7 September 1847 to take charge of the school and orphanage. When the Irish Benevolent Society, which financed the school and orphanage, began to interfere in the operation of the school, the Brothers left by 1852.

"SUITABLE ACCOMMODATIONS"

*Eight --- No house or school can be established till the Br.
Provincial receives from the founder, the documents
necessary to guarantee to the Brothers, a permanent
support and suitable accommodations.* [73]

Rule Eight, requiring "a permanent support and
suitable accommodations" repeats Rules one, two and
three of John McMahon's "Constitutions" above and seems
to be an attempt to prevent a repetition of the "basement
living" in their first four months in Brooklyn, when they
had no house assigned to them for their residence from the
end of May to the end of October, 1858. Two professed
Franciscan Brothers, and eight postulants lived in the
basement of the French De La Salle Christian Brothers'
house at 256 Pearl Street, two blocks from the Christian
Brothers' school at St. James, and three blocks from the
East River in Brooklyn. They finally took charge of the
ill-fated Boys Orphanage at Bedford and Willoughby
Avenues in late October. About half of the brothers
repeated this basement living-experience when they spent
four years residing in the "damp basement" of their St.
Francis Academy on Baltic Street from 1858 to 1862.

In 1877, with only Bernard Matthews, who had come to
California from Ireland by way of Australia, the
Franciscans could no longer conduct the San Ines
"College" with one man, and Archbishop Alemany
requested the Christian Brothers to take it over.

1905 *Constitutions of the Brothers of Penance of the Third Order Regular of St. Francis of Assisi*

The 1905 Constitutions [74] of the Brooklyn Brothers was written to attempt to revise the 1866 Constitutions approved by John Loughlin, so closely modeled on the Irish Christian Brothers' Constitutions. Written at the command of Charles McDonnell by John Doyle, the Brothers' Chaplain, and Linus Lynch, the former Novice Master and Superior General, this Constitution was never approved by the Bishop because it was based on the French Third Order Regular Constitution which provided for priesthood in the community. Chapter Four, Article III, "The Holy Mass," describes priesthood in the Order:

114. Although our Seraphic Father never took on himself the dread dignity of the Priesthood of Christ, nevertheless he surrounded himself with a family of priests who should sanctify themselves and their Brothers in Religion by offering up the unspotted Lamb of God. Those among us therefore who in God's goodness have received the Holy Priesthood, shall strive by the fervor of their preparation to fit themselves for the Sacrifice, and by the fervor of their thanksgiving to bring down many blessings on themselves and on our Institute.

115. Every priest shall say Mass each day for the intention of the Local Minister in order to satisfy for the Mass-obligations which he has received. If he abstain from the daily offering of the sacrifice, he shall notify the Local Minister.

116. Twice every month each priest shall have the right of offering up the Holy Sacrifice for his own private intentions; but he shall not receive any stipend for these Masses.

117. All the Brothers who are not priests shall hear the Community Mass every day, unless those who may be obliged to serve the private masses of the priests. [75]

Although these Constitutions were never approved, they shed light on the period when the Brooklyn Brothers were trying to join the Third Order Regular in Rome, and are discussed in more detail below in Chapter Seven.

1918 *Rules and Constitutions*

The Brooklyn Brothers Constitutions of 1918 [76] closely copied the 1866 Constitutions which continued to be modeled after the Irish Christian Brothers' Constitutions, with the "End of the Third Order" the same as that of the 1866 Brooklyn Constitutions. This paper-covered Constitutions was replaced in 1924 to conform to the new Code of Canon Law promulgated in 1918.

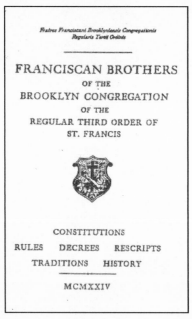

1924 BROOKLYN RULE AND CONSTITUTIONS

On 7 May 1922, Columba Reilly, with Eugene Dunne and Vincent Mulcahy, were appointed a Committee of Three to revise the 1918 Constitutions. [77] At a General Chapter held on 9 April 1923, George Kaupert, V.G., added David McPartland and Jarlath Phelan to the Committee, and the brothers elected Solano Stephens, Philip Lynn, Sebastian Rynne, and Jerome Roese. This Committee of Nine brothers was given the task of "completing the revision of the Constitutions of the Franciscan Brothers."[78] On 26 February 1924, Msgr. Kaupert called a meeting of this Committee of Nine and recommended "certain portions of the new revision for re-adjustment." [79]

David McPartland, the Superior General, reported to the Council on 11 September 1924, that Bishop Molloy had given him "an approved copy of the revised Constitutions". [80] The second page of a letter [81] from Thomas E. Molloy to Brother David [the first page is missing in the Minute Book], raises interesting questions about what the committee had sent to the Bishop, apropos a new form of government. It reads:

> *d. The present form of government has been retained. The changes proposed by your committee have not been adopted since they represent a substantial modification of the Constitutions for which the consent of the Holy See would be required. It does not seem to be desirable to petition the consent for the proposed changes.*
>
> *e. No. 109 relating to "Chapter of Business" seems to be an innovation and would be open to objection except for the fact that the next paragraph - No. 110 - requires the sanction of the Bishop for all legislation.*
>
> *Other changes of lesser importance have been made here and there in the revision as a comparison of the two forms will show, but now this final expression of*

*the Constitutions merits my approval and sanction.
Please submit it to the attention of your Council and
the Brothers of the Community.*

> *With best wishes, I am
> Faithfully yours in Christ,
> signed + Thomas E. Molloy*

There is no information in the Council Minutes about the nature the "substantial modification of the constitutions" concerning the government of the community, which the Bishop would not send to the Holy See. There is also no evidence in the Minute Book of the Council that the "Brothers of the Community," in Chapter, were ever asked to vote on the final revision of the 1924 Constitutions. The possibility that brothers might wish to revise these 1924 Constitutions and Statutes met with vigorous opposition from Columba Reilly after he was elected Superior General in 1925.

These 1924 Constitutions [82] extensively revised the 1866 Constitutions before printing. The long sociological commentary on the "laboring classes and the poor" was taken out and replaced with two articles on the "ends" and "spirit" of the Congregation:

*Chapter I.
(Of the Admission of Novices)*

*Article I. -- Ends of the Congregation.
1. The end of this Congregation of the Regular Third
Order of St. Francis is two-fold. First, the members
shall apply themselves to the work of their own
salvation by making it their earnest care and constant
study to be wanting in nothing of that perfection,
which, by the grace of God, may be acquired by the*

exact observance of the Rule and these Constitutions. Secondly, they shall devote themselves to the religious and literary education of male children and youth, especially the poor.

This chapter continues with the qualifications and duties of the Master of Novices, which are not found at all in the 1866 Constitutions, but are adapted from the 1837 and 1877 Irish Constitutions:

Article 3. -- Master of Novices. Qualifications and Duties.

3. For the office of Master of Novices, a Brother shall be chosen who is a least thirty-five years of age and ten years professed from the date of his first profession.

4. For the office of Assistant Master of Novices, a Brother shall be chosen who is a least thirty years of age and five years professed from the date of first profession.

5. Only Brothers, who by their teaching and example are qualified to train novices in the duties of their state, shall be chosen for these offices. They should be men of tried virtue and have led exemplary lives in the Congregation and be known for their zeal for its progress and interest. They should be men of prayer, mortification, prudence, charity, and meekness, and they should so govern all the movements of their own souls and hearts, as to edify all those under their care. They should be easy of approach, so that the novices may at all times be drawn to him for counsel.

6. They should, above all else, be men of great humility, distrustful of self, relying on God and on Him alone. They shall frequently beg God and our Blessed Lady, her chaste spouse, St. Joseph and Our Holy Founder, St. Francis, to bless them and their charges, and to be the never failing protectors of the novitiate. [83]

FIRST "CHAPTER OF BUSINESS"

The Agenda and Rules of Procedure for the first Chapter of Business to be held on 3 January 1926, were discussed and approved by Columba Reilly, the new Superior General, and his Council on 5, 12 and 18 December 1925. At their meeting of 5 December they voted unanimously that "the Constitutions . . . shall not be amended in any way at the coming Chapter of Business," which was a contradiction of the meaning and nature of what is now recognized as a Chapter of Business. To ensure that the new Constitutions would not be in any way changed, at their next meeting on 12 December, a committee of three consultors was appointed by the Superior General to prepare the Rules of Procedure and Agenda, and these were approved at the meeting of 18 December. However, two of the Rules of Procedure met with vigorous objection from eight brothers of the Community:

5. No discussions allowed.

6. If any matter is put to a vote by the chair, the vote shall be taken by secret ballot without discussion.

These new Rules of Procedure modified what should have been the essential nature of a Chapter of Business, which is to suspend the administrative power of the Superior General and Council during the period of a Chapter, in favor of legislative power of the brothers attending the Chapter, who might wish to revise the Constitutions. These "Rules of Procedure" would not allow the brothers to discuss any motion before voting on it, and would effectively cut off any motion which might revise the Agenda of the Chapter. Rule 1 was also designed to accomplish this purpose by preventing any motions from the floor:

1. A ruling of the chair on a point of order is final.

Anticipating an objection from the brothers, the Council wrote to George Kaupert, the Vicar General, for an interpretation of their right to determine the Rules of Procedure and the Agenda. In a letter [84] to Brother Vincent, the Secretary of the Council, on 26 December 1925, Kaupert ruled that the Superior General and Council had the power to set the Rules of Procedure and Agenda according to Article 109 of the Constitutions, and therefore, he approved them.

At a meeting the day before the Chapter the Council recommended that:

> *The Superior General should have a private meeting with each of the eight Brothers who sent letters of protest concerning the "Rules of Procedure" and "Agenda" prepared and approved by the General Council at a meeting held Dec. 18th, 1925, and to convince them that the General Council or Board of Consultors acted constitutionally in the preparation of the "Rules of Procedure" and "Agenda" for the Chapter of Business as is evidenced by the approval of the Rt. Rev. Msgr. Geo. Kaupert, V.G. as signed below. [85]*

The Chapter of Business was held on Sunday, 3 January 1926 at St. Francis Monastery and the Minutes report that:

> *. . . . No resolutions were passed. The Program of the "Agenda" and "Rules of Procedure" were insisted on and carried out by the Chair. In conclusion, the Superior General closed the Chapter by exhorting the Brothers to observe the approved Constitutions by living up to the requirements of the Religious State, and*

for the comfort of those Brothers who were complaining about the style of collar described in the Constitutions, he exhibited a collar that might be worn on the street dress, namely a Roman Collar with a slit cut from the base to top in the front with a black stock. The Chapter of business was adjourned.[86]

The Agenda for the next Chapter of Business, which followed the elections of 2 August 1928, was again determined by the Superior General and Council and scheduled for Sunday, 23 December 1928. Two of the items submitted by brothers were rejected by the Council and never reached the Chapter. The first suggested a change in the color of the Habit to brown, which was the color of the Franciscan Brothers' habit in Ireland and the Friars Minor, and the second, that Article 173 of the Constitutions be eliminated which required the Librarian to report every two months to the Superior what books had been borrowed by individual brothers. Six items of business were approved for voting:

1. *Shall paragraph 36, sentence 6 which reads "A capuce, large enough to cover the head, shall be worn over the habit in chapel and choir only." be changed to read "A capuce shall be worn over the habit." ?*

2. *Shall paragraph 103, sentence 2 be stricken out which reads "Brothers who come late to the chapel exercises shall, before taking their place, kiss the floor."?*

3. *Shall paragraph 128 be augmented with the following sentence "The Assistant General shall sit at all the meetings of the General Councillors with the right of active voice." ?*

4. *Shall paragraph 158, sentences 4, 5 and 6 which read "A plain white standing collar, which may be celluloid or linen shall be worn. It shall be buttoned in the front. The tie shall be a plain black stock of good material" be changed to read" A Roman collar with a triangular notch Δ in the center shall be worn. Attached to it shall be a black stock." ?*

5. *BOOK OF CUSTOMS- "6:00 P.M. Angelus, supper, visit to the Blessed Sacrament in silence". Shall words "in silence" be stricken out?*

6. *Report of the Superior General as mentioned in Paragraph 109, and Announcements of the Superior General.*

It would not seem that any of the above were major changes in the 1924 *Constitutions and Statutes*, but the Superior General, who had worked on the revision of these *Constitutions and Statutes*, and had seen them through approval by Bishop Molloy, was determined that no discussion be even considered on them. Item Two of the Rules of Procedure approved for this Chapter of Business again read "No Discussions Allowed" on any of the six Agenda items.

CHAPTERS OF BUSINESS ELIMINATED

After the Roll Call, and before any items of the Agenda could be voted upon, the Minutes of the Chapter narrate an extraordinary event by which the brothers lost their right to have a Chapter of Business for the next six years:

Some objections being raised (It was moved and seconded that No 2 of the Rules of Procedure be stricken out. - The Chair did not entertain the motion), on the "Rules of Procedure," the President of the Chapter

*called upon the Secretary to read Msgr. Kaupert's
Letter of Dec. 26, 1925 concerning the duly authorized
approval of the "Rules of Procedure" and the Agenda
prepared by the Board of Consultors for the Chapter of
Business which was held January 3rd, 1926. The letter
having been read, the President, after due consideration
decided that the Chapter of Business was now
adjourned. The Chapter then adjourned sine die.* [87]

The brothers did not have another Chapter of Business
until after the next two terms of office of Columba Reilly.
At the Council meeting of 2 March 1929, Brother Columba
reported on his meeting with Msgr. Kaupert on 27
February 1929:

*[I]t was finally decided that the Chapter of Business
which was adjourned Dec. 23, 1928 sine die, should be
left over until the next administration, and that the
prepared Agenda should be approved by the Rt. Rev.
Msgr. Kaupert, VG, before the opening of the next
Chapter of Business.* [88]

The Chapter of Business, which should have followed
the Chapter of Elections of 2 August 1931, was never held.
At the regular meeting of the Consultors on 16 January
1932, Brother Columba made the following
announcements:

*a) that the Chapter of Business due at Xmas 1931,
was indefinitely postponed.*

*b) that the "Capuce" may be worn at all times with
the permission of Msgr. Cherry, our spiritual Director.*

*c) That Msgr. Cherry ruled that the Assistant
Superior General may, according of custom, sit and
vote with the Board of General Consultors.* [89]

The brothers did finally have a Chapter of Business on 22 December 1934, after the election that Summer of Capistran Cusack as Superior General. Discussion of agenda items was restored, and eight items of business were discussed and voted upon.

VATICAN COUNCIL II

After Vatican Council II, the Community responded to *Perfectae Caritatis* by holding the first of several Extraordinary Chapters to discover the Charism of the Founder and revise its Rule and Constitutions accordingly. In 1964, a document was produced based upon the brothers' Extraordinary Chapters. This was revised in 1976 to reflect the "Franciscan Penitential Life Statement," which was observed until the current *Rule and Life and Constitutions* [90] was approved on 4 October 1989.

The *Constitutions*, which the Franciscan Brothers began to revise after the Second Vatican Council in 1968, was finally approved by the Brooklyn Ordinary, Francis Mugavero, on 19 March 1985. The revised text of these *Constitutions* was resubmitted to the Congregation for Institutes of Consecrated Life and Societies of Apostolic Life, after the approval of the brothers' request for universal suffrage of the life-professed at chapters, as a long-standing tradition of the Community. On 8 September 1989, the Sacred Congregation promulgated the *Decretum Laudis* (Decree of Praise) establishing the Franciscan Brothers as an Institute of Pontifical Right and approved the new *Constitutions* of the Community on the Feast of Our Holy Father St. Francis on 4 October 1989.

John Paul II
as a
Perpetual Memorial

Much as in past centuries, the Franciscan ideal of life even in our times continually draws many men and women desirous of evangelical perfection and thirsty for the kingdom of God. Inspired by the example of Saint Francis of Assisi, the members of the Third Order Regular set forth to follow Jesus Christ by living in fraternal communion, professing the observance of the evangelical counsels of obedience, poverty, and chastity in public vows, and by giving themselves to innumerable expressions of apostolic activity. To actualize in the best way possible their chosen way of life, they dedicate themselves unreservedly to prayer, strive to grow in fraternal love, live true penance and cultivate Christian self-denial.

Since these very elements and motives for living the Franciscan ideal are clearly present in The Rule and Life of the Brothers and Sisters of the Third Order Regular of Saint Francis and since they are clearly in accord with the genuine Franciscan spirit, We, in the fullness of our apostolic authority, determine, declare, and order that the present Rule have the force and importance to illustrate to the brothers and sisters this authentic meaning of the Franciscan life, while bearing in mind what Our Predecessors Leo X and Pius X, with the Apostolic Constitutions Inter cetera and Rerum condicio presented on this matter in their own times.

Since We know how diligently and assiduously the Rule and Life has traveled its path of aggiornamento and how fortuitously it arrived at the desired convergence of different points of views through collegial discussion and consultation, proposals and studied amendments, for this very reason with well-founded hope We trust that the longed for fruits of renewal will be brought to full realization.

We decide, moreover, that this our decision have force from this moment on and be effectively binding both in the present and in the future, everything to the contrary notwithstanding.

Given at Rome, at Saint Peter's
under the ring of the Fisherman,
on the 8th of December, 1982,
the fifth year of our Pontificate.

JOHN PAUL II'S LETTER OF APPROVAL OF
THE RULE AND LIFE

The Brooklyn Franciscan Brothers participated in the revision of the *Rule and Life* with the over four hundred Third Order Regular congregations of men and women throughout the world. Margaret Carney, OSF describes this exciting work in her "Commentary Introduction," to the *Rule and Life*:

The work group responsible for evaluating the proposals, researching the values and principles for the content, and authoring the text itself stabilized their work by reliance on three critical tasks:

1) Insistence upon a return to the proper charism of the founder as imparted to this Order. The work was assisted by the availability of modern research into the writings of Francis and Franciscan history.

2) A rediscovery of the history of the Order.

More that a simple examination of past events was required. This study led to an understanding of the divergent expressions of the charism that exist in contemporary communities/fraternities. We learned that the diversity was not inimical to unity in essential spirit and mission.

3) A world-wide consultation inviting proposals for the text from every congregation.

Brothers and sisters from over thirty countries participated. Nearly two hundred superiors were personally present at the final assembly in March, 1981. Never before in the Order's history have the members exercised such collective responsibility and global communication. [91]

BROOKLYN BROTHERS REGAIN THEIR
IRISH FRANCISCAN CHARISM

The ministries of the Community, after the approval of their Constitutions by the Roman Congregation, returned to the Irish tradition of an **inclusive**, rather than an **exclusive** description of the works of the Franciscan Brothers. This tradition reflects Chapter V: *"The Way to Serve and Work"* of *The Rule and Life:*

> *As poor people, the brothers and sisters to whom the Lord has given the grace of serving or working with their hands, should do so faithfully and conscientiously.*

Thus these *Constitutions* returned the "charism" of the Brothers to a variety of educational and pastoral ministries, when it states:

> *Our apostolate is to live the Gospel. In humility and joy we live in the world to affirm Christ's kingdom of peace. We expend our lives in bringing to fulfillment the love affirmed by the Incarnation. We believe that the Holy Spirit leads us through our varied ministries to one end.*
>
> *Faithful to our Franciscan charism, through our apostolic works in the educational and pastoral ministries of the Church, we proclaim peace as we respond to the needs of society. When we work to establish harmony among people, Christ's peace becomes real and we are free to see all as equal members of His body.* [92]

The brothers have been engaged in many different ministries since their Extraordinary Chapters following Vatican Council II and the approval of their *Constitutions,*

which describe the Charism of the Brooklyn Brothers'
Community:

> *We Brothers of the Third Order Regular of Saint
> Francis form a lay religious institute of pontifical right.
> We observe the life of the Gospel through our prayer,
> apostolic works and fraternity. . . .*
>
> *As non-ordained religious, we make Christ present by
> rebuilding His Church, by sowing seeds of Christian
> consciousness and brotherhood, and by living together
> in peace.*

WRITINGS, RULES AND CONSTITUTIONS
EXAMINED IN CHRONOLOGICAL ORDER

"Letter to All the Faithful," in *St. Francis of Assisi; Writings
and Early Biographies; English Omnibus of* the Sources for
the *Life of St. Francis.* Third Revised Edition, Franciscan
Herald Press, 1992, p. 92.

*Rvle of the Relgious, of the Thirde Order of St. Francis, For both
fexes, making the three vovves, and living together in
Communitie and Cloyster, Vvith certaine other thihgs vvich
the leaf follovving doth shevve, +, IHS, At Brvelles, By Ihon
Pepermans, at the, golden Bible, 1624 [Brussels Rule], from
English Recusant Literature: 1558-1640, Vol 378,* The
Scholar Press, London, 1978.

"Rules of the Christian Brethern," [Clara "Rules"], six-page
manuscript in the Franciscan Brothers Archives,
Mountbellew, 1821.

*Rules and Constitutions, of the, Society, of, Religious Brothers,
to Which is Annexed, The Brief of our Holy Father, Pope
Pius VII, Approving and Confirming the, Institute* [Irish
Christian Brothers, 1832 *Rules*], Joseph Blundell,
Dublin, 1832.

Rules of the Religious Penitents of the Third Order of Saint Francis, with the Ceremonies of Reception and Profession [Irish *Rules* 1837], in the *Irish Catholic Directory*, Gerald P. Warren, 88, Thomas Street, Dublin, 1837.

"In the Name of Our Lord beginneth the rule of the third order of St. Francis, called the order of penance." 25-page manuscript of "Rules and General Rules" for the Loretto community [Loretto 1850 "Rules"], c 1850. From the Mountbellew Archives.

"Constitutions," in a letter from Brother John McMahon to Father James Croke, Vicar General, Archdiocese of San Francisco, Chancery Archives of the Archdiocese of San Francisco, 15 March 1863.

Santa Inez "Constitutions," Propaganda Fide Archives, SC/, 1870-1871, vol. 23, fols. 1314rv to 1316r.

Deus Meus et Omnia. The Rules of, The Third Order of St. Francis, as Contained in the, Bulls of Popes Nicholas IV. And Leo X., The Particular Rescripts Granted, to the Brothers in America, The Ceremonies of Reception and Profession, and, Constitutions, Approved by, the Right Rev. John Loughlin, Bishop of Brooklyn, [Franciscan Brothers 1866 *Rules*] February, 1866.

The Rule of the Regular Third Order of our Holy Father Saint Francis, As contained in the Bull of Pope Leo X., Together With The Approved Constitutions [Irish 1877 Rule], Browne & Nolan, Dublin, 1877.

"Constitutions of the Brothers of Penance of the Third Order Regular of St. Francis " manuscript never approved, 1905.

Rules and Constitutions of the Brothers of the Third Order of St. Francis, Franciscan Brothers of the Diocese of Brooklyn, Blaber & Son, New York, 1918.

Fratres Franciscani Brooklyniensis Congregationis, Regularis Tertii Ordinis, Franciscan Brothers, of the, Brooklyn Congregation, Of the, Regular Third Order of, St. Francis, MCMXXI [Brooklyn *Rule and Constitutions,* 1924], Privately printed, 1924.

Rule and Life and Constitutions, Congregation of the Religious Brothers of the Third Order Regular of St. Francis, Brooklyn, New York, 1989.

Notes

[1] Margaret Susan Thompson, "Charism or Deep Story? Towards Understanding Better the 19th-Century Origins of American Women's Congregations," *Review For Religious,* Vol. 58, no. 3, (May-June, 1999), pp. 230-250.

[2] Rules have a universal character and are approved by the Pope. Constitutions are particular to a specific community and are written by the community and approved by the bishop or the Holy See.

[3] The writing of the "Letter to All the Faithful" is variously placed from 1214, in its earlier version as the *Recensio prior,* to no later than during the two years before Francis' death on 4 October 1226. Other documents similar in tone, such as Francis' "Letter to All Clerics" and his "Final Testament" of 1226, were written in these last years of Francis' life.

[4] *St. Francis of Assisi, Writings and Early Biographies, English Omnibus of the Sources for the Life of St. Francis [Omnibus],* Franciscan Herald Press, 3rd Ed. 1972, p. 91. Two later versions of the "Letter to All the Faithful" are found in *Francis of Assisi, Early Documents,* 3 volumes, New City Press, New York, 1999, Vol. I, pp. 41-51.

[5] *Omnibus,* pp. 92-93.

[6] Raffaele Pazzelli, T.O.R., *St. Francis and the Third Order, The Franciscan and pre-Franciscan Penitential Movement,* Franciscan Herald Press, 1989, p. 104

[7] *Ibid.,* p. 114.

[8] *Ibid.*, pp. 152-154.

[9] *Rvle of the Religiovs, of the Thirde Order of St. Francis, For both fexes, making the three vovves, and living together in Communitie and Cloyster, VVith certaine other things vvich the leaf follovving doth shevve, +, IHS, At. Brvelles, By Ihon Pepermans, at the, golden Bible, 1624.* From *English Recusant Literature: 1558-1640*, Vol. 378, The Scholar Press, London, 1978, notes, pg. iv.

[10] Recusant Catholics lived in hiding in the British Isles or on the Continent. The English books they published in Belgium and other continental countries became known as "Recusant Literature".

[11] Brussels *Rvle*, pp. 18-19.

[12] Brussels *Rvle*, pp. 19-21.

[13] Brussels *Rvle*, pp. 28-29.

[14] Brussels *Rvle*, pp. 32-33.

[15] Brussels, *Rvle*, pp. 42-43.

[16] Brussels, *Rvle*, pp. 46-47.

[17] The distinction between "Rules" and "Constitutions" is sometimes not clarified. The 1877 Irish document has the Rules and Constitutions together, with the "Constitutions" in brackets following each article of the "Rule".

[18] Letter from Benignus Millet, O.F.M. to the author, 2 March 1993.

[19] Although Franciscans, who are not "monks," do not live in "monasteries," the term "monastery" has traditionally been given to the houses of the Franciscan Brothers in the West of Ireland. "Monks of the West" was the popular title given to the brothers in the nineteenth century. The Franciscan Brothers brought this title with them and were incorporated as "The St. Francis Monastery of the City of Brooklyn" in 1868.

[20] PFA, *Lettere e Decreti . . .*, 1830, Vol. 311, Fol. 863v.

[21] PFA, *Rubrica* 12, Prot. N. 21880, February, 1897.

[22] *Rules of the Religious Penitents of the Third Order of Saint Francis, with the Ceremonies of Reception and Profession*, [Irish 1837 Rule] in the *Irish Catholic Directory*, Gerald P. Warren, 88, Thomas Street, Dublin, 1851.

[23] Irish 1837 *Rule,* p. 3.

[24] Irish 1837 *Rule,* p. 6. (The "Reverend Father Director" was a First Order Friar Minor assigned as their superior).

[25] Irish 1837 *Rule,* pp. 4-5.

[26] Franciscan Brothers Archives, Council Minutes and General Chapters, August 2, 1894 to November 19, 1906. Although it was the wish of Bishop Charles McDonnell, "The matter of making the vows only for a time was deferred." p. 5, 2 August 1894.

[27] Irish 1837 *Rule,* p. 5.

[28] Vincent Jordon, O.S.F., "The Order of Penitents, The Third Order Regular of Saint Francis in Ireland," Chapter IV, pg. 4.

[29] Franciscan Brothers Archives, Mountbellew, [FBAM],"In the Name of Our Lord beginneth the rule of the third order of St. Francis, called the order of penance," 25 page manuscript of "Rules and General Rules" for the Loretto community, [Loretto 1850 "Rules"].

[30] Loretto 1850 "Rules," p. 6.

[31] Loretto 1850 "Rules," pp. 6-7.

[32] Loretto 1850 "Rule," pp. 7-8.

[33] Irish 1837 *Rules,* p. 22.

[34] *The Rule of the Regular Third Order of our Holy Father Saint Francis, As Contained in the Bull of Pope Leo X, Together With The Approved Constitutions,* [Irish 1877 *Rule*], Browne & Nolan, Nassau Street, Dublin, 1877.

[35] Irish 1877 *Rule, pp. 17-18.*

[36] Evidence of the abilities of the brother "mechanics" can be seen in the substantial Roundstone Monastery in Chapter One which was built by the brother stone masons and carpenters.

[37] Irish 1877 *Rule,* pp. 19-20.

[38] "Rules of the Christian Brethern," six page manuscript in the Franciscan Brothers Archives at Mountbellew, 1821.

[39] Bernardine Cowan, O.S.F., "The Story of the Irish Franciscan Brothers," Mountbellew, 1955, p. 19

[40] Declan Fox, O.S.F. "History of the Irish Franciscan Brothers," p. 9

[41] *Deus Meus et Omnia. The Rules of The Third Order of St. Francis, as Contained in the Bulls of Popes Nicholas IV, and Leo X, The Particular Rescripts Granted to the Brothers in America, The Ceremonies of Reception and Profession, and Constitutions, Approved by the Right Rev. John Loughlin, Bishop of Brooklyn,* [Franciscan Brothers, 1866 *Rules*], 1866.

[42] *Rules and Constitutions of the Society of Religious Brothers, to Which is Annexed The Brief of Our Holy Father Pope Pius VII, Approving and Confirming the Institute,* [Irish Christian Brothers, 1832 *Rules*] Dublin, 1832.

[43] Irish Christian Brothers, 1832 *Rules*, p. 1.

[44] Franciscan Brothers, 1866 *Rules*, p. 44.

[45] Ibid.

[46] Censuses of Loretto, Cambria County, Pennsylvania, 1850, 1860, and 1870.

[47] Irish Christian Brothers, 1832, *Rules*, pp. 2-3.

[48] Franciscan Brothers, 1866, *Rules*, p. 45.

[49] Seraphin J. Conley, T.O.R., *Third Order Regular of St. Francis of Penance: Resource Manual,* 2nd edition, Convento dei Ss. Cosma e Damiano, Roma, 1994, p. 248.

[50] Francis Caro, O.F.M., who was pastor of St. Joseph's Church in Rossville, Staten Island, was sent to California in early July of 1858, as an Apostolic Visitor by the Franciscan Minister General, to adjudicate a longstanding dispute between the Santa Barbara Franciscans and Bishop Thaddeus Amat, C.M. (*Freeman's Journal and Catholic Register,* July 10, 1858 in the PFA, *Scritt.,* Vol. 985, fols 286r and 287v). After his arrival in San Francisco, Caro wrote to the Minister General on 4 August 1858, to tell of his welcome reception by Archbishop Joseph Alemany and mentions Alemany's high regard for the Santa Barbara Franciscans. (PFA, *Scritt.* No. 1, Vol. 985, fols 81r to 83r).

[51] Franciscan Archives of the Mission of Santa Barbara.

[52] Maynard Geiger, O.F.M., *Franciscan Missionaries in Hispanic*

California, 1769-1848, a Biographical Dictionary, The Huntington Library, San Marino, 1969, pp. 113-120.

[53] Michael Charles Neri, *Hispanic Catholicism in Transitional California: the Life of Jose Gonzalez Rubio, O.F.M., (1804-1876)*, Academy of American Franciscan History (Monograph Series, Vol. 14), Berkeley, California, 1997, p. 87.

[54] *Ibid.*

[55] *Ibid.,* p. 88.

[56] PFA , *Scritture Originale... Congressi Generale,* Vol. 985, fols 364r to 367r.

[57] Francis J. Weber. *California's Reluctant Prelate: the Life and Times of Right Reverend Thaddeus Amat, C.M.,* Los Angeles, Dawson Book Shop, 1964, p. 59.

[58] *Ibid.,* p. 56, n.14.

[59] Ronald H . Bayor and Timothy J. Meagher, *The New York Irish,* Johns Hopkins University Press, Baltimore, 1996, reports that the number of Irish-born and Irish-Americans in Brooklyn in the mid-nineteenth-century provided a large number of children needing the education the Brothers could provide, pp. 554-555.

[60] Maynard J. Geiger, O.F.M., *Calendar of Documents in the Santa Barbara Mission Archives,* p. 199, Document 214, notes the attempt of the Brothers to receive the "Sacred Habit and be professed in the First Order of Our Holy Father St. Francis".

[61] Two letters of Rubio to Loughlin, Nov. 1862 and Nov. 1863, and Loughlin to Rubio, 8 December, 1863, Santa Barbara Archives.

[62] Neri, pp. 44-45.

[63] *Ibid.,* p. 45.

[64] Begun in 1697 for the support of the Jesuit missions of Lower California, "The Pious Fund of the Californias" was created by wealthy donors in Spain and New Spain. At the suppression of the Jesuits in 1767, the income from the capital of this fund, which amounted to about $2 million dollars, was assigned to the Dominicans in Lower California and to the Franciscans in Upper California. As an arm of the Spanish State, the missions in the early

nineteenth century received an annual stipend of $300 to $400 for each priest, and $1,000 for each new mission to purchase bells, tools, seeds, vestments, and the necessary animals and cuttings for the mission ranch.

[65] Neri, p. 43

[66] *Ibid.*, p. 117.

[67] Letter of McMahon to Croke, 15 March 1863, Chancery Archives, Archdiocese of San Francisco.

[68] Maynard J. Geiger, O.F.M., *The Life and Times of Fray Junipero Serra, O.F.M.: Or The Man Who Never Turned Back, (1713-1784)*, Academy of American Franciscan History, Washington, DC, 1959, 2 vols, Vol II, p. 274.

[69] An 1840 letter of Bishop Bouvier of Le Mans, France to Pope Gregory XVI, stating that the De La Salle Christian Brothers require annually $120 for each Brother before they will accept a school, in Angelus Gabriel, F.S.C., *The Christian Brothers in the United States, 1848-1948*, McMullen, New York, 1948, p. 56.

[70] Letter of McMahon to Croke, 15 March 1863.

[71] *Catholic Directories*, 1862-1871.

[72] "Constitutions for the government of the Brothers of the Third Order of St. Francis in the diocese of Monterey and Los Angeles, State of California." PFA, *Scritt*, 1870-1871, fols. 1314rv to 1316r.

[73] PFA, Ibid.

[74] These Constitutions were written at a difficult time in the history of the Brooklyn Brothers' Community, which was attempting to join the Third Order Regular in Rome.

[75] 1905 "French Clerical Constitutions," pp. 30-31.

[76] *Rules and Constitutions of the Brothers of the Third Order of St. Francis, Franciscan Brothers of the Diocese of Brooklyn, 1918*, Blaber & Son, New York City, 1918.

[77] Franciscan Brothers Archives, (FBA), Council Minutes (CM), 1910-1922, p 36.

[78] FBA, CM, 1922-1943. p. 2.

79 FBA, CM, 1922-1943, p. 6.

80 FBA, CM, 1922-1943, p. 10.

81 FBA, CM, 1922-1943, insert between pages 12-13, no date, but before 10 November, 1924.

82 *Franciscan Brothers of the Brooklyn Congregation of the Regular Third Order of St. Francis, MCMXXIV*, [Brooklyn *Rule and Constitutions*, 1924], 1924.

83 Brooklyn *Rule and Constitutions*, 1924, pp. 1-2.

84 FBA, CM, 1922-1943, p. 23.

85 FBA, CM, 1922-1943, pp. 22-24.

86 FBA, CM, 1922-1943, pp.25-26

87 FBA, CM, 1922-1943, p. 28.

88 FBA, CM, 1922-1943, p. 63.

89 FBA, CM. 1922-1943, pp. 103-104. It would seem that it had not been the custom to include the Assistant Superior General as a voting member of the General Council.

90 *Rule and Life and Constitutions, Congregation of the Religious Brothers of the Third Order Regular of St. Francis*, Brooklyn, New York, 1989.

91 *Rule and Life and Constitutions, Congregation of the of the Religious Brothers of the Third Order Regular of St. Francis*, Brooklyn, New York, 1989, pp. 1-5.

92 *Rule and Life and Constitutions*, 1989.

CHAPTER SEVEN

A CRISIS IN THE FRANCISCAN COMMUNITY, AS BROTHERS RESPOND TO A POPE'S "YES" AND A BISHOP'S "NO"

In October 1897, Pope Leo XIII signed the Bull, *Felicitate Quadam*, which required all the many separate Franciscan communities throughout the world to seek affiliation and obedience with one of the four existing Franciscan Orders: the Order of Friars Minor, the Order of Friars Minor, Conventual, the Order of Friars Minor, Capuchin, or the Third Order Regular. In the next ten years, Brothers in Ireland and then America, petitioned to join the Third Order Regular, under the obedience of their Roman Minister General.

The Irish Franciscan Brothers were under the obedience of the Irish Provincial of the First Order Friars Minor since their re-founding in Dublin in 1818, and, therefore, were included in the status of *regulars* under the obedience of a Roman Minister General. Because the so-called Catholic Emancipation of 1829 did **not** emancipate *regular* religious who were under the obedience of a superior outside the British Isles, the Irish Brothers, in order to receive novices and continue in existence, requested Propaganda Fide to transfer their obedience from the Irish Provincial to their local Ordinary, Dr. Oliver Kelly, the Archbishop of Tuam, effectively changing their ecclesiastical standing from a religious community of *regular* status to that of a diocesan institute. The Brothers' Petition, the Archbishop's letter, which Propaganda Fide responded to on 2 October 1830, granting their petition, are shown below:

Memorial of the Monks of Mountbellew, of the
Third Order of St. Francis, to His Excellency
the Most Rév. Mons. KELLY, Archbishop of
Tuam.

MOST REVEREND LORD,—We, the undersigned
monks of the Third Order of St. Francis, con-
stituting the Community of Mountbellew in this
Diocese, humbly implore your Lordship's influence with the Sacred Congregation of the
Propaganda in order that it may be permitted
us by the Apostolic See to transfer our obedience
from the Religious Superior to the Ordinary of
this Diocese, since, as your Lordship knows well,
without such permission our house will come
very soon to be extinguished—the proprietor not
wishing, by reason of the laws, to leave to us any
longer the possession of the place where we
live unless this transfer of obedience is made,
and he no longer permits our religious superior
to visit us ; thus we are no longer like a religious
community.   For this end we have already
presented a petition to the Sacred Congregation,
but without effect.   Yet we hope that with the
present attestation and the recommendation of
your Lordship, we may have better success
another time ; otherwise we shall not know what
to do, for we cannot take another place on lease,
nor find refuge in the other two small houses of
our Order which are the only ones existing in
this country, and which, though poor, are filled
with subjects.   What affects us more is that we
shall not be able to live up to the spirit of our
perpetual vows.   Therefore, we ardently pray
your Lordship to favour us in this lamentable
circumstance by forwarding this humble petityon
with the Holy See, promising you to correspond
to your goodness by attending with more vigour
to the instruction of the poor in the Christian
Doctrine, and in the employments most useful
to them.

> BRO. BONAVENTURE (THOMAS LEE).
> BRO. JOSEPH (MICHAEL GREADY).
> BRO. FRANCIS (JOHN DUFFY).
> BRO. GILES (JOHN CARROLL).
> BRO. PAUL (JOHN WALDRON).
> BRO. DOMINIC (MATTHEW LEE).
> BRO. PETER (PATRICK KIVILEHAN).

Per the Eminent Prefect of Propaganda Fide.

Statement of the Rector of the Irish College regarding the memorial of the monks of the
Third Order of St. Francis.

In the whole of Ireland there are three con-
vents of the Order of St. Francis in which they
take perpetual vows, and lead the common life.

PETITION OF THE MOUNTBELLEW BROTHERS

As a diocesan community since 1830, the Irish Franciscan Brothers had to petition their three ordinaries at the end of the nineteenth century, to allow them to join the Third Order Regular. In a hand-written Memoir, completed when he was fifty-two years in the community, Bernardine Cowan, O.S.F., Superior General and Historian of the Irish Brothers, recalls the two attempts of his community to respond to the Pope's request to return to a *regular* status as members of the Third Order Regular under the obedience of the Minister General of the Order in Rome, and to unite their houses under one central government:

> *In 1898, a movement was started in the two Houses outside the diocese of Tuam* [Clara and Farragher]. *This had for object the Union with the Italian branch* [sic] *of the Third Order in Rome, the authorities of which were favorable and they had secured the good will of the Cardinal Protector. There were a few in Tuam who were really anxious for this Union, and all could see that there was hardly anything else which Clara and Farragher could do if they were to avoid total extinction. For Farragher had just emerged from years of persecution from their late Bishop, and Clara was then in the middle of a similar ordeal.*
>
> *A Petition was therefore drawn up in Clara and brought around secretly to the Houses in the West. Most of the Brothers, some of whom were not allowed to read the document, added their signatures, more out of sympathy with their brethren in Meath* [Farragher] *and Elphin* [Clara], *than of a real desire to become a clerical institute. The document was sent to Rome, and was promptly referred back for comment to the Bishops concerned, who learned for the first time what was afoot. Their reply, to say the least, was unfavorable to*

*the Brothers, and it must have contained something
about our "imperfect religious formation". This letter
was a boomerang, for we had then been 68 years
diocesan. Hence Rome, while giving "non expedit" as
a reply to the Petition, directed the Archbishop [John
MacEvilly of Tuam] to remedy this defect.*

*Accordingly, Br. Francis Costello, Superior of
Annadown, was directed by the Archbishop to write to
all the Houses in Tuam, that each was to send a
delegate along with the Superior to a meeting in
Annadown. This was done, and the meeting reported
back that they had elected a Br. Visitator and Council
of four Assistants; that the Visitator, Br. John Edwards
should visit all the houses and when this was done, the
Chapter should meet again to elect Superiors and
officials of the Houses. The Archbishop agreed to this,
and the Chapter of 1898 came to an end. Not before,
however, the recent Petition [for union with the TORs
in Rome] had been repudiated.*[1]

IRISH BISHOPS PREVENT UNION

Union with the Third Order Regular in Rome was
effectively prevented by the negative response of the
brothers' three Irish bishops. However, with the Chapter
at Annadown in 1898, the brothers in Ireland had achieved
the beginnings of a single, unified Irish community. By
1930, they received Papal Recognition with a centralized
government for the community. Despite the setback
against union with the Third Order Regular in Rome, the
Irish Brothers continued to seek union with the Loretto
and Brooklyn Franciscan communities which had
emigrated from Ireland in the middle of the 19th century.
Bernardine Cowan recalls the attempt of the Brothers to
unite their communities in Ireland and America:

The Triennial Chapter was due in 1901, but, owing to the illness of Br. John, it was postponed to January, 1902. The records of this Chapter are the only ones missing from the Archives. Brother John was re-elected. The chief business on the agenda for the Chapter of Affairs was a proposal to unite, with the approval of the Bishops concerned, all the Franciscans Brothers in Ireland, in Loretto, and in Brooklyn under one central government with separate provinces. Both the American Houses were in favor of the proposal. Loretto was unanimous and Brooklyn very nearly so. The Chapter voted unanimously in its favor, and suspended its sittings until it knew the mind of the Archbishop. When the deputation returned from Tuam, we were delighted to learn that it had been graciously and favorably received by him. Then he had told them to go ahead, and when the necessary documents were ready, he would forward them to Rome with his strong recommendation. [2]

"BIFFED BELOW THE BELT!

Brother Bernardine recalls Archbishop MacEvilly's negative response a few months later:. . *[B]y the time everything was ready, it was found that His Grace had changed his mind in the interval. When reminded that he had told us to go ahead and had promised his support, he asked: 'Have you that in writing?' When told that we had only his word, he replied 'Oh, that was only a transeat!' He then denounced the scheme and its promoters with great abandon. St. Francis might have taken this as a source of perfect joy, but some of his Irish children felt they had been biffed below the belt.* [3]

BROOKLYN BROTHERS SEEK ROMAN UNION

As the Franciscan Brothers approached the 50th anniversary of their arrival in the Diocese of Brooklyn in 1858, their survival as a separate and unique congregation in the American Church resulted from traumatic and painful events between 1900 and 1908. At that time the young community of lay-religious was split by the desire of over three-fourths of them to join the clerical Third Order Regular under the obedience of the Roman Minister General. The movement for Union with the Roman Third Order Regular was promoted by Raphael Breheny and Linus Lynch who were the superiors general of the Brooklyn Brothers from 1900 until 1906. Two "Circular Letters" were sent by Linus Lynch to all the Franciscan Brothers in America, one which promoted priesthood in the Community and the second advocating Union with the Third Order Regular in Rome. These events led to the separation of the two superiors and over twenty-five brothers from the Brooklyn community to the small Spalding, Nebraska community which had received acceptance from the Third Order Superior a year before. The creation of the Sacred Heart Province of the Third Order Regular resulted from this Spalding community.

In 1900, Raphael Breheny was elected Superior General of the Brooklyn community and began a movement to give stability to the brothers by also seeking to join the Roman Third Order Regular. When his plans were not approved by Charles McDonnell, the second bishop of Brooklyn, he resigned his office in October of 1904, a little over a year into his second term as Superior General. Linus Lynch, the Novice Master, was elected Superior General on 29 October 1904, to **complete** Raphael Breheny's term of office. He continued Brother Raphael's work of seeking union with the Third Order Regular in Rome.

With the approval of McDonnell, and the help of John Doyle, D.D., he prepared new constitutions, based on the Constitutions of a diocesan Third Order community of priests of the Archdiocese of Albi, France, which had been suppressed by the "iniquous laws" of France. The Constitutions of these priests were sent to the brothers when they tried to be received into the Brooklyn community. Because this French community was primarily clerical, the Bishop agreed that they could be received only for a time until they made their own foundation. The French community decided instead to go to the Diocese of Matto Grosso in Brazil.

Doyle had been a curate at St. Patrick's in Huntington from 1901 to 1905, who frequently said Mass for the novices in Centerport. He was appointed the chaplain of St. Francis Monastery and a faculty member of the College when Linus Lynch was elected Superior General. An alumnus with high honors from St. Francis College in Brooklyn, Doyle attended the North American College in Rome, and completed his course in Theology at the Pontifical Atheneum of the Urban College, "De Propaganda Fide". He would later join the Third Order Regular Province in Loretto in 1910, where he founded the Seminary, and would later be elected provincial of the Sacred Heart Province. [4]

BISHOP OPPOSES PRIESTHOOD FOR BROTHERS

Since their re-foundation in Ireland in 1818, the brothers had always been a community of lay religious, depending on priests from the First Order as their chaplains, or going to the local parish for Mass and the sacraments. The new 1905 French constitutions were not approved by Bishop McDonnell, who believed that the inclusion of priesthood would prevent the brothers from continuing as teachers in the parish elementary schools. Taking another approach, Linus, Lynch, prepared two "Circular Letters" for the brothers,[5] one advocating the inclusion of priesthood in the community, and the other advocating union with the Roman Third Order Regular. In early 1906, these small pamphlet-sized circular letters were given to all the Brooklyn brothers and sent to the brothers in Loretto, Pennsylvania, and Spalding, Nebraska.

The first "Circular Letter," which was probably written in late 1905, advocated the inclusion of Priesthood in the community. The fourth paragraph of the Introduction states the question: "Is it advisable to have Priests in the Institute of Brothers of Penance of the Third Order Regular of S. Francis of Assisi?" [6] Chapter I of this "Circular Letter" advances the argument that Priesthood is sanctioned by the Third Order Rule and long-standing Custom:

> *Before the destruction of Monastic Institutions in Ireland, there was in that country some fifty-three houses of Brothers of the Third Order Regular of S. Francis of Assisi. . . . In each of these Monasteries there were Priests, who, professing the Third Order Rule and living in obedience, without property and in chastity, ministered to the spiritual needs of their Brethren in Religion.* [7]

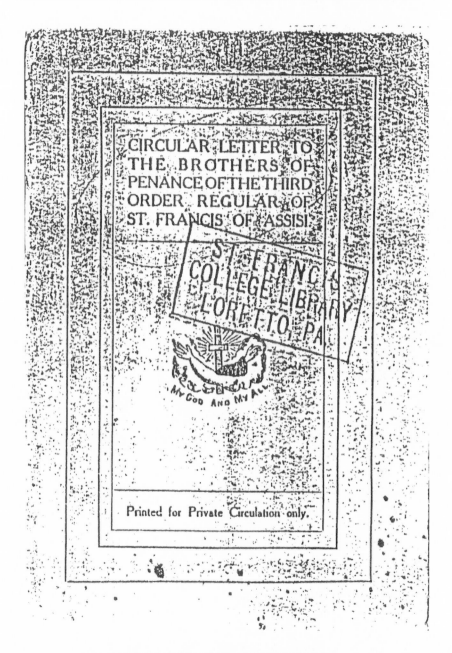

CIRCULAR LETTER TO THE BROTHERS OF PENANCE OF THE THIRD ORDER REGULAR OF ST. FRANCIS OF ASSISI.

MY GOD AND MY ALL

Printed for Private Circulation only.

FIRST "CIRCULAR LETTER":
PRIESTHOOD IN THE COMMUNITY?

The "Circular Letter" continues with the claim that a Father Smyth who lived in a Monastery of the Third Order in the town of Dalkey near Dublin, and a Father Dillon, who was a professed religious of the Mountbellew community in its early years, were clerical members of the **Third Order Regular:**

> *The last Priest of the Third Order Regular in Ireland died only some fifty years ago [1855], in the Franciscan Convent of the Friars Minor at Merchant's Quay, Dublin. This priest, Father Smyth, belonged to a Monastery of the Third Order in the town of Dalkey, near Dublin. Attached to this monastery there was a school for the education of the youth of the surrounding district, and in this school the Franciscan Brothers taught. But at length, for some cause, of which history is silent, they were obliged to disperse. Some four or five went to a small house in Jamestown, County Longford, and then returned to the Monastery at Mount Bellew, where they lived and died as members of that community. Father Smyth remained at Dalkey for some time after his brothers had left; but, he, too, was at length forced to leave the retreat he loved so well. He rested in Dublin at the Convent of the Friars, and there, falling sick, passed to his eternal reward.*
>
> *Moreover, it is an indisputable historical fact that a Father Dillon was one of the professed Religious of the Mt. Bellew community in its early days. This Brother Dillon, priest of the Third Order Regular at Mt. Bellew according to the testimony of Brother Peter Kevelaghen of Brooklodge (who was professed at Mount Bellew under the Provincial of the First Order, who lived there with this Father Dillon),"was a Brother at Mount Bellew; became a Priest of the Order there, and lived and died there." [8]*

However, evidence from more current documents and contemporary research, suggest that Owen Smyth and Michael B. Dillon were **priests of the First Order** under the obedience of the Provincial of the Irish Province at Adam and Eve's Convent on Merchants Quay in Dublin. In a letter from Bernardine Cowan to Pascal Kelly, dated 1 December 1945, he states that *Young's Catholic Directory of 1821* gives May 1820 for the foundation of "Mt. Alvernia near Milltown, under the immediate direction of Rev. Mr. Dunn of Adam and Eve's Convent; Mr. Owen Smyth, Superior and Mr. Dillon, Local Director, and eight other religious subjects." Father Owen Smyth was a Friar Minor who served as Superior of the brothers at Milltown and Dalkey before he returned to Adam and Eve's Convent before he died. [9]

MICHAEL B. DILLON, O.S.F.

Father Michael B. Dillon, regarded by the Irish Brothers as one of the founders of Mountbellew, may have been related to the landlord Christopher Dillon Bellew. His signature "on behalf of the monks, Michael B. Dillon," is attached to an agreement, dated 19 December 1822, between the Brothers and the landlord Christopher Dillon Bellew, regarding the care of the chapel (then newly built) and the cemetery at Mountbellew in Galway.

Bernardine Cowan believes that Dillon was recalled from Mountbellew by the Provincial of the Friars Minor and returned to Milltown where he died in 1828. He states that, "I have seen the tablet in Milltown Church stating that he [Fr. Michael B. Dillon], died in 1828." The actual date of his death is given on a marble plaque, hidden behind a radiator, on the south wall of the old Church of S.S. Columbanus and Gall in Milltown, which reads: "Pray for the soul of the Reverend Michael B. Dillon, O.S.F.,[10] who departed this life on the 23 June 1828, aged 33 years, whose remains are deposited in this Church, R.I.P."[11]

Less than a month later, Michael B. Dillon was prayed for with seven other Friars at the Chapter of the Irish Province of the First Order Friars Minor "held in the place of refuge of the Dublin community," on 16 July, 1828:

> *Defuncti ab ultimo capitolo provinciali, quorum notitia ad nos pervenit, sunt sequentes: illustrisimus et reverendissimus dominus... V. P Michael B. Dillon*[12]

IRISH FRANCISCAN BROTHERS AS A COMMUNITY OF LAY- RELIGIOUS

Bernardine Cowan, in a four page message of congratulations and history, "Ad Multos Annos," sent to the Brooklyn community at its centenary celebration in 1958, states very clearly that the Irish and American Franciscan Brothers, as educators of youth, were no longer a clerical community as they had been before their suppression in the troubles of the Penal Laws, but were a community of lay religious since their re-founding in 1818:

> . . . .*engaging in a special activity for which the Irish province had been noted in pre-Reformation days. For Franciscan historians tell us that in every Monastery of the Third Order Regular, and there were numerous in Ulster and Connacht, there was a special portion called the School set apart for the purpose of Catholic Education. This important work was carried on by the Friars in addition to their pastoral activities, for in those days they formed a canonically established Clerical Institute.*

However, Bernardine Cowan makes clear that the Franciscan Brothers, after their revival in the nineteenth century, were a lay Institute, whose lay character had been confirmed by the Holy See:

> *In the early days of the last century some Brothers were engaged in teaching Christian Doctrine under the jurisdiction of the Friars Minor in the Dublin diocese. The Third Order Regular had thus revived after the Penal Days, but as a lay Institute; and this lay character has maintained ever since, having been confirmed by the Holy See as being the better suited to the secondary end of our Institute.* [13]

Patrick Quinn, T.O.R. also states that the Irish Franciscan Brothers were exclusively laymen in the nineteenth century:

> *[T]he Third Order Regular would once again flourish in the west of Ireland. Their growth and success was a response to the desperate need for education and to stave off the new evangelization effort launched by the Bible Society. While the membership of the pre-Reformation Third Order Regular was predominantly clerical, its re-emergence brought an exclusively lay membership.* [14]

However, the "Circular Letter" continues with other cogent arguments for priesthood in the community. It cites its inclusion in the Rule of the Third Order in all provinces except Ireland and America; claims that "many spiritual benefits" will be derived from the presence of priests in the community; believes that "many temporal benefits" will also accrue to the institute; states that the "intellectual development of our professed members" will take place;

that priesthood will prevent "desertions from our ranks"; will give us "prestige as a teaching Institute" and "admission into a certain class of society," with a "steady income from our own Priests." [15]

Chapter III of the "Circular Letter" narrates the difficulties which might be experienced by the introduction of Priesthood into the Community and argues against each one: that "discord and strife between those who are Priests and those who are not"; that it will "hinder the work of education in parish schools, the object and end of our Community"; that it is an "innovation"; that Priests "will usurp the power of government," and "will snatch it from the hands of those who have been thus far the stay and support of the Institute". The author of the "Circular Letter" continues with the claim that we have "not given sufficient time and earnestness to the spiritual development of the younger members," and, that Priesthood would open to us "the procuring of postulants. We cannot get the youth of America to join us: because we have not the Priesthood." Perhaps the most startling statement of Linus Lynch, in light of the 25 young postulants, who had just arrived from Ireland in the late Spring of 1903, and whose Novice Master he had been from 1900 to 1904: "We cannot continue to import vocations, because the ecclesiastical authorities, both here and in Ireland, do not want it."

(Printed for Private Circulation Only)

"Our eyes are not closed to the spirit of the times."
Leo XIII., Encyclical "Immortale Dei."

✠

Letter

To the Brothers of Penance

of the

Third Order Regular of St. Francis

On Union with Their Own Order Under the Jurisdiction of Their Own General in Rome

✠

Dear Brothers in S. Francis: Peace and Blessing in Jesus Christ.

1. In a few short months we shall be celebrating the fiftieth anniversary of our advent into the Diocese of Brooklyn. It should be a time of rejoicing for us: a time of rejoicing in the Lord for all the benefits which He has bestowed on us. It is a celebration which recalls the past, emphasizes the aspirations of the present, and anticipates the success of the future.

2. But as we look over the history of our Order in the past, we are forced to confess that there are many things there to cause us regret. We see our beloved Order split up into many petty observances. In America, Ireland, Italy, France, Spain, Portugal, Belgium, England, and Germany there exist congregations of Franciscan Brothers of the Third Order Regular, but each existing by itself. Between them there is not even the tie of a mutual spirit. And the result has naturally been that the Order has been weakened and in certain localities brought to almost certain destruction.

3. To-day, however, the spirit of Unity—the spirit of Jesus Christ has become more and more prevalent. Nor is it limited to the Catholic Church, the root and center of all religious union: it has found its way into the various sects of Protestantism. Serious minds amongst these sectaries have been confronted by evidences of decay in their various organizations; and they have instituted an investigation to discover its causes. Their conclusion has been that the fundamental cause of their failure has been and is the spirit of dissent, so prevalent amongst them. Consequently they are advocating the union of all the sects into one grand Brotherhood, which will be for the betterment of the whole and the advancement of each particular branch. This same spirit of union has always been the strength of the Church of Jesus

"SECOND CIRCULAR LETTER" ADVOCATING "UNION WITH THEIR OWN ORDER UNDER THE JURISDICTION OF THEIR OWN GENERAL IN ROME"

The argument of the "Second Circular Letter" [16] begins with the need for unity under one Superior General in Rome. Citing the wish of Pope Leo XIII to unite the many factions of the Franciscan orders, the author gives an historical sketch of the development of the Third Order Regular "with a Rule perfect in all its details and obliging all its members by the command of the Roman Pontiff." Chapter II of the "Second Circular Letter" cites reasons advising union with the Third Order Regular which "will preserve us in the spirit of the Order; will preserve Regular Discipline; will give us the Holy Priesthood; will give us the privilege of making Solemn vows; will give canonical establishment to our community and will elevate it from the rank of a mere tolerated community, to the enviable position of a province of a Regular Order canonically recognized by the Holy See."

Pride in an organization with a history going back to 1448, with the wisest of canonical regulations in their Rule and Constitution, is compared by Lynch "with the meager Constitutions and elementary Rule, which we possess, we certainly must be forced to admire the Roman Rule and to long for its possession." The possibility of new fields of activity outside the diocese, would be open to the community if it could join the Roman Third Order Regular, and Brother Linus argues, that we would solve "the many difficulties we have in procuring vocations."

Citing *"a certain "Circular Letter," which was placed in the hands of you all some time since* [probably in late 1905 or early 1906], *must convince you of this . Even those outside our community have spoken of the impossibility of continuing the present state of artificial propagation which is in vogue amongst us. Our own graduates, who know and appreciate the difficulties*

*under which the community is laboring will tell you,
when there is a question of novices and postulants, that
the time for the procuring of such in this country is
past. And if we speak of procuring of vocations from
other countries, they merely smile and answer: 'When
a man needs to go to Florida in order to keep life in his
body, we must judge that the term of his life is not far
off.'"* [17]

As he was writing these Circular Letters, Linus Lynch
was also busy writing to Rome, and sent the first of many
letters to the Third Order Regular in Rome. He wrote first
to Donald [sic] Zec, thinking him to be the Minister
General, and began the process of introduction and
explanation of the young Brooklyn community: [18]

> *St. Francis College*
> *Brooklyn, New York*
> *February 3, 1906*

Rev. Donald Zec
Most Rev. Father:

*My voice is the voice of a son seeking his Father, the
voice of one who believes he will find in you the
legitimate head of the Third Order Regular of Saint
Francis of Assisi.*

*For many years I have desired to write to you to learn
the origin, progress and present state of our Order in
Rome; but there were many things to hinder me in
satisfying this desire. Now, however, as the Superior of
our Congregation, that long desire and opportunity has
at last come and eagerly I embrace it.*

*Perhaps you do not know of our existence, or at least
you have no knowledge of the story of the origin and*

development of our congregation. . Our Congregation took its origin from the Congregation Franciscan Brothers in Ireland. Fifty years ago a few Brothers came here from Ireland to lay the foundation of this Congregation under the jurisdiction of the Ordinary of the place.

In our Congregation at present there are 65 Brothers with simple Perpetual vows, 30 with temporary vows, 18 novices and 2 postulants. The secondary end of our Congregation is the education of youth in parish schools. At present there are 14 parish schools under our direction, 2 select schools and a college.

We are not, however, content with our present state. Indeed, it would seem that we have no canonical status since our Constitutions were never approved by the Apostolic See. The community is, therefore, exclusively diocesan, and we do not even have one house outside the Diocese of Brooklyn. Considering all this, we are not pleased with the present state of our Congregation and, a future does not seem to be possible. Hence, we desire union with you, so that professing the same Rule, we may form one Order.

There are, however, some difficulties in the way; because, the Third Order of Saint Francis in Rome is a clerical institute while in our Congregation the sacerdotal element is not found: our community is lay. Indeed, some of our Brothers at first did not want union with you, because they feared the effects of the introduction of priests. At present, however, all or nearly all are convinced of the necessity of having our own priests, and are content, indeed anxious to obey the Rule in this.

Hence, they have planned to remodel our constitutions and to introduce the sacerdotal element.

This remodeling of the constitutions [based upon constitutions from a diocesan community of French TOR priests, discussed above], *has already been done, and the new constitutions are now in the approbation* [being reviewed by the Bishop], *we will immediately have our own priests and the way to union with you will be open; if, however, he refuses this approbation, it will become necessary for us to seek union with you without priests.*

Hence, I would ask you, Most Reverend Father, to answer these questions:

1. *If the Bishop approves our new constitutions, will it be possible for us to send some of our Brothers to Rome to make their theological studies, and can they live there with you?*

2. *If, however, he refuses this approbation, what should we do to have union with you immediately?*

With best wishes, I remain your humble brother in Jesus through Mary,

Signed - Brother Linus Lynch, O.S.F.

BISHOP OPPOSED TO UNION

Over the next four months Brother Linus' painful education in the difficulties of achieving the desired union would become evident in the many letters going to and coming from Rome. The two "Circular Letters" did convince more than three-fourths of the 65 life-professed Brothers of the community of the need to seek union with the Third Order Regular in Rome. Therefore, in the spring of 1906, a petition was prepared by Linus Lynch seeking union with the Third Order Regular in Rome. This was signed by 51 Brothers, 78% of the professed Brooklyn

Brothers, and sent on 13 May 1906, to the Minister General in Rome, without the knowledge of Bishop Charles McDonnell. The Latin Petition, from the Archives in Rome, is shown below and translated on the next page:

SECRETARY'S COPY OF LATIN PETITION (EXCERPT)

PETITION

OF THE BROTHERS OF PENANCE OF THE THIRD ORDER REGULAR
OF SAINT FRANCIS OF ASSISI UNDER THE JURISDICTION OF
THE ORDINARY OF THE DIOCESE OF BROOKLYN TO THE MOST
REVEREND MINISTER GENERAL OF THE THIRD ORDER REGULAR
IN ROME

Most Reverend Father:

We, the undersigned Brothers of the Third Order Regular of Saint Francis of the Brooklyn Congregation under the jurisdiction of the Ordinary of the Brooklyn Diocese, anxious for the furtherance of our Order and approaching you as the recognized Head of the entire Third Order Regular, beg and beseech you that you deign to give heed to our requests for union.

We desire and pray for union with our Regular Order under your jurisdiction in the city of Rome, so that, in possessing the one Rule and the one Spirit of our Seraphic Father, we may constitute one Order.

Names of the Brothers

1. B. Linus, Superior	22. B. Alexis	43. B. Bernardine
2. B. Jerome, Asst.	23. B. Pacificus	44. B. Ferdinand
Superior	24. B. Juniper	45. B. Lawrence
3. B. Austin	25. B. Cyril	46. B. Raymond
4. B. Paul	26. B. Liquori	47. B. David
5. B. Sebastian	27. B. Cosmas	48. B. Ignatius
6. B. Dominick	28. B. Pius	49. B. DeSales
7. B. Silvester	29. B. Aquinas	50. B. Solano
8. B. Joseph	30. B. Alphonsus	51. B. Casimir
9. B. Matthew	Liquori	
10. B. Anthony	31. B. Stephen	
11. B. Joseph E.	32. B. Eugene	
12. B. John	33. B. Victor	
13. B. Angelus	34. B. Benedict	
14. B. Leo	35. B. Bonaventure	
15. B. Bruno	36. B. Jarlath	
16. B. Aloysius	37. B. Kevin	
17. B. Joachim	38. B. William	
18. B. Angelo	39. B. Leopold	*St. Francis Monastery*
19. B. Michael	40. B. Silverius	*Brooklyn, New York,*
20. B. Raphael	41. B. Augustine	*U.S.A.*
21. B. Simon	42. B. Louis	*May 13, 1906*

When Brother Linus had obtained the 51 signatures above, he wrote the following letter to accompany the Petition to Father Angelus DeMattia, the Minister General of the Third Order in Rome [English translation]: [19]

Brooklyn, New York
May 14, 1906
Saint Francis College

The Most Reverend Father Master Angelus DeMattia,
Minister General of the Third Order Regular of
Saint Francis of Assisi in Rome

Most Reverend Father:

"Joyfully will I rejoice in the Lord and my soul will be glad in my God" because my eyes have seen this day. With this letter I am sending you our formal petition for union with the Third Order Regular under your jurisdiction. I hope, therefore, that the time is ripe for the fulfillment of our desires and that we may see our congregation united with the Third Order Regular of Saint Francis under your jurisdiction. Hence, I beg you to hear our petition and to act as quickly as possible and arrange all that is required for the union both with your General Curia and the Holy See.

Hoping you are well, I kneel before you as the legitimate head of the entire Third Order Regular of Saint Francis to ask your blessing.

Always your son and devoted brother,
In Jesus through Mary,

(signed) Brother Linus Lynch, O.S.F.

"COLLECT AND FETCH"

Charles McDonnell learned of these circular letters when he received his copy of the Petition. He ordered Linus Lynch, in a rather hortatory letter,[20] "in virtue of holy obedience to collect and fetch me" all of these circulars and the Petition and bring them to his office:

367 Clermont Avenue
Brooklyn, New York
May 15, 1906

Dear Brother Linus:
As Superior of the Franciscan Brothers of this Diocese by appointment of the Holy See, I hereby command you in virtue of holy obedience to collect and fetch me every copy of the two circulars distributed among the Brothers and also the Latin document you had the Brothers sign at the same time as the Petition to myself.

(SEAL)

+ Charles Edward
Bishop of Brooklyn
Superior of the Franciscan Brothers
of the Diocese of Brooklyn

The Petition had already been mailed to Rome two days earlier, but the circular letters were obediently delivered to the Bishop. [21] In order to prevent the Brothers from achieving their desired union, Charles McDonnell immediately sent his Chancellor, George W. Mundelein, to Rome. Mundelein had been a brilliant student in the Pontifical Atheneum of Propaganda Fide with many influential friends in Rome, including Giovanni Bonzano, who was a fellow student, personal friend, and later,

Apostolic Delegate to the United States. Archbishop Bonzano, who was very influential in promoting Mundelein's ecclesiastical career, presided at the Eucharistic Congress in Chicago in June 1926. With the help of Bonzano, Mundelein, by then Cardinal Archbishop, had won the Eucharistic Congress for his Chicago archdiocese three years earlier.

George Mundelein's influence in Rome can be seen in his election in 1907 to membership in the ancient Roman Academy of the *Arcadia* for a Latin essay he wrote defending the Pope's condemnation of Modernism. The *Arcadia*, an exclusive literary society of the Roman clerical nobility, gave Mundelein entree to the highest levels of the Roman Church. Young Monsignor Mundelein was entirely successful in preventing the Brooklyn Brothers from their desired union with the Roman Third Order Regular when he traveled to Rome for that purpose in 1906. Shortly after the Brothers' Petition was received in Rome, Daniel Zec, T.O.R. wrote to Charles McDonnell informing him of the request for Union, seeking his "favor and good will": [22]

Your Excellency:

The General Council of my Order has received a Petition from the Brothers of the Third Order presently residing in the Brooklyn Diocese, - said petition seeking union with our Regular Order. The Holy Apostolic See has decided that I, as procurator general of the entire Third Order, seek the favor and good will of your Excellency. So, humbly and fraternally, I asked that our Protector, Cardinal Vanutelli, favor us with the reply that he finds the request acceptable and foresees no objection to the possibility and likelihood of bringing about the desired union.

*I trust I will receive an answer as soon as possible,
since I must reply to the Apostolic See.*

*Humbly and dutifully, I am
Your servant in the Lord.
At Rome, June 4, 1906, No. 2 "Miranda street"
On the part of the undersigned Cardinal Protector of
the Third Order Regular of St. Francis, I find no reason
why the union in question should not be studied and
scrutinized by the Sacred College of Bishops and
Regulars. It is my earnest hope that all will proceed
smoothly to the satisfactory and speedy disposition of
the matter of union.
At Rome, June 4, 1906*
[signed]: *Procurator General Vincent Cardinal
Vanutelli*

However, Daniel Zec did not obtain the "favor and good will" he hoped for, and the movement for Union certainly did not "proceed smoothly". George Mundelein's considerable influence in Rome would effectively prevent the Brooklyn Franciscan Brothers from joining the Roman Order.

On 2 August 1906, the General Chapter for the election of a Superior General was held in the Chapel of Our Lady of the Angels in Centerport, Long Island, under the presidency of Charles McDonnell. Although Linus Lynch, elected Superior General on 29 October 1904, was **completing** a year and two months of the term of Raphael Breheny, who resigned in his second term as Superior General, the Bishop declared that Linus Lynch required a two-thirds majority for re-election. When the brothers did not object, the fourth ballot, short of the two-thirds majority by **two votes**, did not result in a vote the

President said was necessary to re-elect Linus Lynch to a second term. The Bishop declared a deadlock and appointed Vincent Mulcahy, a Brother strongly opposed to the Union, as his Vicar of the community with full powers of superior until the next election to be held in October. The existing Consultors were to retain their office, "by whom the Vicar was to be guided." [23]

Nonetheless, influenced by the "Circular Letters," five Franciscan Brothers in Spalding, Nebraska, were successful in seeking union with the Order in Rome. With the approval of their Bishop, Richard Scanlon of Omaha, Nebraska, they sent their petition on 20 November 1906, and were granted union with the Third Order Regular by a letter of Father DeMattia, Minister General, on 8 December 1906. Raphael Breheny, who had gone to Rome in October to press for the union of the Brooklyn Community, urged the Minister General and his Council to quickly approve the petition, despite the small number of five brothers who signed it. He correctly predicted that more brothers from Brooklyn would eventually join the small Spalding community.

Despairing of achieving union with the Order in Rome, twenty-five brothers, including Linus Lynch, who still wished to be part of the Roman Third Order, were released from their vows of poverty and obedience, but not chastity, by Charles McDonnell at a special chapter at their summer monastery in Centerport, Long Island on 14 July 1907. [24] These brothers had all written similar letters in May and June of 1907, stating that they had believed they were entering a valid Third Order community when they joined the Brooklyn Community, but now, **"I realize that I was deceived"** They all requested entrance to the Third Order Regular in the new community in Spalding, Nebraska, under the jurisdiction of the Minister General.

Bernardine Dillon's Latin letter, similar in text to all the other unfortunately-worded letters, may reveal why the brothers who remained with the Brooklyn community were so bitter against those who left, and would never discuss the details of those days.

An English translation of this letter is given below: [25]

> *From: St. Francis College*
> *Brooklyn, New York*
>
> *My dearest Father:*
>
> *After mature consideration of this matter with my spiritual director, I wish to express my desire to enter the Third Order Regular of St. Francis of Assisi under your jurisdiction.*
>
> *The reasons which persuade me to this action, are as follows:*
>
> *1. On account of the conditions prevailing in this community, such conditions undoubtedly known only to those who live in it themselves, which make for impediments to the spiritual life. Such being the case, and of my own free decision, I seek to enter the Third Order Regular under your jurisdiction.*
>
> *2. So also to better renounce worldly things, and not to fail to trust more firmly in the Lord, I seek to be admitted to the solemn vows of religious life.*
>
> *3. Formerly, when I entered this community, I thought that I was entering the Third Order Regular of St. Francis. More recently, however, **I realize that I was deceived.** This community, which professed to be a valid Third Order community, is in fact, only **a diocesan sodality,** and should not even be called the Third Order Regular of St. Francis.*

Deeply moved by these reasons, I explain my intention to you in all humility, and hoping in God, I request that your permission be granted to me to enter the order to which I will dedicate my whole heart and soul along with other men like myself.

Your most humble Brother,

26 May 1907   *[signed]* <u>*Bro. Bernardine*</u>

The expected departure of these Brothers did not go unnoticed in the secular press. In the "Catholic Church Notes" column of *The Brooklyn Citizen* we read:

It is said that fourteen [sic] *of the Franciscan Brothers have left the order established in this diocese to go West, where they might become priests of the Third Order of St. Francis.* [26]

After the arrival of these twenty-five Brothers to the small Third Order Regular community in Spalding, Nebraska in the summer of 1907, Stanislaus Dujmovic, T.O.R., the General Delegate of the Roman Order to the new community in Nebraska, requested the usual testimonial letters for the brothers who were to receive the Habit of the Third Order Regular. Vincent Mulcahy, the Bishop's Vicar of the Brooklyn community, responded in a rather cold, impersonal letter, "By command of the Most Reverend Bishop," "TO WHOM IT MAY CONCERN," not to Father Dujmovic:

SAINT FRANCIS MONASTERY
Brooklyn, New York

December 11, 1907

TO WHOM IT MAY CONCERN:

Whereas Reverend Father Stanislaus, General Delegate of the Third Order Regular, now residing at Spalding, Nebraska, U.S.A., has sought information from me concerning the natals, customs, life, fame, condition and education of Philip Lynch, James Driscoll, James Phelan, Michael Murphy, John Campion, Thomas Lewis, Patrick Conroy, Charles Brown, Patrick McCarthy, Thomas Byrne, Edward English, all of whom professed perpetual vows in the Franciscan Brotherhood in the Diocese of Brooklyn; and Patrick Hogan, James Lynch, Joseph Segourn, Michael McNamara, Patrick Donaghue, John Fitzgerald, Peter Gormley, all of whom professed temporary vows for the space of three years in the aforesaid Brotherhood; and William Barry, Patrick Smyth, who were novices in the same aforesaid Brotherhood, I hereby testify, as far as I know, that no impediment, as specified in the Decree of Pope Pius IX concerning the admission of novices, exists concerning all the persons mentioned above.

Brother Vincent, O.S.F., Superior

By command of the Most Reverend Bishop,

George Kaupert, V.G.
Brooklyn, New York December 14, 1907
(SEAL) [27]

Twenty-seven Brothers were given the Habit of the Third Order as recorded by Stanislaus Dujmovic, who lists them as Brothers or Clerics:

CONVENT OF THE IMMACULATE CONCEPTION
SPALDING NEBRASKA
JANUARY 1, 1908

This morning, after the Conventual Mass, having passed eight days in the Spiritual Retreat, as it is prescribed in the Constitutions of the Third Order Regular, and received the Holy Communion, the following Brothers were received to the habit of our Order according to the Ceremonial, by Father Stanislaus Dujmovic, General Delegate. They were all affiliated to this Convent in Spalding, being now the only one existing in this country:

Brother 1. Osbelt, Francis, with the name: William
Brother 2. Fielding, Michael, with the name: Joseph
Brother 3. Yunck, William, with the name: Francis
Brother 4. O'Rourke, James, with the name: Alexander
Brother 5. Mangan, Thomas, with the name: Timothy
Brother 6. McCaffrey, Thomas, with the name: Joseph
Brother 7. McCarthy, Patrick, with the name: Angelus
Cleric 8. Breheny, Edward, with the name: Raphael
Cleric 9. Lynch, Philip, with the name: Linus
Cleric 10. Phelan, James, with the name: Simeon
Cleric 11. English, Edward, with the name: Benedict
Cleric 12. Lewis, Thomas, with the name: De Sales
Brother 13. Byrne, Thomas, with the name: Aquinas
Cleric 14. Dillon ,James, with the name: Bernardine
Cleric 15. Campion, John, with the name: Leopold
Brother 16. Thornton, Michael, with the name: Bonaventure
Cleric 17. Murphy, Michael, with the name: Cyril

Cleric 18. Hogan, Patrick, with the name: Edward
Cleric 19. Lynch, James, with the name: Bernard
Cleric 20. Segourn, Joseph, with the name: Damien
Cleric 21. McNamara, Michael, with the name: Nicholas
Cleric 22. Donaghue, Patrick, with the name: Louis
Cleric 23. Fitzgerald, John, with the name: Chrysostom
Cleric 24. Gormley, Peter, with the name: Alban
Cleric 25. Barry, William, with the name: Camillus
Cleric 26. Smyth, Patrick, with the name: Hugh

In fidem . . .

Friar Stanislaus Dujmavic

Note: Charles Brown, considered above in the testimonial letters of the Bishop of Brooklyn, was received in the Order and made profession of simple vows in Rome on January 1, 1908, with the name Brother Victor.

Fr. Stanislaus

DISPENSATION FOR THE SPALDING BROTHERS FROM POPE PIUS X

The Brooklyn brothers who joined the Spalding brothers immediately increased their small community and were able to open a college (elementary and high level school) in Spalding. Although they were preparing for entrance to the Third Order Regular, and would ordinarily have had to complete a year of novitiate before their profession, the Third Order Regular Minister General and Procurator General requested and received a special dispensation from Pope Pius X, on 29 November 1907, which permitted the professed brothers to be received and professed in their new community without the year of novitiate. "This personal favor of the Holy Father to the brothers, who had left Brooklyn to enter the Order, brought great consolation to them; for it was the supreme approbation of the Roman Pontiff of their act; and they set themselves to the work of preparing for their vows."[28] This special dispensation also permitted the newly arrived brothers to conduct the college at Spalding which they had just opened. In 1908, Eugene Garvey, the Bishop of Altoona, Pennsylvania, approved the petition of the twenty Loretto brothers, [29] and on 22 May 1908, a Rescript approving their request for union was granted. Most of the brothers in Spalding eventually joined the Loretto community, which together, became the Sacred Heart Province of the Third Order Regular, the first Third Order Regular Province in America.

The "Yes" of the bishops of Spalding and Loretto for Union with the Third Order Regular, and the enthusiastic acceptance of these two communities of Franciscan Brothers by the Roman Minister General and his Curia, with the approbation of the Supreme Pontiff, Pius X, created the Sacred Heart Province of the Third Order Regular in America.

POPE PIUS X'S DECREE AGAINST PRIESTHOOD FOR BROOKLYN BROTHERS

To complete the separation of the Brooklyn Brothers from the possibility of Union with the Third Order Regular and to prevent any of them from desiring or entering the Priesthood, a Decree was obtained from Rome, dated 22 November 1908:

DECREE

*Since for the religious education of the Catholic people
it is especially desirable that the Institution, called
"Franciscan Brothers" founded for this end in North
America, may by no means lose its laic nature; and
since, from the access to the Third Order Regular of St.
Francis, a great danger threatens lest the Institution
"Franciscan Brothers" not only be deprived of suitable
increase, but even, as is evident from lamentable
experience, be daily lessened in number and lose
internal peace, the Sacred Congregation of Religious
has decreed that the following be adopted:*

*(1) That the Religious Body called the "Franciscan
Brothers" having observed their simple vows can, and
truly ought to be, regarded as belonging to the religious
family - the same as the Brothers of the Third Regular
Order, and are, therefore, the true children of St.
Francis.*

*(2) That the Franciscan Brothers of Brooklyn cannot
pass over to any other Institute, not even a regular
Institute, without the express license of the Holy See.*

*(3) That ascent to Hold Orders is interdicted to those
who belong to the Institute of Franciscan Brothers, or
who thereafter shall belong thereto, without the special
license of the Holy See; that this be communicated by
the Bishop of Brooklyn to the proper Ordinaries of the
actual or future brethren of the said Institute.* [30]

The Brooklyn Brothers were also pleased that the same
Pontiff, Pius X, approved their request for the Rescript
enjoining them from access to the Priesthood and union
with any Regular order without the approval of the Holy
See. This document gave them a measure of peace which

was badly needed at this difficult time in their history, but would be a continuing hurdle for any brothers who would leave the community to go for the priesthood.

The next quarter-century would be a stressful time for the young Brooklyn Community with the declining numbers of brothers, loss of some of their schools, difficulties in governance with an Ordinary not concerned with their troubles, and neglect of the education of their young brothers beyond the level of normal school. There would seem to be a suspicion of higher education beyond the high school, normal-school levels. As will be reported below, brothers did not attend St. Francis College until the 1930s, when Thomas E. Molloy insisted that Franciscan Brothers had to be trained to assume teaching and administrative positions at St. Francis Prep and the College. When Molloy, a former student of St. Francis College, became the third Bishop of Brooklyn in 1921, his affectionate regard for the Community became evident in his support for the Brothers' Fund Raising Drive for a new Monastery and College.

"COMMUNITY A DIOCESAN SODALITY?"

To counter the claim of some of the brothers that the Community was, as some of them would later claim in their letter to the Minister General, simply a "diocesan sodality," the Brooklyn Community sought and was granted a "Certificate of Aggregation" from Dionysius Schuler, the Minister General of the First Order Friars Minor, dated 23 February 1905. [31] The Loretto Community also sought affiliation with the First Order which was granted in 1906. [32]

FR. DIONYSIUS SCHULER,
Minister-General of the Whole Order of
Minorites To the Ven. Cong. of Brothers
of the III Order in Brooklyn of
the Diocese of Brooklyn
Health and Seraphic Benediction

Desiring to second the laudable solicitude of your soul towards the Seraphic Order, from which, as the documents which you have forwarded to us give ample proof, you have received both Habit and Rule of Life; and anxious to satisfy in as far as we can the petition which you have lately sent to us; led moreover, by the hope that your piety and charity may be increased from day to day by these new favors and graces, and that the virtue of the Seraphic Spirit may produce through you more abundant fruit; by the tenor of the present document we unite you all and all your Brothers who may hereafter be received by you, and declare you all united to our Order, from which you take both Name and Habit; but, however, to this end that, according to a decree of the S. Cong. of Indulgences and Relics, given on the 28th day of August, 1903, you may receive all and only the indulgences directly granted by the Roman Pontiffs to the First and Second Orders, and that your churches may have the same indulgences which the churches of the aforesaid Orders enjoy.

Farewell and be mindful of our Seraphic Order in your prayers to God.

Given in Rome at St. Anthony's, the 23rd day of the month of February,1906

[Seal] Fr. Dionysius Schuler,
Qui Supra

A BISHOP'S "NO" PRESERVES THE
YOUNG BROOKLYN COMMUNITY

Despite this setback for Union, the "Will of God" for the young community can be seen in the decision of Charles McDonnell, who believed, as their Ecclesiastical Superior, that the Brooklyn Franciscan Brothers were intended to be a community of non-clerical religious dedicated to teaching. His firm "No," to their attempt at Union with the Third Order Regular Roman community, although a difficult obedience to accept at that time, effectively preserved the existence of the Brooklyn Franciscan Brothers as a unique, non-clerical Third Order Regular community dedicated to teaching young men and boys.

"ST FRANCIS COLLEGE OPENING"

The brothers who remained after the departure of those who went to Spaulding, tried to reassure the parents who would be sending their sons to St. Francis College. Under a banner headline, "ST FRANCIS COLLEGE OPENING-- The fiftieth year of St. Francis College will begin Monday. A very competent faculty has been selected. Day scholars and boarders will be received as usual." [33] "Owing to the departure of several of the Brothers for the West during the early part of the Summer, there will be many changes in the faculty. The last two years of the College course will be in charge of secular priests assigned to the College by Bishop McDonnell. Father [Jose] Glenn, will be professor of junior year philosophy and will also act as chaplain [of St. Francis Monastery]. Father John McClancy, will be professor of senior year philosophy. Dr. [John] Doyle, former chaplain of the College, [and promoter of the Union of the Brothers with the Roman Order], is now stationed at the Church of Our Lady of Good Counsel on Putnam Avenue." [34] "Four of the students who graduated from the College in June, sailed on the 5th of October to begin theology studies. Messrs, Woods, Balon, Rogers, and Molloy, [35] of the Class of '07 of St. Francis College, are to enter the American College in Rome." [36]

Of the 51 members of the Community who signed the 1906 Petition for Union with the Third Order Regular in Rome, only half left for Spaulding. The almost 40 brothers who remained were divided in their loyalties. Their continuing dependance on Ireland for vocations will be discussed in the next chapter.

Notes

[1] Bernardine Cowan, O.S.F., "Thirty, Forty, Fifty Years - and Two!", [manuscript], Mountbellew, Galway, 8 November 1946, pp. 13-14.

[2] Cowan, "Thirty, . . . " p. 17.

[3] *Ibid.*

[4] *Mariale,* 'Saint Francis Seminary, 50th Anniversary," 1962, pp. 36-37

[5] Authorship of these "Circular Letters" was not printed in either document.

[6] "Circular Letter to the Brothers of the Third Order Regular of S. Francis of Assisi," privately printed, late 1905-early 1906, p. 1.

[7] *Ibid.,* pp. 2-3.

[8] *Ibid.,* p. 3.

[9] Bernardine Cowan, O.S.F. to Pascal Kelly, O.S.F., 1 December, 1945, [From the Friars Minor Franciscan Archives in Killiney, sent by Benignus Millet, O.F.M. to the author, 2 March 1993].

[10] "O.S.F.", (Order of St. Francis) was a common religious designation for all Franciscans in the English-speaking world in the 18th and 19th centuries. John McMahon used the initials "IIIrd O.S.F." after his name on his Rescript request letter to Rome in 1859, to distinguish his membership in the Third Order Regular of St. Francis .

[11] V. Rev. John J. Meagher, P.P. Dalkey, "Notes made by . . . . *re* Franciscan Brothers," Meagher was the Pastor of the Milltown Church, historian of the Dublin Archdiocese and a friend of Benignus Millet,O.F.M., Archivist of the Irish Friars Minor, who sent his four pages of "Notes" to this author from the Franciscan Archives in Killiney, 2 March 1993.

[12] *Liber Dubliniensis: Chapter Documents of the Irish Franciscans, 1719-1875*, edited by Anselm Faulkner, O.F.M., Franciscan Friars, Killiney, 1978, p. 229.

[13] Bernardine Cowan, O.S.F., "Ad Multos Annos, The Irish Franciscan Brothers of the Third Order Regular offer fraternal greetings and congratulations to their brothers in the diocese of Brooklyn on this happy occasion: the Celebration of the Centenary of their foundation," four -page manuscript letter, 1958, Franciscan Brothers Archives.

[14] Patrick Quinn, T.O.R., "The Third Order Regular of St. Francis in Ireland," *ANALECTA TOR*, XXIV/ 153, (1993), pp. 247-263, p. 262.

[15] "Circular Letter. . . . pp 1-9.

[16] "Letter to the Brothers of Penance of the Third Order Regular of St. Francis: On Union with Their Own Order Under the Jurisdiction of Their Own General in Rome" ["Second Circular Letter"], privately printed, 1906.

[17] "Letter to the Brothers . . . ." p. 9.

[18] Archives of the Curia of the Third Order Regular, SS. Cosmas and Damian, Rome.

[19] Archives of the Curia of the Third Order Regular, SS. Cosmas and Damian, Rome.

[20] Archives of the Sacred Heart Province of the Third Order Regular,

Loretto, Pennsylvania.

21 Copies of these Circular Letters, found in the Archives of the Sacred Heart Province of the Third Order Regular in Loretto, were kindly shared with the author by the former Archivist, Bonaventure Kiley, T.O.R.. They were deposited in the Archives by John Doyle, who believed that Charles McDonnell's letter of obedience to Linus Lynch did not apply to him.

22 Archives of the Curia of the Third Order Regular, SS. Cosmas and Damian, Rome

23 Minutes of the Council and General Chapters, Archives of the Franciscan Brothers , 1894-1910.

24 "Account Book - St. Francis Monastery, 1904-1930," p. 107, indicates that on 22 July 1907, most of these brothers received train fare (between $20 and $45) for the trip to Spalding, Nebraska, Archives of the Franciscan Brothers.

25 Third Order Regular Curia Archives, SS Cosmas and Damian, Rome.

26 *The Brooklyn Citizen,* 6 July 1907, p. 3.

27 Archives of the Sacred Heart Province of the Third Order Regular, Loretto, Pennsylvania

28 Archives of the Province of the Sacred Heart of the Third Order Regular, Loretto, Pennsylvania.

29 "At present our community consists of twenty members. We are engaged in the work of Christian education, and conduct a college for the education of young men and boys, having an attendance of from 90 to 100 students." Document accompanying their request for union with the Roman Third Order Regular, dated 29 December 1907.

30 *Franciscan Brothers of the Brooklyn Congregation of the Regular Third Order of St. Francis, Constitutions, Rules, Decrees, Rescripts, Traditions, History,* 1924, pp. 123-124.

31 "Community Prayers, . . . ", St. Francis Monastery, Brooklyn, NY, 1951, pp. 98-99.

[32] *Mariale*, [St. Francis Seminary Yearbook - 50th Anniversary, 1962], Loretto, Pa., p. 31.

[33] *The Brooklyn Citizen*, August 31, 1907, p. 5.

[34] *The Brooklyn Citizen*, Sept, 7, 1907.

[35] Thomas E. Molloy, who would be ordained in Rome, at the Basilica of St. John Lateran on 19 September 1908, would be ordained an auxiliary bishop on 3 October 1920. Upon McDonnell's death, Molloy was named the third Bishop of Brooklyn on 21 November 1921.

[36] *The Brooklyn Citizen*, October 12, 1907.

CHAPTER EIGHT

BROTHERS IN THE TWENTIETH CENTURY:
IRISH OR AMERICAN?

After the departure to Spalding of twenty-seven brothers, including Raphael Breheny and Linus Lynch, the two former superiors general, the approximately forty brothers who remained in the Brooklyn community in July of 1907, began to reassess their numbers and plans for the future. The incomplete Minutes of the Council for that period reveal their concerns about vocations, the necessity of leaving some of their schools, their precarious finances, and internal and external struggles for discipline and control of the Community.

The "Records of Council Meetings and Other Community Matters," were copied by Celestine McGarry, Secretary General, on 29 April 1943, from the Original Records as kept by the Secretary, Athanasius O'Donoghue, Dec 11, 1910 - Dec. 15, 1922. Brother Celestine notes that "These records were kept in an ordinary school copybook. Many pages were torn from the original book, and in several instances there were errors in names. Every effort has been made to correct such errors and the family name has been added to the religious name to clarify matters". Of special note , there are no Community records for the period, (August 1906 to December 1910), although Brother Paul Hill, the Secretary at that time, did not die until March 1911. Likewise, in the present book there are no detailed results of the elections of 1909, 1912, and 1922. The Minutes (if any), for the periods July 1916 to January 1917 and November 1917 to August 2, 1918, are lacking."

Brother Celestine also notes what we now consider an archival disaster: "In accordance with directions from the Superior General and the General Consultors, the old Monastery 'Minute' books have been transcribed in the following pages and **the originals have been burned**. In keeping with Canonical requirements regarding such matters, each page has been marked with the Monastery seal and signed by the Secretary."[1]

The gradual evolution of a formation program for the young Americans who began to be attracted to the Community after the First World War, resulted in the relocation of the Novitiate from Brooklyn to Smithtown Branch, Long Island, and the opening of a residential Juniorate for young men of high-school age. The novitiate program was relocated to Wyandanch in South Huntington in 1949, to Upper Brookville, Oyster Bay in 1961, and currently, has returned to Brooklyn to Trinity Friary on Gold Street near St. James Cathedral.

After a half-century in America, the Brooklyn Brothers were still depending on Irish vocations to fill their novitiate and were even considering reopening a training school for postulants in Clifden, Ireland. In 1876, Jerome Magner, the Superior General, began to regularly send a brother to Ireland to "stimulate vocations among the Irish youth". An example of two vocation advertisements are shown on the following pages:

The Brooklyn Daily Eagle criticized the Brothers for continuing to seek candidates from Ireland instead of seeking young American men. This criticism mirrored the ambivalence of some of their alumni on the brothers still seeking vocations from Ireland, as we read in the "Second Circular Letter," discussed above in Chapter Seven.

St. Francis' Training School

FOR

YOUNG TEACHERS,

MOUNT BELLEW, CO. GALWAY.

This Institution which is in connection with the Franciscan Monastery, Mount Bellew, Co. Galway, has been established by Brother Jerome, O.S.F., Superior of the Franciscan Brothers Brooklyn, New York, with the sanction and approbation of His Grace the Most Rev. Dr. MacEvilly, Lord Archbishop of Tuam, and of the Most Rev. Dr. Loughlin, Bishop of Brooklyn, for the purpose of affording to talented young men, religiously disposed, facilities for preparing themselves to take an active part in the meritorious and much-needed work of Catholic Education in America.

The Franciscan Brothers of Brooklyn, besides conducting St. Francis' College, which is chartered and empowered to confer degrees, have charge of five Academies with an average attendance of about 3,000 boys, besides seven or eight of the largest parochial schools in the city, having an average attendance of about 5,000 pupils. Each of these Schools affords employment to eight or ten, and sometimes to fourteen Teachers.

St. Francis' Monastery and College of Brooklyn having been in existence for nearly thirty years, the Brothers are widely known and respected, and have frequent applications from Bishops and Priests through the states to open Academies and Schools. It is with the view of satisfying this demand Brother Jerome has instituted the Training School at Mount Bellew, where young men between the ages of fifteen and twenty-five who wish to join the Franciscan Order, and to devote their lives to the honour and glory of God and the education of the American youth, will receive religious training and a liberal education in science and literature, preparatory to their departure for the Novitiate at Brooklyn.

Besides the young men who went out with Brother Jerome last August to enter the Novitiate, there are at present in the Training School several others prosecuting their studies with success.

Applications for admittance can be made to Brother Jerome, O.S.F., President of St. Francis' College, Brooklyn, N.Y.; or to the Superior of the Franciscan Monastery, Mount Bellew, Co. Galway.

Send for Circular, &c.

N.B.—St. Francis' Training School must not be confounded with St. Francis' Academy. Although both are conducted in the same Institution, they are entirely distinct departments; the former being used exclusively for the preparation of members for the Order in connection with St. Francis' College, Brooklyn, while in the latter young gentlemen are prepared for professional examinations, Civil Service appointments, and Mercantile pursuits.

106

ST. FRANCIS TRAINING SCHOOL,
MOUNT BELLEW, CO. GALWAY [2]

"THE WILDS OF GALWAY -
THE BEST PLACE TO TRAIN TEACHERS DEVOTED
TO THE EDUCATION OF AMERICAN YOUTH?"

The continuing practice of seeking postulants in Ireland was debated in the public press when Jerome Magner responded to a reporter's questions when *The Brooklyn Daily Eagle* published a letter and article critical of the brothers' custom of seeking young men for their "St. Francis Preparatory Training School" in Mountbellew, County Galway, Ireland.[3] The advertisement, which Jerome Magner placed in a Dublin newspaper in early Summer, 1891, briefly told the history of the community and requested young men, to prepare themselves:

> *"to take an active part in the meritorious and much needed work of Catholic education in America, particularly in the United States.*
>
> *The Franciscan Brothers of Brooklyn beside conducting St. Francis College, have charge of five academies or seminaries, with an average attendance of 3,000 boys, beside fourteen of the largest parochial schools in the city, having an average attendance at present of upward of 8,000 pupils. Each of these schools afford employment to twelve, sometimes to fifteen teachers. They have also several schools in other dioceses, such as that in Jersey City, diocese of Newark; in Roundout, diocese of New York; in Clontarf, Minn, diocese of St. Paul, etc.*
>
> *St. Francis Monastery and College of Brooklyn having been in existence for thirty-two years, the brothers are widely known and respected and have frequent applications from bishops and priests throughout the states to open seminaries and schools. It is with the view of satisfying this demand that Rev.*

Brother Jerome has instituted the training school at Mountbellew, where young men, between the ages of 15 and 25 who wish to join the Franciscan order and to devote themselves to the honor and glory of God and the education of American youth, will receive religious training and a liberal education in science and literature preparatory to their departure for the novitiate at Brooklyn.

Beside the young men taken out in 1887 by Rev. Brother Jerome himself, every year since, numbers have been sent out from the preparatory training school, Mountbellew, who are now professed brothers of the order, and actively engaged in spreading the faith of Christ in the new world.

Applications for admittance can be made to Rev. Brother Jerome, O.S.F., president of St. Francis College, Brooklyn, N.Y., or to the superior of the Franciscan monastery, Mountbellew, County Galway, who can supply all necessary information."

When the Dublin newspaper reached New York, a caustic letter was sent by "American" [4] to the *Brooklyn Daily Eagle* which criticized the Franciscan Brothers' practice of continuing to seek vocations in Ireland:

To the Editor of the Brooklyn Daily Eagle:

"Some time ago a Protestant congregation in New York imported a minister from Europe. The reverend gentleman was stopped at the landing stage by the federal officials. And under the operations of the contract laws the congregation had to pay a fine of $1,000 before Uncle Sam would let him in. We may have a little experience like that here in Brooklyn. The fast trip of the <u>Teutonic</u> landed files of the Irish papers here up to August 13, and in some of them are items of special Brooklyn interest."

After quoting the advertisement above, the author of the anonymous letter writes:

> "*I don't like it at all. It is wrong from the very start. The brothers have been here now, if I remember right, since May, 1858, and thirty odd years ought, in all conscience, be long enough to develop a native source of supply. We Catholics are proud of our parochial schools and make many sacrifices to keep them up. I see by the Eagle Almanac for this year that the official figures of the board of education show that our parochial schools saved local taxpayers last year $515, 950. We are going to keep up our schools, but I am free to say that I don't think that the wilds of Galway is just the place to train the best material to be devoted to the education of American youth. The idea is all wrong and we ought not to have any Cahansly business [5] in this quarter. We have scores of talented young men and women graduating from our colleges and convents every year. Why can't we have them for our own? There is no lack of native supply.*" "*American*"

"WE CAN'T GET THEM IN THIS COUNTRY."

The reporter interviewed a number of persons who felt that the brothers, as members of a religious order, "do not come under contract to receive pay at all, but under vows, one of which is that of perpetual poverty." Brother Jerome, head of St. Francis College in Butler Street, and of the Order in this city, explained this fully and the workings of his Order to a reporter this morning. Asked why the Franciscans recruited their brotherhood from Ireland instead if in this country, Brother Jerome said:

"Because we can't get them in this country. The graduates of our American parochial schools do not enter religious orders. If they did we should not be at the expense of maintaining a training school in Galway."

"Are not nearly all the teachers in the parochial schools of the city members of your order that have been secured in this way?" the reporter asked.

"Certainly they are," Brother Jerome replied, "and serving without compensation. There are a few lay teachers, but the salaries are small and the places are chiefly filled by ladies teaching the primary classes. Our lay teachers are both Catholic and Protestants. We have Protestants in this college teaching mathematics, gymnastics and branches having nothing to do with religion and we find them very satisfactory."

"But do none of the graduates of your parochial schools take up teaching as a profession?" the reporter asked. "A few," replied Brother Jerome, "and they become teachers in the public schools of the city or else in Catholic colleges. But the public schools do not allow a boy to teach until he is 21. He is graduated from our schools at 16 or 17, and before he is 21, he drifts into business and stays there. I put two teachers into the public schools this year. Our boys who wish to teach can pass the examinations readily, and when they have obtained their certificates they usually have influence enough to secure places." [6]

The Brooklyn Brothers continued to depend on young men from Ireland for most of the postulants admitted to the Community. In addition to the advertisements seen above, direct recruitment was still fostered by regularly sending a brother to Ireland. Jerome Magner again went to Ireland in October 1902 and returned on the "Lucania" from Queenstown on Saturday, 5 April 1903. The death of John MacEvilly on 26 November 1902, [7] and the appointment to Tuam of John Healy, the Bishop of Clonfert, who was a friend of Brother John, must have prompted thoughts of another attempt at a union of the Irish and American communities, which was not to happen.

A letter of Cardinal Loque, recommending Brother Jerome, was published in *The Leader*, a Dublin paper on 21 March 1903 and mentions that he "still has room for some more zealous youths":

> *Br. Jerome, who has been in Ireland since last Oct. looking for candidates for his Order, is going to return on the "Lucania" Cunard Line from Queenstown on Sat. April 5th, and though he has a good number of zealous youths going with him to the Novitiate and House of Studies at Centerport, Long Island, he still has room for some more and it is not yet too late to apply to him at the Franciscan Monastery Clara, Kings Co.*
>
> *Cardinal Loque says of Br. Jerome and his mission:*
>
> *"I have great pleasure in recommending the mission of Rev. Br. Jerome, Superior of the Franciscan Brothers, United States of America, who has come to Ireland in quest of subjects for his Order. I wish Br. Jerome every success in his mission which has a great and important object - the offering to young men who feel they have a vocation, an opportunity of working successfully for the Glory of God and the salvation of souls by imparting to the young a solid Catholic Education which will go far to shield them from the dangers of a very dangerous age."* [8]
>
> *+ Michael Card. Loque*
> *Armagh, Jan 30th 1903*

"INSULA SANCTORUM ET DOCTORUM."

It is marvellous how, notwithstanding the manner in which this country is handicapped in matters educational, it is still regarded by foreigners, the Land of Scholars. The latest proof of this comes from America—The greater Ireland beyond the seas. Rev. Br. Jerome, O.S.F., is now in Ireland on a recruiting mission in the interests of his community—The Franciscans. He wants healthy young men (18 to 20) of good education and character, suitable to take up education—the chief work of the Franciscans. It is hoped that many of these may ultimately join the Order, which has charge of the principal Catholic educational establishments in Brooklyn, as well as the other States. Their College—over twenty Professors—has power to confer Degrees and annually a goodly number of B.A.'s pass through. It is not a little strange that while the accredited representative (he has Introductory Letters from the Bishop of Brooklyn) of the Franciscans has received well-nigh thirty applications within the past few months, only three of these came from Ulster—Belfast, Portadown, and Enniskillen. We do not encourage emigration in any form, but we think it right to say that if Ireland in days of old could spare sons to obtain for her the proud title of Land of Scholars, surely she can still sen dmen to retain that title. Letters addressed: Rev. Br. Jerome, O.S.F., Franciscan Monastery, Clara, will receive prompt attention.

"INSULA SANCTORUM ET DOCTORUM "-
ISLE OF SAINTS AND SCHOLARS [9]

Brother Jerome was able to bring back twenty-five young men, which immediately forced the Community to move the Novitiate from the top floor of the Monastery at 41 Butler Street to the Summer Monastery at Centerport. The transfer of the Novitiate [10] had been decided on 17 September 1901, but the large number of young men who arrived with Brother Jerome made it a necessity in late Spring of 1903. [11] At the 30 March 1903 meeting of the Council, furniture and repairs for the Novitiate at Centerport were entrusted to the Superior.

The ambivalence of the Council on the nature and location of a formation program is evident when the possibility of a training school for postulants in Clifden, Ireland was discussed on 5 April 1903, but was "deferred until Brother Jerome's return from Ireland, who is expected home Monday, 13 inst." [12] The possibility of such a "training school" is surprising considering the earlier decision of John MacEvilly, the Archbishop of Tuam, that the Irish Brothers could not unite with their American confreres. However, the death of MacEvilly on 26 November 1902, while Brother Jerome was in Ireland, changed the Irish and American Brothers' hopes for a more friendly archbishop in Tuam: [13] The brothers continued to seek vocations in Ireland until the Great War closed access to Europe.

After the departure of 27 Brothers to Spaulding in 1907, the Novitiate was returned to the Monastery at 41 Butler Street in 1909. The Council met on 26 February 1911, to discuss the need for vocations and decided to again send a brother to Ireland:

A meeting was called today to consider ways and means of getting postulants. A quorum being present, it was decided to advertise for candidates in several papers. A motion was put, moved and carried that some Brother go to Ireland next July to get candidates for the Order.

As the Summer of 1911 approached, the Council met on 12 June and tried to have its resolution of 26 February implemented:

A resolution was proposed, seconded and agreed on by a majority of the Consultors to form a committee to petition the Rt. Rev. Bishop to allow a Brother to go to Ireland for postulants.

The Brother Superior [Stanislaus Ryan], *refused to put the resolution to the Consultors to vote on.*[14]

However, the Consultors continued their resolve to send one of their members to Ireland, and on 1 July they met again, with Msgr Kaupert, the Vicar General, presiding, and voted on sending one of the consultors to Ireland, who it turned out was not the Superior:

The consideration of getting postulants from Ireland was discussed. A Brother to be sent to Ireland immediately to get candidates for the Order. Brother Gerard Lynne was selected to go.

Vote: Brother Gerard Lynne 5
   Brother Stanislaus Ryan 3 [15]

Three days later, on 4 July, the Consultors met again and the tone of the Minutes indicates their unhappiness with the Superior:

At this meeting the names of the Brothers for perpetual vows were merely mentioned by the Superior. The cases were not considered singly or collectively by the Consultors. No vote was taken to decide the presentation of their names to the general council. [16]

On the evening of the next day, Brother Stanislaus tried to overturn the decision of 1 July, when he was not selected to go to Ireland:

> Bro. *Stanislaus Ryan called a meeting tonight and endeavored to over-rule the decision of the majority of the Council: the decision of the Rt. Rev. Bishop and his representative, Msgr. Kaupert, on the matter of the selection of Brother Gerard to go to Ireland for Postulants. He was defeated in his purpose of making his own selection, as the Consultors adhered to their original decision to send Bro. Gerard Lynne.* [17]

The Council's difficulties with the Superior came to a head in the meeting of 28 July 1911, when they were called to decide on the admission of Brothers to perpetual vows:

> *After the formal opening, the following members of the Council objected, as the proceeding was irregular: Brothers Ignatius Culhane, David McPartland, Athanasius O'Donohue, and Vincent Mulcahy stated that the candidates' names were not presented to the Council, according to custom and Constitution. Meeting adjourned. No decision on candidates.* [18]

On the next day, the consultors met and passed on the candidates for vows: each got 8 votes; Brother Leonard McNamara was rejected. [19] On 30 July, the *"General Council* (all life professed present at Centerport [20]), *were called to vote on candidates for vows. 44 present."* [21]

> *Bro. Clement Garvey passed for perpetual vows 26 votes*
> "   *Adrian Doyle*   "   "   "   "   *38*   "
> "   *Ivo Dunne*   "   "   "   "   *42*   "
> "   *Maurice Farrell*   "   " *Three year vows 42* "

SUPERIOR GENERAL RESIGNS

On the Feast of Portiuncla, 2 August 1911, "Brother Stanislaus Ryan resigned as Superior" and "Brother David McPartland, the Assistant, was appointed by Msgr. Kaupert and the Consultors to fill the unexpired term." [22] Although the Minutes of 5 August 1911 indicate that Brother Ambrose Canavan and Egidius Mason "were to be sent to New England for postulants,"[23] subsequent Minutes record that a "vote of thanks was given to Brother Domnus Carroll for his successful work in getting postulants in Ireland.[24]

While the Council Minutes do not indicate the country where postulants might have come from, we do learn that two young men: James Boyhan (28 December 1911), and Robert Ford (14 January 1912), were sent their passage money to come from Ireland to Brooklyn as postulants. Seven young men: Sebastian Rynne, Francis Croke, Anthony Boyhan, Fidelis Hance, Benedict McDonald, Bernardine O'Sullivan and Leo Gardner, were received to the Habit on 31 July 1912.[25] With the exception of Fidelis Hance, who sounds German, the others all had Irish names. Robert Ford, who received his passage money to America in January, 1912, never entered the Community. Vocations to the Community continued to grow. On 9 March 1913, five young men were passed for admission who were all Irish: Camillus Dooley, Bonaventure Dunne, Felix McNamara, Paul Vaughan, and Lawrence McBeath. On 14 March 1914, three young men were passed to receive the Habit, including a Casimir Szypicki, who did not make it to profession.

ST. ANTHONY'S BOARDING SCHOOL

During the six years the Novitiate was in Centerport (1903-1909), the brothers opened a primary school for boys. In the words of an advertisement in *The Brooklyn Daily Eagle*:

> *St. Anthonys Boarding School for boys is at Mount Alvernia, Centerport, L.I., two miles from Greenlawn Station. The school is in a picturesque spot overlooking a lovely bay. Boys under 15 years are received. In its work the school corresponds to a grammar school and fits pupils for entrance to high school departments attached to the colleges. Exceptional opportunities are offered to backward pupils, who were neglected in their early school days by providing for them special tutors. As St. Anthony's School is under the immediate care of the Franciscan Brothers, religious training will not be neglected, while physical and intellectual education receive the closest attention.* [26]

The closing of eight of the brothers' schools: St. Stephen's, St. Charles Borromeo, and Our Lady of Mercy in 1923; St. Joseph's, St. Vincent de Paul's and St. Paul's in 1928; St. Peter's, 1933; and Sacred Heart in 1935, [27] and the opening of St. Francis Xavier's, on President Street in 1914, and the relocation of St. Leonard's Academy from Williamsburg to 26 Brevoort Place in 1925, put new pressure on the Community to find, train and keep vocations.

With the closing of Ireland as a source of vocations during and after the Great War of 1914-1918, the Franciscan Brothers were forced to plan a more permanent formation program. The community again moved its novitiate from the top floor of 41 Butler Street to the new

Mount St. Francis which they opened at Smithtown Branch in 1929.

MOUNT ST. FRANCIS NOVITIATE

Except for the six years the novices used the Centerport monastery [1903 -1909] and the one year at St. Leonard's Academy in Williamsburg [1909-1910], the space on the top floor of St. Francis Monastery in Brooklyn was always inadequate for a formal novitiate. When the young men moved to their new Mount St. Francis Novitiate in the mansion of the Mills Estate in Smithtown Branch, Long Island on 13 February 1929, a whole new era of preparation of the novices began. No longer were the novices, as the youngest members of the community, the dish washers, waiters and house cleaners for the life-professed brothers at the Monastery, but they were finally able to devote time to their spiritual studies as required by canon law.

The Mills Estate was part of the property of the original patent obtained by Richard "Bull" Smith from the local Indian tribe. [28] The Mills house was built between 1826 and 1840, by his great-great-grandson, Sam "Stevens" Smith, sheriff of Suffolk County. The house and farm passed to the Mills family who were descendants of Richard Smith. The family made its fortune during the Civil War by the sale of buttonwood for ships' masts and black walnut wood for gunstocks. The estate was still a rural farm without electricity when the Community purchased it on 13 October 1928. "While the records of Suffolk County name the Brothers as owners, there is no record of the sale of the land to them. . . . As manifested by Governor Al Smith's disastrous presidential campaign in 1928, anti-Catholic feeling was strong in America, especially rural America during the 20's, and discretion dictated that little public attention be drawn to the purchase. Only four or five years earlier, the Ku Klux Klan had burned a cross at Camp Alvernia in Centerport." [29]

The practice of seeking young men of high school age as aspirants for religious communities began in the 1920s with the opening of high-school-level seminaries and juniorates by dioceses and religious orders. The Franciscan Brothers opened a "day juniorate, the first in the diocese," at St. Francis Preparatory School in 1923. "Eleven years later, (actually ten years - on 13 September 1933), it was transferred to the new St. Anthony's Boarding Juniorate built at Smithtown Branch." [30] The opening of St. Anthony's Juniorate for high-school-age boys, on the apple orchard of that same rural, eleven acre Mills estate, allowed the brothers to concentrate their formation program at one location, at St. Johnland Road and Landing Avenue, between Kingspark and Smithtown Branch, on the North Shore of Suffolk County, Long Island. They were able to seek young men from their own elementary and high schools, and other schools in the Diocese of Brooklyn.

Although the brothers had given up hope of obtaining vocations from Ireland, they still valued the spirit of those Irish-born men whom they placed in charge of the Novitiate and the Juniorate: **Ferdinand Kiely** from Tipperary, Ireland, was Master of Novices for 20 years before his death on 1 December 1935. **Capistran Cusack,** who was born in Limerick, became the Novice Master in 1937, after his term as Superior General. He also served as Master of Postulants and teacher of English Grammar to the novices and postulants until his death on 2 August 1962. **Brendan O'Brien,** from Tipperary, was Master of Novices and Assistant Superior of St. Anthony's Juniorate until his death on 7 October 1950. The writer remembers Capistran and Brendan as holy men whose edifying lives were inspirations to the young men they directed. Although he was not from Ireland, **Bernard Costa**, who was born in Procida, Italy, was Master of Novices for 12 years. His vivacious personality and love of prayer impressed his charges. He was especially remembered for his devotion to St. Anthony of Padua.

THE NEW JUNIORATE — BEGUN AUGUST 31, 1933.

ST. ANTHONY'S JUNIORATE

Through the hard work and academic qualifications of the first brothers, especially **Celestine McGarry,** the founding principal, the State of New York certified St. Anthony's as a four-year high school on 17 December 1936. The Juniorate never had more than forty or fifty young men who were seeking entrance to the Franciscan Brothers.

In 1957, when the counties of Nassau and Suffolk on Long Island were separated from the Brooklyn Diocese, the Diocese of Rockville Centre was created. In response to the request of Edgar P. McCarren, the Superintendent of Schools of the new Diocese, the Community opened St. Anthony's as a day-high school in September 1958, to serve the boys of the neighboring towns. [31] To accommodate the new day-students, the Juniorate boys took up residence in the Mills house at the edge of the property in September of 1958, and their dormitory in the Juniorate building became classrooms and Guidance Department offices. By September 1968, the Juniorate boys made their last move to a new building at Camp Alvernia in Centerport, traveling by bus each day to the high school, a distance of about ten miles. In keeping with a new formation program philosophy, that thirteen and fourteen year-old adolescent boys should not be accepted to religious life until they were mature enough to understand the implications of what they were undertaking, the Juniorate program ended in June 1969. [32]

When Bishop Molloy gave the community the nine acre Collins Estate which had been donated to the Brooklyn Diocese, the Novitiate program moved to Wyandanch, South Huntington, Long Island in 1949. The brothers purchased additional property to assure privacy, expanding St. Francis Novitiate to thirty-two acres with four buildings - Molloy Hall, St. Louis Hall, and Collins

Hall, all used as residences for the over forty novices and professed brothers. St. Mary's Cottage, across from the chapel, was used as the chaplain's residence and the laundry room. The first-year novices spent their days in the study of theology and the second-year novices studied secular subjects with Brother professors from St. Francis College. They were also very involved with manual labor, raising much of their food by tending pigs, turkeys and chickens, and begging in their habits in the Hunt's Point Market from the vendors who were very generous with their surplus vegetables and potatoes.

"LA SALVA"
ST FRANCIS NOVITIATE, OYSTER BAY

In 1961, St. Francis Novitiate was moved to the Wheeler estate in Oyster Bay to again seek isolation for the novices from the incursions of visitors onto the Collins estate in Wyandanch. This beautiful property, called *La Salva,* was used by the Community for the many young men who were seeking entrance to the community during this time. In more recent years, as fewer postulants were seeking entrance to the Community, it became St. Francis Center, which served groups of high school students and adults for retreats and conferences.

In 1962, The Brother Columba Reilly Scholasticate was opened in the five-story house at 82 Pierrepont Street in Brooklyn Heights to accommodate the large number of young brothers who were attending St. Francis College full-time at either the Science Building on Butler Street or the new College at 180 Remsen Street. Before this time, brothers attended the college part time in the afternoons and Saturdays, after teaching a full day's schedule in their parish schools.

BROTHER COLUMBA REILLY SCHOLASTICATE[33]
82 PIERREPONT STREET, BROOKLYN HEIGHTS

The mansion had been built in the 1890s for the Baer family, and was expanded in the early 1930s to house the Palm Hotel. An elevator, restaurant and large lobby were part of the expansion to accommodate the hotel. During the Second World War the quality and reputation of the hotel declined and its purchase by the Community for a religious House of Studies was welcomed by the brothers' neighbors on Pierrepont and Henry Streets. With the decline in the number of young brother-scholastics, this house was sold by the Community in 1975. Currently, young men who are completing their undergraduate education before acceptance to the Community, live in pre-novitiate friaries to live community life for two or more years with a group of professed brothers. This gave young men the opportunity to observe religious life and to be observed by the professed brothers. This paradigm was the custom in the earliest monasteries of the Community in Ireland and America when postulants and novices lived in the monasteries and were observed in their daily lives by the life-professed brothers who voted on their entrance to profession. This custom ended in the early 1940s, when the young temporary professed brothers did not all live at St. Francis Monastery at 41 Butler Street, and the brothers who voted on them might never have lived with them.

Brother Jerome Roese Hall, the first pre-novitiate, was opened in 1970 on 73rd Street in Our Lady of Angels Parish in Brooklyn. Other pre-novitiate communities were established in Sunnyside, Ridgewood, and Woodside, Queens. Currently, the pre-novitiate is at Trinity Friary, 200 Gold Street in Brooklyn.

BROTHER CHARLES RYNNE
LAST IRISH-BORN MEMBER OF THE COMMUNITY [34]

Daniel Colman Rynne, born in Ennistymen, County Clare, on 2 October 1899, the brother of Brother Thomas Rynne, received the Habit on 25 March 1915, with the name Brother Charles. When he died on 21 April 1982, after more than four-score years of life, and 67 years of service in the Franciscan Brothers, the Community Necrology notes that his death:

*marked the end of an era which spanned the first
century and a quarter of the Franciscan Brothers of
Brooklyn. He was not only the senior member of the
Congregation but also the last of the Irish-born
Brothers. He crowned the long line of those noble
pioneers who left Erin and helped Catholic emigrants
take root on the distant soil.*

His eulogist affectionately continues his memory with
Brother Charles' favorite last word on any event of note:

*In addition to history, algebra or religion, his
students learned lessons in discipline, attention and
respect for Irish tenacity when he deemed a situation
"desperate".* [35]

Charles Rynne's death marked the end of a long
history of dependence on Ireland for vocations and
Community identity, when the last of the brothers, known
affectionately as "FBI," or "Foreign Born Irish," departed
this life.

VATICAN COUNCIL II PROMPTS THE
COMMUNITYTO RETURN
TO THE SPIRIT OF THE FOUNDER

The Extraordinary Chapter of Affairs convened by the
Community in response to Vatican Council II in 1968,
began a twenty year process leading to the completion of
the Congregation's revised *Constitutions* in 1989. On the 8th
of December 1982, Pope John Paul II ratified the new *Rule
and Life* of the Third Order Regular, which had "traveled
its path of *aggiornamento* and how fortuitously it arrived at
the desired convergence of different points of views
through collegial discussion and consultation, proposals

and studied amendments . . . . We trust that the longed for fruits of renewal will be brought to full realization." [36]

The "collegial discussion and consultation" was extensive. As was reported in Chapter Six, the Franciscan Federation of Brothers and Sisters of the Third Order Regular worked for many years to achieve *The Rule and Life* approved by Pope John Paul II.

As the Community prepared for its 140th Anniversary in1998, it was able to celebrate its establishment as a Congregation of Pontifical Right with the approval of its revised Constitutions. This international approval complemented a global awareness as the Brothers helped establish a Franciscan presence at the United Nations and fostered inter-Franciscan dialogue with other organizations. It was evident that the Franciscan Brothers had moved beyond their nineteenth century Irish and twentieth century American roots and had entered into collaborations with other Franciscans throughout the world. Brother Thomas Grady's Letter of Promulgation of the new Rule, Life and Constitutions best expresses the history of those times: [37]

> *Dear Brothers,*
>
> > *"We are the brothers of our Lord*
> > *Jesus Christ, when we do the will*
> > *of the Father through the Holy Spirit."*
> > *- St. Francis, Letter to the Faithful*
>
> *For over twenty years we have worked together to discern and describe the will of God for us. We affirmed our understanding as a Chapter body in 1982 when we endorsed a renewed Constitutions and a decision to seek pontifical approbation. In the same year, our Holy Father Pope John Paul II ratified the new Rule and Life of our Order. Subsequently our Constitutions were*

approved by Bishop Francis Mugavero, Ordinary of the Diocese of Brooklyn, in 1985, and finally by the Holy See on September 8th of this year.

Each of these steps engaged us in a process larger than ourselves. Requesting pontifical recognition culminated a movement begun by our Brothers in 1859 when our congregation was established as a diocesan institute "pro tempore." Participating in the revision of our Rule engaged us in a collaborative process of understanding the charism of continuous conversion which we share with congregations of our Order across the globe. Renewing our Constitutions involved all of us in a reflection on and articulation of our particular vocation as Franciscan Brothers within the Universal Church and the entire Franciscan family.

Acknowledging with humble gratitude all who have brought these efforts to fulfillment, it is my privilege to promulgate these texts on the Feast of Saint Francis, October 4, 1989.

The Rule and Constitutions, together with our Directory, Policy Book and History are presented here as a definition of our way of life. From these words which describe God's will for us, let us draw inspiration and encouragement to move from understanding to action and "to the will of the Father" in the spirit of St. Francis and the Brothers who preceded us. In living these words "as spirit and life" we will be blessed with interior peace, apostolic zeal and fraternal love as we journey toward a new century extending "peace and goodness" throughout God's creation.

With personal and prayerful best wishes, I am,
Fraternally yours in Saint Francis,
    Brother Thomas Grady, O.S.F.
    Superior General

Notes

[1] Archives of St. Francis Monastery

[2] *The Irish Catholic Directory and Almanac for 1888,* James Duffy, Dublin, 1887, p. 106.

[3] *The Brooklyn Daily Eagle,* 21 August 1891, p. 4, "FOR TEACHERS, The Search of the Brooklyn Franciscan Brothers, Why They Maintain a Training Institute in Galway".

[4] Although we do not know the identity of "American," his knowledge of the Brothers' history and schools suggests that he may have been one of their graduates.

[5] Abraham Cahan, (1860-1951), editor, writer and political leader was a member of the "People's Will Party," which was responsible for the assassination of Tsar Alexander in 1881. Escaping the Russian police, he moved to New York City in 1882, where he became a leader of Yiddish-speaking radical unionists, and launched *The Jewish Daily Forward* in which he advocated the rights of immigrants seeking to organize industrial unions. *The Encyclopedia of New York City,* edited by Kenneth T. Jackson, Yale University Press, 1995, pp. 175-176.

[6] *The Brooklyn Daily Eagle,* 21 August 1891, p. 4. One week later Patrick Ford's *Irish World* repeated the full text of the *Brooklyn Daily Eagle* article on 29 August, 1891.

[7] Liam Bane, *The Bishop in Politics, Loyal Friend, Bitter Foe, Life and Career of John MacEvilly,* Westport Historical Society, 1993, p. 158.

[8] *The Leader,* 21 March 1903, Article with Letter of Michael Cardinal Loque, Archbishop of Armagh and Primate of Ireland.

[9] (Belfast newspaper, early Spring 1903).

[10] Minutes of "Council Meetings and General Chapters, August 2, 1894 to November 19, 1906," September 17, 1901, pp. 223-224.

[11] *Ibid.,* March 9, 1903 and March 30, 1903, pp. 233-234.

[12] *Ibid.,* April 5, 1903, p. 234.

[13] Bernardine Cowan, O.S.F., "Fifty Years in a Monastery, Br.

Bernardine Cowan, O.S.F., 1878-1969," pp. 11-12.

14 Records of Council Meetings and other Community Matters, as Kept by the Secretary General, Brother Athanasius, Dec. 11, 1910 - Dec. 15, 1922, p. 1.

15 *Ibid.*, p. 2-3

16 *Ibid.*

17 *Ibid..*

18 *Ibid.*, pp 3-4.

19 *Ibid.*, p 4.

20 The practice of submitting all candidates for vows to the whole community continued until the 1940s. It was a custom which evolved in Ireland when all the brothers lived in the same monastery and the novices and junior-professed were observed on a daily basis by the life-professed brothers.

21 "Records," p. 4.

22 *Ibid.*

23 *Ibid.*, pp. 4-5

24 *Ibid.*, p. 8.

25 *Ibid.*, p. 7.

26 *Brooklyn Daily Eagle Education Section*, September 5, 1907.

27 John K. Sharp, *History of the Diocese of Brooklyn, 1853-1953,* Vol. II, p. 211.

28 Richard "Bull" Smith [or Smythe as he spelled it] received ten square miles from Lion Gardner of Gardiner's Island in 1663. To expand his ten square miles, legend tells us, he wished to buy a tract of adjoining land from a local Indian chief. The Indian said he did not wish to sell the land, but seeing the lively activity of one of Smith's bulls remarked that he would give Smith as much land as he could ride around between sun and sun on the back of a bull. After training one of his bulls, he rode it all day and laid claim to a great territory near the town of Huntington. Smith was ever afterward known as "Bull" Smith. In Henry Isham Hazelton, *The Boroughs of Brooklyn, and Queens, Counties of Nassau and Suffolk, Long Island, New*

York, 1609-1924, Lewis Historical Publications, New York, 1925, Vol II, pp. 804-808.

[29] Lorna Strachan, CSJ, "A History of Saint Anthony's High School, 1934 to 1984," p. 1.

[30] John K. Sharp, *History of the Brooklyn Diocese, 1853-1953,* Vol. 2, pp. 210-211.

[31] Strachan, "History . . . .", p. 12.

[32] The current practice of the Church as expressed in Canon 643. 1, is that persons who have not completed the seventeenth year of age may not be admitted to the novitiate of religious communities.

[33] Watercolor by E. M. Russell, 1978, (Donated by Patrick Russo).

[34] "San Fran, 1983," Yearbook of St. Francis Preparatory School, p. 6.

[35] "Necrology of the Congregation of the Brothers of the Third Order Regular of St. Francis," Saint Francis Monastery, Brooklyn, New York, 1999.

[36] "John Paul II as a Perpetual Memorial," Letter approving the revised *Rule and Life of the Brothers and Sisters of the Third Order Regular of Saint Francis,* 8 December 1982.

[37] "Rule and Life of the Brothers and Sisters of the Third Order Regular of Saint Francis " and "Constitutions of the Franciscan Brothers of Brooklyn" October 4, 1989, p. 2.

CHAPTER NINE

"THE SAINT FRANCIS MONASTERY
OF THE CITY OF BROOKLYN":
A LEGAL CORPORATION AS STEWARD
OF ITS FRANCISCAN IDENTITY

The Franciscan Brothers' community was created a legal corporation in New York State when "The St. Francis Monastery of the City of Brooklyn" was incorporated on 2 June 1868, by Chapter 851 of the Laws of 1868 of the New York State legislature.[1]

Most of the text of the original 1868 document is standard language of incorporation, with the names of the founding members, the name of the new corporation, the statement of power to sue and be sued, to own property, to receive money by will or gift, the composition and number of the board members, and their ability to fill vacancies in the board when necessary.

The text of the Act of Incorporation reveals some of the history of the early community, giving the name of John Loughlin, the first Bishop of Brooklyn, and the secular names of the four brothers who completed the original five-member board:

CHAPTER 851

AN ACT TO INCORPORATE

"THE ST. FRANCIS' MONASTERY,"

of the City of Brooklyn

Passed June 2d, 1868.

The People of the State of New York, represented in Senate and Assembly, do enact as follows:

Section I. John Loughlin, Robert Magner, William Butler, Miles Coén, and Jeremiah Fruin, and their associates and successors, shall be, and they are hereby constituted a body corporate and politic by the name of "The St. Francis' Monastery," of the City of Brooklyn, and by that name shall have perpetual succession, and may sue and be sued in any court of competent jurisdiction; and may take, receive, hold and enjoy by gift, grant, devise, bequest or otherwise any real estate or personal property within this State, not exceeding Fifty Thousand Dollars, subject however to the provisions of existing laws.

Section II. The object of said corporation shall be the education of children, those able as well as those unable to pay, and the visiting and assisting of poor.

Section III. The persons named in the first section of this act, shall be the first trustees of said corporation, and all vacancies by death, resignation, refusal to act, or removal of any of said Trustees, or otherwise, in the office of the Trustees shall be filled by the election of persons who shall be members of the "St. Francis' Monastery." The said Board of Trustees shall fill such vacancy without unnecessary delay, and at least three votes shall be necessary for the election of any Trustee. There shall be at least one meeting of the Board each year.

Section IV. The business of said corporation shall be managed by a Board of five Trustees, who shall elect from their number a President, a Secretary and a Treasurer.

Section V. The Board of Trustees of said corporation shall have power to make and establish such By-Laws, Rules and Regulations for the managing and directing the Officers of the said corporation, as from time to time shall be necessary or expedient.

Section VI. This act shall take effect immediately.

Office of the Secretary of State.

I have compared the preceding with the original law on file in this office, and do hereby certify that the same is a correct transcript therefrom, and of the whole of said original law.

GIVEN under my hand and seal of office, at the City of Albany, this twenty-first day of July, in the year one thousand eight hundred and sixty-eight.

H. A. NELSON
Secretary of State

1868 Charter for "The Saint Francis Monastery"

The short paragraph of Section II, on the "Object of the said corporation," reveals an historical dichotomy between the "monastic" charism of the Franciscan Brothers who arrived in Brooklyn in 1858, and a fundamental change in that charism, when they described their "Object" in their Charter a decade later in 1868.

*Section II. The Object of said corporation shall be the education of children, those able **as well as those unable to pay**, and the visiting and assisting of the poor.*

The education of children, "unable to pay," was a unique characteristic of the Franciscan Brothers who came to Brooklyn from Ireland in 1858. The Irish Brothers 1837 *Rule and Constitutions* stated: "The mechanics, and every other individual, to be employed in their different pursuits of industry [carpentry, coopering (barrel-making), and stone cutting, as well as farming], for the support of the Monastery," permitted the teaching Brothers, "who will devote themselves, in a particular manner, to the instruction of poor male children," to be able **to teach without receiving a fee for tuition**. This commitment of the Irish Franciscan Brothers to free education of poor male children and young men continued a long tradition. Each Third Order Regular monastery, especially in the West of Ireland, had a section of the friary devoted to schoolrooms, where poor boys received a primary education, and young men of the parish received education in useful trades of "mechanism". [2]

A young man who requested entrance to the Irish Franciscan Brothers was examined on "his life, conduct, and vocation, and his abilities for teaching, catechising, mechanism, etc." [3] The Irish community's long-standing custom of receiving young men who might not be teachers, but who would have other talents useful to the Monastery, such as "mechanism," was unique to the Irish Franciscan Brothers and was not found in other nineteenth-century Irish communities of teaching brothers.

John McMahon, who was the Superior of the Brooklyn Brothers from 1858 to 1862, sheds more light on this tradition of the Irish community when he tried to establish a college in Santa Ines, California in 1863. In a letter [4] responding to two letters of James Croke, the Vicar General of the Archdiocese of San Francisco, he writes how the Brothers would support themselves while teaching **"poor male children gratuitously"**[author's emphasis].

The object of our vocation is to teach poor male children gratuitously; we can establish wherever we are needed or required, if we get the use of a house and salary sufficient to find us in food and clothing. In dioceses when Brothers are needed they get in addition to this, aid in the way of lands, colleges, pay schools, etc. to form and educate young teachers. This accounts, in a great measure for whatever property the Brothers possess.

The brothers did establish a "pay school" in St. Francis Academy on Baltic Street in Brooklyn in 1859, but difficulties between John Loughlin and the brothers about accommodation and their work in their first year in Brooklyn, may have made them feel not "needed or required," and prompted half of them to seek to join the First Order Franciscans in Santa Barbara, California before the end of 1859. By 1862, the Bishop had still not moved to have the community incorporated, nor had he transferred the ownership of St. Francis Academy to the brothers. In

California, John McMahon would still describe the "object of our vocation is to teach poor male children gratuitously." This "object of our vocation" would seem to contradict the new *Constitutions* the Brooklyn Community would receive from John Loughlin in 1866.

Two years before the Brooklyn Franciscan Brothers were incorporated in 1868, a decade after their arrival in the diocese, they received a new *Constitutions,* [5] approved by John Loughlin and printed two years earlier in 1866. Most of this *Constitutions* was taken directly from the 1832 *Rules and Constitutions of the Society of Religious Brothers,* [6] known as the Religious Brothers of the Christian Schools, founded by Blessed Edmund Rice in Ireland. As shown above in Chapter Six, whole paragraphs of this Irish Christian Brother's *Constitutions* were imposed on the young Brooklyn Franciscan Brothers' community. The inclusive, monastic charism which the Franciscan Brothers brought with them from Ireland was radically altered by this 1866 *Constitutions*, which permitted the possibility of free education for the majority of their students only in the parish schools. Although we do not know when this process of changing the Brooklyn Brothers' *Constitutions* began, it may have started shortly after their arrival in Brooklyn and may have been a factor in their desire to travel to California by the Fall of 1859. This fundamental change in the identity of the Franciscan Brothers was accomplished by changing their Irish monastic-style *Constitutions* to match the Irish Christian Brothers' *Constitutions.*

Although "the religious and literary education of **poor male children**" was given as the secondary "end" of the Franciscan Brothers, these new 1866 Constitutions would make it difficult to educate only poor children, because the elimination of the inclusive, monastic-charism of the community no longer permitted them to accept young men as novices who could not be teachers. Those brothers, who as farmers and carpenter-builders, supported the teaching brothers in the Irish Franciscan monasteries, were now considered to have an avocation *"foreign to the end of our Institute, and contrary to the benevolent intentions of our pious and zealous founders."* [7]

Because of their immigration in the mid-nineteenth century to the urban part of the City of Brooklyn, surrounding the docks of the East River, the rural, monastic character of the Franciscan Brothers' communal life was no longer possible. In contrast, over half of the Irish brothers who went to the rural community of Loretto, in the hills of Cambria County, Pennsylvania in 1847, were still able, through the next half century, to engage in the traditional monastic activities of an agricultural community, such as farming and practices of "mechanism" in carpentry and stone cutting. [8] Was this the rural, agricultural style of life which John McMahon and the five brothers who traveled with him across the continent to Santa Barbara, California in 1862, still trying to find - and were they seeking to restore the secondary "end" of their institute, "the religious and literary education of poor male children," which John Loughlin would take from them when he imposed the Christian Brothers' 1832 *Rules and Constitutions* on them four years later?

ST. FRANCIS ACADEMY

In 1859, John Loughlin purchased a former Protestant church and public school at 300 Baltic Street for use as St. Francis Academy and the brothers' residence. By March, 1862, three months before he left for California, John McMahon purchased a residence at 41 Butler Street, which became the first of the connected buildings on Butler Street behind the Academy. These buildings would be Saint Francis Monastery and the home of the brothers for the next century. Two years after the new *Constitution* was printed in 1866, and the Monastery was incorporated in 1868, the bishop finally transferred the Baltic Street Academy building and plot of land to the Franciscan Brothers.

MONASTERY AND COLLEGE BUILDINGS (1890)

ST. FRANCIS MONASTERY AND COLLEGE (c.1880)

CREATION OF ST. FRANCIS COLLEGE IN 1884

Although the Brothers elected their superior general and council at their triennial chapters, the canonical governance of the brothers and their legal governance by the five-member board of trustees of "The St. Francis Monastery of the City of Brooklyn," were not the same. John Loughlin, the Ordinary of the Brooklyn Diocese, as the ecclesiastical superior of the brothers, was named the "President" of the Board of Trustees of "The St. Francis Monastery" in 1868. By 1884, Brothers Jerome Magner, the Superior, Paul Hill, the Assistant Superior, Fidelis Carrier, Consultor, and Isidore Garvey, Consultor and Treasurer, completed the five-member "The St. Francis Monastery" board when the College Charter was granted.

Although St. Francis Academy had offered college-level courses before 1884, "Students completing their high school studies frequently took college-level courses, though they did not receive a diploma to attest to the fact. On 8 May 1884, the original 1868 Charter was amended to reflect the creation of St. Francis College as a degree-granting institution. As the legal board of the community, "The St. Francis Monastery" Corporation received a number of powers vis-a-vis the new College: to establish a "Literary College in the City of Brooklyn, under the title of St Francis College, and appoint twelve persons of full age, citizens of the United States and the State of New York, whom it desires to manage and direct the said college." [9]

With the amended Charter of 8 May 1884, prominent clerics and laymen were elected to the St. Francis College Board of Trustees by the five trustees of "The St. Francis Monastery of the City of Brooklyn".The new trustees of the College were: The Rt. Rev. John Loughlin, Bishop of Brooklyn; Rev. William J. Hill, Rector of St. Paul's; Rev. James S. Duffy, Pastor of St. Agnes Church; Dr. John Griffin, D.D.; John L. Deveney, L.L.B; Robert Magner, (Brother Jerome); James Carrier, (Brother Fidelis); Patrick Garvey, (Brother Isidore); and Joseph Hill, (Brother Paul).[10]

FIRST MEETING OF ST. FRANCIS COLLEGE BOARD

In less than a month, after these nine persons presented their certificates of election to the Clerk of the County of Kings (Brooklyn), they held their first meeting of the new Board on Monday, 2 June 1884, and assumed the following powers and duties as trustees of St. Francis College:

1. To make such bylaws as they shall deem proper for the management of the College,

2. To prescribe the course of study and discipline to be pursued and observed by the students attending the college,

3. To have the power to confer diplomas, literary honors and degrees as is possessed by the Universities and Colleges of the State of New York, and

4. To adopt a seal for the use of the College. [11]

Seal of St. Francis College [12]

A circular seal for the college was designed using some parts of the Third Order Regular Seal of the Franciscan Brothers. It consisted of a cross surmounted by the crossed arms of Christ and Saint Francis on clouds in a circle, inside a circular band on which the words "Sigillum Collegii Sti. Francisci, Brooklyn, N. Eb." [Seal of the College of St. Francis, Brooklyn, New York]. The Seal was approved by the College Trustees on 25 May 1885.

The Trustees continued to meet in June of 1884, but decided not to award degrees that year. [13] At its busy first meeting the new Board addressed other duties:

> *It named the Bishop as its President, and Brother Paul Hill as Secretary. The Trustees also created a Board of Examiners to determine the fitness of candidates for "literary honors or degrees," naming: "Fathers Hill and Duffy; Doctor O'Connell, Pastor of St. Michael's Church; Dr. Griffin; Prof. Paul Martin of St. Francis College; and Brothers DeSales and Paul."*
>
> *"The Prospectus for the College and a body of Rules and regulations presented by Robert Magner, O.S.F. were ordered to be read. Certain changes were deemed necessary, and were made accordingly."*
>
> *"The Rt. Rev. Bishop suggested that the words 'obscene' and 'profane' should be inserted with reference to language, as matters deserving of expulsion from the College; the 'Severest Penalties' relating to breaches of minor points of Discipline, was changed so as to read 'severe penalties.'"*
>
> *"Rev. Father Hill thought the Greek Course rather limited, while he considered the Mathematical Course too heavy."*
>
> *"At the recommendation of the Right Rev. Bishop it was resolved to have several copies of the Prospectus,*

Course of Studies, Rules and Regulations, printed and to have each member of the Board, furnished with a copy."

Mr. Deveney moved that Rev. Father Hill be made Vice President of the Board of Trustees; it was seconded and carried unanimously."

"Mr. Deveney then moved that the Superior of St. Francis Monastery, be, by his office, President of St. Francis College. It was so resolved, all agreeing." [14]

The trustees then concerned themselves with the design of a diploma and decided to "procure copies of diplomas already in use and take whatever was considered good and suitable in each."

"The Secretary was advised to notify the absentees when the next meeting would take place." [15]

This request to the Secretary indicates that more than nine members were elected to the first Board of the College. Daniel Ambrose, M.D. who was among the laymen elected by the Monastery Board, was removed and replaced by Joseph P. O'Connell, D.D., Pastor of St. Michael's on 25 May 1885, on account of Dr. Ambrose's "protracted stay in Europe" and "long continued absence from the United States". [16]

At its annual meeting, usually in late May or early June, the College Board approved the names of students for graduation from the Academy and, from 1885, and thereafter, the names of the scholars recommended by the Board of Examiners for the conferral of degrees by the College. On 25 May and 8 June 1885, the College Board approved the first six graduates to receive the Bachelor of Arts degree from St. Francis College:

"The president of the Examining Board submitted the names of six young men who had successfully passed the examinations: Michael H. Carey; Michael J. Flaherty; Thomas J. O'Connor; Daniel J. O'Connor; John A. Conway; and Michael J. Murray. . . . Dr. O'Connell moved that the six young men who had successfully passed examination, be, and they were accordingly declared worthy, to receive the degree of A.B." [17]

"HONORARY DEGREES" AWARDED

At the same College Board meetings of 25 May and 8 June 1885, an interesting process of awarding "honorary degrees" to clerics and laymen became evident:

"On motion of Rev. Father Duffy to confer the honorary degree of M.A. on the following gentlemen: Rev. M. G. Fleming; Rev. John J. Barry; Rev. Hugh Cassidy; Rev. William J. Doherty; Rev. James McCusker; Rev. Michael J. Kilaby; Rev. James O'Neil, O.P.; Rev. Peter H. Plunkett, (afterwards withdrawn).

Also nominated by Father Duffy were these laymen: John L. Deveney, LL.B.*(who was a member of the Board); John Green; James J. Calwell, Esq; Edward A. Doyle; Hugh McTurnan; and Eugene Curran. It was seconded, and being put, was carried.*

"Rev. Father Duffy moved that the degree of Ph.D. be conferred on Prof. Martin [of St. Francis College and a member of the Board of Examiners]; *it was agreed to."*

"On the recommendation of Brother Jerome Magner, Thos. J. McGowan; Edward A. Doyle; and Edward A. Rorke, received the Master of Arts degree."

The next paragraph from the minutes reveals some ambiguity about the Board's thinking on the nature of an "honorary degree," where an examination would be required for the gentleman's "fitness to receive the degree of Ph.D.":

> "It was agreed that Prof. Thos. F. Wilford, A.M., be accorded an examination and if he should be found successful, that his name be presented to the Board for the decision as to his fitness to receive the degree of Ph.D. [18]

On 8 June 1885, five more names were added to the M.A. honors list:

> "The following names were added by unanimous consent to those already approved of for the degree of M.A.: James McGee, LL. B.; John J. Conway, M.D.; Eugene A. Curren, Esq.; Eugene F. O'Connor, LL.B.; and Rev. Paul McClancy, of the diocese of Hartford." [19]

In subsequent years the Board of the College would seem to consider "applications" a requirement of persons for "honorary degrees," and would not award an honorary degree if the person had not requested it either verbally or in writing :

> "It was moved and seconded that Rev. John A. Conway; Rev. Thos. O'Connor; Rev. Michael H. Carey; Rev. Michael J. Flaherty; Doctor William E. Sullivan; and Rev. Joseph P. McGinley receive the degree of Master of Arts; amended to read, if personal **application,** or by written request, be made by them who had not applied, viz, all but Rev. J.P. McGinley and Dr. W. Sullivan, put and carried as amended.

*"Rev. Father Hill moved that Mr. Cusick, a gentleman of culture and refinement, at present engaged as principal of a public school in the City of Brooklyn, upon direct **application**, be awarded the degree of M. A. Mr. L.J. Deveney seconded the motion. The chair put the question, calling for the ayes and nays. It received a unanimous vote."*

BACHELOR OF ARTS GRADUATES AWARDED "HONORARY" MASTER OF ARTS DEGREES

In 1890, the Minutes of the "Acts of the Trustees" reveal a strange practice in awarding "Honorary" Master of Arts degrees to alumni of the College, many of whom were members of the clergy:

*"On motion of Brother Paul, being duly seconded, it was agreed that an addition to the By-laws be made entitling the **graduates who had received an A.B. two years before, to make application for the honorary degree of A.M.** It was agreed to by a full vote"* [20]

Implementation of Brother Paul's motion, to award the "Honorary" Master of Arts degree to College graduates two years after their Bachelor's degree, was done in 1891:

"On motion of Brother Jerome, being duly seconded, it was resolved unanimously to confer the Honorary Degree of Master of Arts on Secundo Marchisio, Professor of Latin in St. Francis College; Rev. William Joseph Donaldson, S.T.L.; Rev. Thomas Joseph Baxter, S.T.L.; and Rev. Francis A. McArtner, S.T.L., all three graduates of the College, and on Louis Thomas McGinn; and Thomas Francis Farrell, also graduates of the College." [21]

TRUSTEES REAPPRAISE THEIR "HONORARY DEGREES"

The Trustees continued to award "Honorary Degrees" from 1885 until 1906, when the New York State Regents issued new regulations curtailing this practice. The Board realized that the nature of its "Honorary Degrees," and "rules respecting the conferring of degrees," needed clarification, and appointed a Special Committee to prepare a report and recommendations for action by the Board:

To the Honorable The Board of Trustees of St. Francis College

The undersigned members of a Special Committee appointed to consider and report rules respecting the conferral of degrees beg respectfully to report the following as regulations which should govern the granting of degrees by the College:

I The bachelor's degree in arts, science, philosophy and literature, and the doctor's degree in philosophy shall not be conferred honoris causa.

II No degree shall be conferred on examination without the completion of a prescribed course in which one year at least has been spent in regular attendance at the college.

III Inasmuch as under the rules of the Regents of the University of the State of New York, no institution hereafter chartered is to be empowered to confer any honorary degree or any degree on examination, without residence, it is deemed judicious that no honorary degree should be conferred upon any candidate not of distinguished merit, and that in general the grant of such degrees should be conferred to persons of whose fitness the authorities of the college are especially cognizant either through ancient association with the college as students or because of notable services rendered to the church, the community, or the state in maturer years.

Signed: M.G. Flannery; Bro. Raphael, and John Greene."[22]

BISHOP McDONNELL RESIGNS FROM THE COLLEGE BOARD

At this same meeting a letter was read from Charles McDonnell, resigning from the Board.[23] As reported in Chapter Seven above, on 15 May 1906, McDonnell had written to Linus Lynch, the Superior of the Franciscan Brothers, ordering him to "collect and fetch" all the "Circular Letters" and the Petition for Union with the Roman Third Order Regular and bring them to him. Whether he was indicating his anger with the brothers or his disinterest in the College is not known, but since his installation as Ordinary of the Brooklyn Diocese on 2 May 1892, Charles McDonnell had attended only four meetings of the St. Francis College Board.[24] At his first attendance of the Board on 15 June 1893, the new Bishop arrived late and, after taking the chair, proceeded to lecture the College Board of Trustees on the strong requirements he would implement before the acceptance of St. Francis College graduates to the diocesan seminary.

The St. Francis Monastery Board also received and approved the annual reports of the Academy and College for transmission on, or before, the fifteenth of July of each year to the Board of Regents of the University of the State of New York, showing "the number of students attending the College, the number of classes or grades into which such students are divided, the course of study pursued by each of such classes or grades and other facts concerning the College or its management as the Board of Regents may by resolution require." [25]

Section III of the 1868 Charter of Incorporation specified that vacancies in the Board be filled by persons who were members of "The St. Francis Monastery," guaranteeing that, with the Bishop as President, only Brothers would be elected to membership on the Monastery Board.

> **Section III.** *The persons named in the first section of this act, shall be the first trustees of said corporation, and all vacancies by death, resignation, refusal to act, or removal of any of said Trustees, or otherwise, in the office of the Trustees shall be filled by the election of persons who shall be members of the "St. Francis Monastery." The said Board of Trustees shall fill such vacancy without unnecessary delay, and at least three votes shall be necessary for the election of any Trustee. There shall be at least one meeting of the Board each year.*

The "St. Francis Monastery" Board of Trustees was also charged with approval of financial transactions of St. Francis Academy and College, and the election of new members to the College Board when necessary. The minute books of the Monastery Board and the College Board reflect actions on these powers through the end of the nineteenth century and through the first half of the twentieth century.

Although he was the Dean of the College, Columba Reilly did not himself have an A.B. degree. To solve the lack of an academic degree the Board acted to confer a degree on him. At the regular annual meeting of the Board of Trustees of the College, Columba Reilly, after recommending three candidates for the Bachelor of Arts degree, which were approved unanimously, was himself nominated for a degree. "Brother Jarleth [Phelan], President of the College, recommended Philip C. Reilly (Brother Columba), [based on] (Advanced Academic Diploma 100 points, City College, Columbia College, St. Francis College), for the Degree of Bachelor of Arts. It was regularly moved, seconded, and adopted that the Degree of Bachelor of Arts shall be conferred on Philip C. Reilly (Brother Columba)." [26]

BISHOP MOLLOY'S CONCERN FOR THE COLLEGE AND SCHOLASTIC STUDIES FOR THE BROTHERS

Brothers did not attend their own St. Francis College for academic degrees until the mid-1940s. Prior to this time most of the brothers attended one year of "Normal School" after their graduation from high school, which was considered enough education to equip them for the elementary school classroom. This custom of not providing higher education for the brothers would come back to haunt them when Thomas E. Molloy, their own alumnus, criticized them for not having brothers academically prepared to teach at the College.

On 6 December 1930, the Franciscan Brothers' Council became concerned about "educational courses of the Brothers, including the Brothers temporarily professed," and appointed Eugene Dunne and Jerome Roese a "Committee of Two" to report at the next meeting of the

Consultors. The Council may have been anticipating the Bishop's appointment of James Sullivan, Ph.D. as Dean of the College, pro tem. Among the reasons given by the Bishop was the lack of brothers academically prepared to teach or be administrators in the College and St. Francis Prep. [27] The Committee of Two prepared a detailed "Report of Studies" on the "scholastic standing of all members of the community who are not professed twenty-five years." [28] They reported that "seven Brothers are pursuing college graduate courses - four at St. John's, three at Fordham. Two Brothers are pursuing undergraduate work at Fordham." However, they reported no knowledge of the "nature of the work being pursued in graduate fields by any of the temporary professed nor whether any temporary professed are pursuing undergraduate work." They recommended "that all temporary professed holding high school diplomas be obliged to pursue at least two semester credit hours of work per term."

The committee reported that:

"The condition of those pursuing college work is wholly satisfactory and commendable."

"The status of the men who should be pursuing high school work is very unsatisfactory and discouraging."

"Of fourteen cases examined but two are in a position to receive their diplomas in 1931 - Brother Bonaventure who lacks one subject, and Brother Francis who lacks two subjects. Of the remaining twelve only four have passed nine subjects in the aggregate. The remaining eight have no high school credit. This shows a wonton lack of industry in self-improvement when one considers that classes in high school work has been in organization and open to these men for the past six or seven years."

RECOMMENDATIONS

1. That classes in English four years and American History be organized and started in February, 1931 and that any of these fourteen as well as any of the temporary professed who have not credit in these subjects be obliged to attend. This will allow a registration of at least fourteen or fifteen in each class."

2. "That our men be obliged to utilize their time more generously in self betterment educationally than by novel and newspaper perusal. "This can be accomplished by compulsory class attendance. It is futile to assert that certain ones will never grasp the work. They will, if they are serious-minded toward themselves and their community, at least learn something."

3.   "That classes in each subject be for two hours a week from four to six. The passing mark under this method will be 75. The committee recommends that the Superior appoint a Brother with full powers to assign Brothers to classes. This appointee will be responsible for attendance at classes of each man under twenty-five years professed. This appointee will make a report in June to the Superior and his council. This report will include the work of those pursuing both college and high school work. All results shall be individualized."

"The committee believes that the high school work being pursued in cycles should be continued for some time during the summer months."

It seems ironic that the Franciscan Brothers' academies and many of their elementary schools in the nineteenth century were reported as having outstanding curricula with strengths in mathematics, music, and public speaking, but that in the first half of the twentieth century a significant number of brothers needed to be persuaded to seek education beyond the "Normal School" level, and some to go beyond "novel and newspaper perusal" to finish high school.

"THE COLLEGE IS NEITHER FRANCISCAN NOR CATHOLIC"

In 1931, Thomas E. Molloy, as president of the Board of Trustees of the College and "The St. Francis Monastery," was aware that Columba Reilly, as president, was the only Franciscan Brother associated with the College. He also learned of a number of non-Catholic teachers on the faculty. He appointed Rev. James A. Sullivan, Ph.D. as dean and five priests as professors. The Bishop's intervention in the governance of the College was, in hind sight, instrumental in the school's survival, but was not appreciated by the Community at that time. They felt that their rights as owners and administrators of St. Francis College had been usurped by the Ordinary and they wrote a petition in 1933, "requesting the removal of the present Dean of St. Francis College - Rev. James A. Sullivan - in order that the General Consultors of Saint Francis Monastery may appoint a competent Brother to fill this important office." The Bishop knew well that the brothers were not ready to appoint an academically competent Franciscan Brother as Dean of the College, nor were they yet ready to assign brothers to teach at the collegiate level. His strong response to their request is given below in its entirety: [29]

THE CHANCERY
DIOCESE OF BROOKLYN
75 GREENE AVENUE
BROOKLYN, N. Y.

Aug 21, 1933

Reverend General Consultors,
Franciscan Brothers,
St. Francis' Monastery,
Brooklyn, New York.

Reverend dear Brothers:

Allow me to acknowledge receipt of the
formal petition presented by your Committee requesting the "removal of the present Dean of St. Francis'
College - Rev. James A. Sullivan - in order that the
General Consultors of Saint Francis' Monastery may appoint a competent Brother to fill this important
office".

First of all I must say that I heartily
indorse your disposition to preserve through legitimate authority the letter and spirit of your approved
Constitutions.

In the present instance I hasten to
assure you that the original appointment of Father
Sullivan was made by me and as Bishop of this diocese
and Superior of your Community I so acted and provided
any necessary dispensation required in the circumstances.

Secondly, it is perfectly proper and
indeed laudable for you to endeavor to direct your
own College in administration and teaching just as
soon as you have available qualified Brothers for
these purposes.

Presently, you must admit that, judged
by the personnel of teaching staff, the College is
neither Franciscan nor Catholic in the full sense of
the terms.

THE CHANCERY
DIOCESE OF BROOKLYN
75 GREENE AVENUE
BROOKLYN, N. Y.

-2-.

Last June, for instance, the teaching
staff was composed as follows:

    (a) Brothers   2

    (b) Priests   5

    (c) Lay   16

and half of the lay teachers were non-Catholic.

Thirdly, Doctor Sullivan's term of of-
fice, as well as I can learn from your own Brothers,
laymen, and the diocesan school office, has been most
efficient and successful.

In fact, he has been super-generous with
his talents, energies and even personal means.

It is hardly considerate, therefore, to
consider a peremptory removal from office in his case.

Fourthly, the diocese can well use
Doctor Sullivan's services at any time and really made
a great sacrifice in giving him to the College.

In view of this fact and also to promote
the proper development of a Brothers' collegiate teaching and administrative staffs, I now decide as follows:

Doctor Sullivan will remain as Dean of
St. Francis' College until June 1935 unless the diocese
will require his services earlier.

In the meantime, you may prepare and
equip Brothers for the College teaching staff and administrative office.

Presently, I am quite satisfied you have
no such qualified Brothers.

-3-.

In 1935 (June) if you have a Dean and Brother teachers who will satisfy diocesan regulations and the State Educational Department, I shall approve their appointment.

I shall then withdraw Doctor Sullivan and most likely all other diocesan priests teaching in the College.

If the Brother teachers or administrative officers are not satisfactory, as above indicated, I shall take due action. In the meantime I shall direct the scrupulous observance of the following:

1. All Brothers should be counseled for the harmony of the Community to eliminate from private and public discussion the present Deanship.

2. A more cooperative attitude should be shown Doctor Sullivan during the remainder of his term of office.

3. The appointment of any future Brother Dean or college professor should not be made without my previous knowledge and approval.

4. The present lay Staff should gradually be replaced by Brothers or competent Catholic laymen so that by 1935 the Staff may be thoroughly Catholic.

Wishing you every blessing in the right solution of this problem and in your other religious duties, I am

Sincerely yours,

+ Thomas E. Molloy

BISHOP OF BROOKLYN.

BISHOP MOLLOY'S 1933 LETTER
TO THE BROTHERS

Thomas E. Molloy's 1933 letter describing St. Francis College as **"neither Catholic nor Franciscan,"** must have come as a shock to the Community. The effect his words had on the brothers served as a wake-up call which began to move the Brothers' Council and "The St. Francis Monastery" Board to see that the young brothers were educated beyond the Normal School level so that they could become teachers at the secondary level and professors in the College.

JAMES A. SULLIVAN, Ph.D., DEAN, CAPISTRAN CUSACK, O.S.F., SUPERIOR GENERAL, AND COLUMBA REILLY, O.S.F., PRESIDENT–ST FRANCIS COLLEGE,C.1935[30]

The Bishop's requirement that: "All Brothers should be counseled for the harmony of the Community to eliminate from private and public discussion the present Deanship."

and that: "A more cooperative attitude should be shown Doctor Sullivan during the remainder of his term of office," must have been observed, because the consultors learned to work with Dr. Sullivan and saw that in his five years as Dean he accomplished much of what the Bishop had hoped for in sending him to the College in 1931. Not only was the Bishop the President of the College Board of Trustees, but he was also the College's most famous alumnus, who felt that his Alma Mater was in danger of foundering.

In a comprehensive four page latter to the Franciscan Brothers Council [31] the Bishop set forth a number of goals which needed to be addressed before the College could act independently of the Brothers Council and apply for Middle States Accreditation.

280 WASHINGTON AVENUE
BROOKLYN, N.Y.

June 22nd, 1935.

Reverend General Consultors,
    St. Francis Monastery,
        Brooklyn, N. Y.

Reverend dear Brothers:

Permit me to bring to your attention that last Sunday, June 16th, a conference was unexpectedly arranged for me and held at your Juniorate in Smithtown, Long Island, and some questions relating to St. Francis' College were discussed.

At this conference there were present Right Reverend Monsignor Patrick J. Cherry; Very Reverend Brother Capistran; Reverend Brother Fidelis and myself.

The chief topics of consideration were the Deanship of St. Francis College; the membership of the administrative and teaching staffs of the College and desirable improvements in the living accommodations of the Reverend Brothers at the Monastery.

I feel that these matters should now be presented formally to your attention.

In this connection I shall first of all recall to your attention my letter to you under date of August 21st, 1933.

In that communication among other things I indicated that in 1935 (June) if you would have a qualified Brother Dean and Brother teachers who will satisfy diocesan regulations and the State Educational Department, I should approve their appointment and withdraw Father Sullivan from the College.

I also called attention to the fact that judging by the personnel of the teaching staff at the time, your College was neither Franciscan nor Catholic in the fullest sense of the term.

This observation was based upon the composition of the teaching staff which was as follows:

    a) Brothers...2.
    b) Priests....5.
    c) Lay.......16,
and I understood at the time that one-half of the lay teachers were non-Catholic.

280 WASHINGTON AVENUE
BROOKLYN, N.Y.

- 2 -   6/22/35.

Rev. General Consultors.

        Now we have reached June, 1955, and what are conditions of the
College in relation to my recommendations, requirements and directions
as presented in my letter of August, 1933?

        You have presently, I believe, no Brother Dean prepared,
experienced and qualified who will satisfy diocesan regulations and the
State Department of Education to take Father Sullivan's place.

        Then again, in reference to the personnel of the teaching staf
I find that in comparison with the statistics of 1933 the membership has
become relatively less representative of your Brotherhood even though it
shows some increase in Catholic teachers.

        In these circumstances I am absolutely convinced that the
withdrawal of Father Sullivan at this moment would be harmful to the
efficiency, standardization and proper functioning of your College.

        As I indicated in my letter of August 21st, 1933, I still be-
lieve that it is perfectly proper and indeed laudable for you to endeavor
to direct your own College in administration and teaching just as soon as
you may have available qualified Brothers for this purpose.

        To effect the realization of this reasonable and fitting progra
I shall submit now the following directions and recommendations:

    #1.
        Father Sullivan will continue as Dean during the scholastic year
1935-1936.

        Even though I should prefer that his term should be prolonged unti
1937, I shall not insist upon this greater extension.

        You should now designate a Brother who will be associated with
Father Sullivan during the coming scholastic year and who will observe
closely the policy and administrative procedure of the present Priest-Dea
so that a Brother may be properly prepared and appointed in 1936 to take
the place of Father Sullivan.

    #2.
        Before the Priest-Dean is relieved by the assignment in 1936 of a
Brother-Dean, the Board of Trustees of the College at a regular meeting
should see that the Brothers number at least ten and that they are compete
in view of the standards of our diocesan School Office and the Board of Re
gents.

280 WASHINGTON AVENUE
BROOKLYN, N.Y.

- 5 -   6/22/35.

Rev. General Consultors.

#2-cont'd.

The Board of Trustees should then petition me in a formal, written statement for the withdrawal of the Priest-Dean.

In making this reference to the Board of Trustees of the College, I wish to call attention to the fact that the Brothers should have the clear idea that the College is a legal corporation and that the direction of its educational activities belongs to the College Trustees and not to the Community Council.

All matters, therefore, pertaining to the Faculty, administration, teaching and finances of the College should be referred to the judgment and decision of the Board of Trustees of the College.

#3.

You should make a real beginning in the Fall of this year to have representative number of Brothers of College training on the staff.

In this matter it must be imperatively required that no Brother should be so honored unless he holds a College Degree.

The Brothers on the Faculty should number next September at least six.

If you will be able to realize this condition, announcement should be made at once so that the lay teachers thus relieved may have an early notice with the prospect of looking elsewhere for employment.

#4.

In September of 1936 at least four additional Brothers, each with a College Degree, should be added to bring the number of Brothers to the required minimum of ten, otherwise the title of a Brothers' College cannot reasonably be applied to your institution.

#5.

A really serious effort should be made by the Board of Trustees of the College to have the College affiliated with the Middle Atlantic States Association, for without this affiliation the candidates for medicine and law are suffering unexpected handicaps on graduation.

This registration should be accomplished by Summer of next year, if possible, and if not surely by June of 1937.

230 WASHINGTON AVENUE
BROOKLYN, N. Y.
- 4 -   6/22/35.

Rev. General Consultors.

#6.
    In reference to the finances of the College, the College accounts
should be kept distinct from any other funds and all such resources should
be listed under the College ownership and control, since this arrangement
is the proper legal requirement of a distinct legal corporation.

    A separate, careful listing, moreover, of college assets, invest-
ments and liabilities undoubtedly will be required for recognition and
approval by the Regents of New York State and the Middle Atlantic States
Association.

    I wish, therefore, to have the Reverend General Consultors consider
these directions and recommendations and prepare to render them effective
at the earliest possible moment, for unless we build up our educational
system in a thorough, efficient, systematic manner, we shall reduce our
educational work to an unbecoming superficiality or mediocrity, which not
only would reflect discredit upon Christian schooling but also impose
injustice upon our students.

    Finally, I am sympathetically disposed towards your proposed program of im-
proving housing conditions and accommodations of the Brothers in the Monastery.

    This program, however, represents a distinct undertaking in itself
and a special appeal for funds should be made throughout the diocese for the
fulfillment of this worthy purpose.

    The ordinary income of the College could not be expected to be used in
this regard.

    While we all understand that in a religious spirit you have taken upon
yourselves a serious program of self-denial and self-sacrifice, still we all
recognize that you should be assured of a clean, decent human habitation,
besides of course the proper facilities of a Community dwelling.

    I should be very glad to offer every expression of reasonable and
helpful cooperation for the realization of this worthy objective.

    I wish then to offer to you my sincere congratulations and thanks for
your successful completion of another year of Christian teaching in the Parish
Schools and in your own High School and College for the moral and religious
benefit of our Catholic boys and young men.

    I shall also express the hope that you and your Reverend Brothers
will enjoy a restful and pleasant Summer.

                            Sincerely yours,

                            Thomas E. Molloy

                            BISHOP OF BROOKLYN.

THOMAS E. MOLLOY TO
GENERAL CONSULTORS; JUNE 22ND, 1935.

Less than a year later, 18 June 1936, he asked that the
Board of the Trustees of the College meet and act on a
number of recommendations he then felt the College's
Board was prepared to accomplish:

280 WASHINGTON AVENUE
BROOKLYN, N. Y.

June 18th, 1936.

To the Board of Trustees,
         St. Francis College,
                 Brooklyn, N. Y.

Gentlemen:

        Allow me to bring to your attention that as President of your Board
and as Bishop of the diocese, I instituted in the Fall of 1931 a program of
special diocesan interest and aid to promote the progress of St. Francis
College.

        The chief feature of this plan was to offer the services of Reverend
James A. Sullivan in the capacity of Dean pro tem.

        I made this initial assignment with the distinct understanding that
I should be disposed to recall Doctor Sullivan whenever I decided that the
interests of the diocese necessitated such an action.

        I now find that particular parish requirements and an important
special diocesan undertaking will make very desirable if not actually necessary
the discontinuance of his duties in the College.

        I shall, therefore, make effective his withdrawal from the College
as of June 30th of the current year.

        I have good reason to know that Doctor Sullivan's work at the
College has been very faithful, constructive and successful.

        Under his capable and conscientious leadership the collegiate depart-
ment of St. Francis College has realized a notable degree of scientific
organization and standardization as well as of efficient and effective functioning.

        It is therefore with great reluctance that I proceed to deprive the
College of his services.

        I am greatly relieved, however, in the circumstances by the belief
that the Board of Trustees, as the legally responsible, authoritative body of
St. Francis College, will zealously endeavor to preserve the benefit of
Father Sullivan's fine work by maintaining the required qualifications in
administrative and teaching personnel, and his high standards of admission
requirements; of teaching and study courses; of discipline and equipment in
the College.

280 WASHINGTON AVENUE
BROOKLYN, N. Y.

- 2 -   6/18/36.

Board of Trustees.

To insure the future realization of these desirable and necessary features, I shall submit to the Board the following urgent recommendations:

First.
The Board of Trustees may well consider undertaking, through proper college officials, the registration of the College with the Middle Atlantic States Association.

The academic and future professional interests of the students seemingly require this affiliation.

To realize this program there are very definite college requirements of faculty personnel, equipment and finances, which the Board of course may readily determine.

Second.
Preparation should be made at once to have in due time the majority of the teachers in the College members of the Franciscan Brotherhood, yet no Brother should be admitted to the Faculty who does not possess a collegiate degree attained in a Catholic College or University.

Third.
All lay teachers should be practical Catholics and if possible residents of the diocese.

The non-Catholic teachers therefore presently on the staff should be replaced during the Summer, unless legal contractual agreements already made will prevent this accomplishment.

Fourth.
It would be well for the President of the College to be himself a college graduate.

Fifth.
In reference to the finances of the College, the College accounts should be kept distinct from any other funds and all such resources should be listed under the College ownership and control, since this arrangement is the proper legal requirement of a distinct legal corporation.

A separate, careful listing, moreover, of college assets, investments

280 WASHINGTON AVENUE
BROOKLYN, N.Y.

– 3 –   6/18/36.

Board of Trustees.

and liabilities undoubtedly will be required for recognition and approval
by the Regents of New York State and the Middle Atlantic States Association.

Sixth.
The Board will now submit to me the name of a Brother ór Brothers
equipped for the office of Dean.

The qualifications of such candidates should be clearly and
completely set forth.

In this matter it is essential of course to consider only such
Brothers who will be able and disposed to preserve and promote the standardization and efficiency of the College as now achieved, and who will insure
to the students of the present and future that they will be guaranteed an
education of genuine collegiate grade; of thoroughly Catholic spirit, motive
and purpose and of such scientific excellence and cultural influence as will
surely merit the approval of the Church and of the Department of Education of
the State of New York.

Frankly, I must confess that only for such a type and standard of
education do I wish to be now or in the future personally and officially
responsible for St. Francis College.

Assuring you of my very sincere appreciation of your valued counsel
and cooperation in this very important work of advanced Christian education,

I am

Sincerely yours,

BISHOP OF BROOKLYN.

THOMAS E. MOLLOY'S 1936 CHARGE TO THE BOARD [32]

The Bishop's intervention was both successful and prophetic. His recommendations for the future of the College gave the Board a blue print for the next twenty years. The Board met and began the process of implementing his recommendations and addressed a "Resolution" of their appreciation to Father Sullivan and the Bishop, acknowledging that "under Dr. Sullivan's leadership [the college] has realized a notable degree of scientific organization and effective functioning" and that for his "long, faithful and useful service for the growth and purpose of the College," the Board expressed its "heartfelt thanks". [33]

Although the Board of Trustees began to try to prepare the college for Middle States Association review and accreditation, the Second World War brought much of their activity to a grinding halt. The number of students declined drastically and at one point only forty-five young men were in attendance. [34] After the War the numbers of students increased significantly. In 1946, over six hundred young men, most of whom were returning veterans, crowded the halls of the college, and evening school became a necessity, with classes beginning at 8 A.M. and ending at 8 P.M. [35]

COLLEGE BOARD SEPARATES FROM MONASTERY BOARD

Bishop Molloy's recommendation number 5, in his 18 June 1936 letter to the Board of Trustees of the College was prescient: "In reference to the finances of the College, the College accounts should be kept distinct from any other funds and all such resources should be listed under the College ownership and control, since this arrangement is the proper legal requirement of a **distinct legal corporation.**" However, the College was fortunate that it was not yet a "distinct-legal corporation" at that time. Its continued existence during the Second World War was maintained only because the salaries of the brothers of St. Francis Prep and three elementary schools were still deposited into the "common pot" of St. Francis Monastery's treasury. The Monastery dining room did not distinguish college, high school or elementary brothers at their common table.

COLLEGE'S 1957 ABSOLUTE CHARTER

After the War the increasing numbers of students utilizing the generous "GI Bill" pushed the College toward expansion of its facilities and a reappraisal of its corporate role as a part of "The St. Francis Monastery". The requirement that elections of new College Trustees be by members of the "St. Francis Monastery Board," would guarantee control of the College Board by the Franciscan Brothers until 10 April 1957, when St. Francis College received an Absolute Charter from the Education Department of the State of New York. The new College Charter, an Act dated 19 February 1957, separated the College from the Monastery Board by creating a new, legal, corporate entity subject to the Regents of the University of the State of New York.

The earlier Charters were amended to have St. Francis College incorporated as a separate, legal, corporate body by the Regents of the University of the State of New York. This action was taken on the recommendation of the Associate Commissioner of Education of the New York State Education Department. [36] The Franciscan Brothers were not doing anything unusual by this action. In the 1950s, many religious communities across the United States were separating their schools of higher education from their corporate control on the recommendation of their state education departments and the advice of their own legal counsels.

Among the amendments to the earlier Charters in this 1957 Charter, was one which eliminated the power of the Trustees of St. Francis Monastery to appoint the Trustees of the College, and an interesting Section II of the 1868 Charter, which eliminated a part [in brackets] of the "Object" of The St. Francis Monastery which "shall be the education of children, [those able, as well as those unable to pay], and the visiting and assisting of the poor."

Although the phrase, "those able, as well as unable to pay" was removed from the "Object" of "The Saint Francis Monastery" corporation when the Charter was amended in 1957, the spirit of the original 1868 Charter has been preserved in the Franciscan Stewardship and commitment of St. Francis College and the other schools of the Franciscan Brothers to provide many scholarships for needy and worthy students.

CENTENNIAL FUND RAISING: BROTHERS STILL CONCERNED ABOUT THE COLLEGE

Despite the legal separation of the College from "The St. Francis Monastery" Corporation a year earlier, a fund raising campaign for the St. Francis Monastery at the 1958 Centennial of the Brothers' arrival in Brooklyn, reveals that the Development Office was planning a campaign to benefit all the institutions of the Community, with St. Francis College listed as its first priority. [37] As reported in Chapter Four, the efforts of the brothers to build a new college **and monastery** in 1922, had the enthusiastic support of Thomas E. Molloy, but only the new College was built with the monies raised. In 1958, a letter from Bryan J. McEntegart to all the pastors of the Brooklyn diocese regarding two fund raising campaigns for St. John's University and **St. Francis College**, indicated that the Bishop perceived the 1958 St. Francis Monastery Centennial Development Campaign as primarily benefiting the College.

At a Council Meeting 24 June 1959, the Consultors were presented with the results of the year-long Centennial Campaign. They were told that "Mahoney, Weilert and O'Brien" had resigned from directing the Campaign because they felt that there is "no definite objective," following the Centennial Dinner held on 24 May 1958 at the St. George Hotel. Other topics discussed included the anticipated negative response of the brothers to a campaign exclusively for St. Francis College. The Consultors were also presented with possible places for relocating St. Francis College, but were ambivalent about raising funds for the College as well as the Community. [38] The fraternal concern of the Franciscan Brothers toward their new College in Brooklyn Heights is revealed in a meeting on 27 October 1964, when "The St. Francis Monastery" ceded the property of "The St. Francis Monastery" in "Tax Block #402" at Butler and Baltic Streets, to St. Francis College. [39]

"BUNDY" MONEY [40] AFFECTS THE COLLEGE'S
CATHOLIC AND FRANCISCAN IDENTITY

St. Francis College's Mission Statement and its Catholic and Franciscan identity began to change a decade after it received its Absolute Charter:

In its <u>1967-1968 Catalog</u>, the General Objectives of the College clearly stated the College's Catholic and Franciscan identity:

General Objectives
As a Catholic College, St. Francis participates in the realization of the general objective of the Church itself by directing the student so that he may attain the end for which he was created.

*Specifically, the College aims to produce graduates
with trained minds, disciplined wills, cultural interests,
a consciousness of social responsibilities, sound physical
and mental health, and a vocational purpose.*

In six more paragraphs, this catalog spells out the expectations it holds for its graduates, such as "trained minds . . . with the Catholic view of man and his destiny;" who "with disciplined wills . . . order their lives not only according to the Natural Law but also to the Divine Positive Law". Theology was still in the course of studies of the College when the Catalog read: "This end is sought through studies in ethics and theology, guidance, and liturgical and sacramental opportunities for growth in charity, and the example and influence of religious men who live according to the teachings of the Gospel in true Franciscan tradition."

Through Franciscan philosophy it was hoped that graduates would acquire "cultural interests to appreciate what is true and beautiful," and have refined personalities, who, after the example of St. Francis, interpret creation as reflecting the infinite beauty and wisdom of God." It was expected that graduates with a consciousness of social responsibility would "understand cultural and civic relationships in the light of Catholic teaching, knowing when to act in order to preserve or change them." A program of health education and intercollegiate and intra-mural athletics would help graduates to attain sound physical and mental health and recognize "their obligations to perfect whatever special gifts Divine Providence has bestowed upon them."

In the 1968-1969 and 1969-1970 Catalogs, the almost two pages of "General Objectives," reflecting the College's Catholic and Franciscan traditions, were reduced to one paragraph:

General Objectives

As a result of its history, location, and sponsorship, St. Francis College is concerned with the liberal education of students in the Metropolitan Area. By virtue of its Franciscan religious and cultural traditions, the College is committed to principles of Christian thought and education. The College regards as its primary function the systematic introduction of qualified students to the larger world of the mind. To provide a setting for such larger awareness the College offers pre-professional and pre-graduate training in the arts, the sciences, and business.

By the 1970-1971 Catalog, the College's "Franciscan religious and cultural traditions" and "principles of Christian thought and education" were completely eliminated:

General Objectives

As a result of its history, location, and sponsorship, St. Francis College is concerned with the liberal education of students in the Metropolitan Area. The College regards as its primary function the systematic introduction of qualified students to the larger world of the mind. To provide a setting for such larger awareness the College offers pre-professional and pre-graduate training in the arts, the sciences, and business.

FRANCISCAN AND CATHOLIC

As presidents and boards of trustees of Catholic colleges and universities in the United States examine the Catholic identity of their institutions, and discuss how John Paul II's *Ex Corde Ecclesiae* will affect their relationship to the hierarchical Church, it is interesting to report how St. Francis College has successfully restored its Franciscan spirit and the Catholic tradition of its founders. [41] Each classroom, office and public room now has a Franciscan San Damiano crucifix on its walls.

THE CRUCIFIX WHICH SPOKE TO ST. FRANCIS

SAN DAMIANO CRUCIFIX

The Mission Statement of the <u>1999 -2001 Catalog</u> of the College restored its historical identity:

Mission Statement

St Francis College is a private, independent, co-educational college that welcomes students from all walks of life, providing a superior liberal arts education at an affordable price. The St. Francis student benefits from small classes taught by professors who are committed to provide an education in an atmosphere of support and friendship. By integrating liberal arts and pre-professional programs, the College promotes the development of the whole person. Both the Franciscan Heritage and the Catholic tradition establish a cornerstone of academic excellence, social responsibility, and mutual respect throughout the entire College community.

Efforts to restore the "Franciscan Heritage and Catholic Tradition" of the schools of the Community will be discussed in the next and final chapter of this history.

Notes

[1] State of New York, Office of the Secretary of State, *Chapter 851, An Act to Incorporate "The St. Francis Monastery" of the City of Brooklyn, June 2ⁿᵈ, 1868*, Franciscan Brothers Archives.

[2] Patrick Quinn, T.O.R., "The Third Order Regular of St. Francis in Ireland," *ANALECTA TOR*: XXIV/153 (1993), pp. 247-263, p. 253.

[3] Irish 1837 *Rule*, p. 6.

[4] Letter of John McMahon to James Croke, 15 March 1863, Archives Archdiocese of San Francisco.

[5] *The Rules of The Third Order of St. Francis, as Contained in the Bulls of*

Popes Nicholas IV, and Leo X . . . .Approved by the Right Rev. John Loughlin, Bishop of Brooklyn, Privately Printed, 1866.

6 *Rules and Constitutions of the Society of Religious Brothers; to which is annexed the Brief of Our Holy Father Pope Pius VII, Approving and Confirming the Institute,* Dublin, Joseph Blundell, 1832.

7 *The Rules of the Third Order . . .,* 1866, p. 44.

8 Federal Censuses for 1850, 1860 and 1870 for Cambria County, Pennsylvania.

9 "The St. Francis Monastery, By-Laws of the Board of Trustees," Brooklyn, N.Y., 1957, p. 8.

10 "Acts of the Trustees, St. Francis College and Academy, 1884-1957," 2 June 1884, p. 3, Archives of St. Francis Monastery,

11 "The St. Francis Monastery, By-Laws of the Board of Trustees," p. 8.

12 "Acts . . . , 25 May 1885," p. 6, and insert with Seal.

13 "Acts. . . , 12 June 1884," p. 5

14 The Superior General of the Brothers would be the President of the College until the early 1930s.

15 "Acts of the Trustees. . . , 2 June 1884," pp. 3-4.

16 "Acts. . . , 25 May 1885," p. 7.

17 "Acts . . . ., 25 May and 8 June, 1885", pp. 7 & 9.

18 "Acts . . . . , 25 May 1885", p. 8.

19 "Acts . . . . , 8 June 1885, p. 9.

20 "Acts . . . . , 11 June 1890" pp. 21 and 22.

21 "Acts . . . . , 19 June 1891" p. 26.

22 "Acts . . . ., June 11, 1906, pp. 78-79.

23 "Acts . . . ., June 11, 1906, p. 80.

24 "Acts. . . . , June 15th, 1893, pp. 35-37; June 15th, 1897, p. 49; April 14th, 1998, p. 53; and June 12th, 1905, p. 72.

25 "St. Francis Monastery By-Laws," pp. 8-9.

26 "Acts . . . ., June 13, 1922, p. 117.

[27] Although not expressed in writing in 1931, a 1933 letter of Thomas E. Molloy to the Council, explains his concern with the academic condition of the college and his reasons for Dr. Sullivan's appointment as Dean, pro tem, "Minutes of Chapters and Consultors of the Franciscan Brothers," 21 August 1933, pp. 148-150 FBA.

[28] "Minutes of Chapters and Consultors . . . , January 10, 1931., p. 89.

[29] Thomas E. Molloy to the Consultors of the Franciscan Brothers, [21 August 1933], "Minutes of the Chapters and Council of the Franciscan Brothers ," between pp. 148-150, FBA.

[30] Franciscan Brothers Archives

[31] Thomas E. Molloy, to the Reverend General Consultors, St. Francis Monastery, June 22nd, 1935.

[32] Thomas E. Molloy to the St. Francis College Board of Trustees, 18 June 1936, "Acts of the Board of Trustees of St. Francis College," pp. 177-179. FBA.

[33] "Acts of the Board of Trustees of St. Francis College," 2 July 1936, pp. 180-181.

[34] James Adams, "The Student Body: Lifeblood of St. Francis," in *St. Francis College: the First Hundred Years, A Collection of Essays*, p. 16.

[35] *Ibid.*

[36] "The St. Francis Monastery, By-laws of the Board of Trustees," 1957, Preamble, p. 2.

[37] "Projects Planned for Development Program," July 30, 1958.

[38] "Minutes of Chapters and Council Meetings Franciscan Brothers," 24 June 1959 and "Franciscan Brothers Parish Appeal, September 1958 - June 1959".

[39] "Acts of The St. Francis Monastery, 27 October 1964.

[40] The granting of funds to New York State colleges and universities began a process of secularization of those institutions which accepted "Bundy Money." Religious symbols in the classrooms and Catholic Theology and Philosophy in the curricula of these schools were removed by trustees and administrators who mistakenly believed these actions were required to qualify for these grants.

[41] "The Franciscan Charism in Higher Education," *Spirit and Life: a Journal of Contemporary Franciscanism,* Vol. 2, 1992, is entirely devoted to essays exploring the efforts of Franciscan colleges and universities to discuss and identify their Franciscan identity.

CHAPTER TEN

FRANCISCAN SPIRIT IN THE BROTHERS' SCHOOLS IN THE THIRD MILLENNIUM

Colleagues, alumni, students, parents and friends of the Franciscan Brothers have expressed their perception of the Franciscan Spirit they see in the Brothers' work in the schools and ministries of the Community. This Franciscan Spirit, expressed in calligraphy below, can be found in both the Irish and American Constitutions of the Community: [1]

THE spirit of this Congregation is one of faith, humility, poverty and fraternal charity united with great simplicity of character, with fervent piety and zeal, seeking sanctification rather in the perfect manner of discharging ordinary actions than in things extraordinary in their nature.

"SPIRIT OF THE CONGREGATION" [2]

"EDUCATION WITH A FRANCISCAN TWIST" [3]

At a meeting, "Celebrating Our Franciscan Vocation," at St. Francis Center in Oyster Bay on November 1, 2000, Dr. Frank Macchiarola, President of St. Francis College, shared with the brothers and guests his vision of how the "Brothers preserved and augmented this Franciscan Spirit" at St. Francis College:

During my formative years as a college student, I had the opportunity to study at a Franciscan School, St. Francis College, Brooklyn. I had gone to learn things that were explicitly cited in the college catalogue - the liberal arts education with a major in history - but in the time I was there I learned a great deal more that was not noted in the official literature of the college. I learned about the Franciscans and the special charism of the Order. It was what I learned that was to change the way I saw life and its meaning.

SIMPLICITY

The President of St. Francis College continued with: *"three things that I saw in the Franciscans at St. Francis College that would challenge and inspire me for the rest of my life. The first was simplicity. In a period of time when people saw things in more complex ways, the Franciscan sense of what they were to do in their lives was extremely simple. Their lifestyle, the things that they enjoyed, their interactions with students and others all had as their foundation the fact that the simple life was the best life. . . . "*

HUMILITY

"The second characteristic that had its impact upon me was the humility that seemed to be a universal quality of the Brothers. It is not that many of them did not appreciate the levels of excellence that they had attained in their own lives. Many of them were accomplished scholars with advanced degrees. Many possessed extraordinary talents as musicians and artists. But these talents and accomplishments were seen as gifts from God. This is not to be confused with

some who see themselves - rather than their talents - as God's gifts.

Though these Brothers may have had rank and distinction in the outside world, humility marked the way of life within their community. They even surrendered their worldly identity to take names that parents would not visit upon their children - names like Celsus, Celestine, Athanasius, Anthelm, Camillus, and Benignus. In these religious names they lost their identity within their own families."

RESPECT FOR OTHERS

"The third of the Brothers' qualities was their sense of respect for others. I often say that the Franciscan Brothers did not discriminate on the basis of race, religion, creed or ability. But it is extraordinary to think that in a school setting, academic achievement is placed in such a position as not to be the basis of discrimination. And yet it was just that which marked the way the Brothers dealt with us. It was important to strive toward excellence and we were all expected to do just that. But you were important not because of what you did, but because of whom you were.

The simple, humble and respectful life of the Brothers taught a lesson that could never be found in texts or could not simply be preached. The lessons were taught by example and the examples were all around us. It is not an accident that the charism of the Franciscan Brothers has left an enduring mark on so many of us who were educated in their schools. Today, in times of great trouble in the spiritual life of this city, they offer an example that is worth recalling and emulating."

"INVITE STUDENTS INTO YOUR COMMUNITY!"

Dr. Joseph Castellano, an Assistant Principal at St. Francis Preparatory School, commented at that same meeting: "You practice a person-centered approach to life and education. Your philosophy influences your co-workers." He challenged the Brothers "to teach more about Francis; to have a wider presence in school events; to pray with faculty and students; to invite students and co-workers into your community."

Speaking to the brothers, Maureen Scharen, parent and Mothers Guild President at St. Anthony's High School, complimented the Franciscan Brothers: "You allow the individual to be him/herself and you encourage all by stressing that each individual can make a difference. In the 60s 'entering' meant to the novitiate or seminary and was widely accepted. Today, you need to approach and invite a student."

"I challenge you to talk more about your life and to invite students to be a Brother," was suggested by Gregg Rannazzosi, President of St. Anthony's High School's National Honor Society and an active member of various campus ministries.

"ST FRANCIS: A COLLEGE OF VALUE AND VALUES"

In the 2000-2001 Annual Report of St. Francis College, Dr. Macchiarola wrote that "the Franciscan Brothers founded the College with a mission to serve the working poor, many of them recently arrived immigrants."[4] The tuition and fees of $10,180 in 2002-2003, coupled with state and federal student aid grants, makes the College's tuition the "least expensive of all four-year private colleges in

New York State, with more than 90% of our students receiving some form of financial aid, including academic and/or athletic scholarships, and state and federal grants. The number of students on academic scholarships during 2001-2002 was 896, up from 776 in 2000-2001, 625 in 1999-2000, and 449 in 1998-1999. Spending for academic scholarships in 2001-2002 was $4,649,395, up from $3,585,209 in 2000-2001, and from $2,303, 576 in 1999-2000."[5]

In an essay about the Catholic Mission of the College, the President wrote: "In addition to low tuition, our mission also requires significant student aid and scholarship assistance to students so that even the most economically disadvantaged students can afford to come here. Our Catholic mission requires that we do the best we can to make the college available to families and students who understand what we are about and who want to be part of a community which supports religion and worship while providing a college education. For many Catholics, a college education that is founded on a system of values is very important. We like to think of St. Francis as a college of value and of values." [6]

On 1 November 2001, St. Francis College sponsored a full-day workshop on "What Does It Mean To Be Franciscan?", an ongoing series of workshops sponsored by the "Franciscan Institute at St. Francis College." The "Rhodes Consultations on the Church-Related College," funded by the Lilly Endowment, supported the four speakers who presented both philosophical and practical aspects on how a Franciscan college might identify and claim its Franciscan heritage and present this to its faculty, administration and students.

"STUDENTS MUST BE INSPIRED BY A
LARGER VISION"

Colleges must not only evaluate their students in the core curriculum and their competence in their specific field of study, "but in the end, students must be inspired by a larger vision, using the knowledge they have acquired to discover patterns, form values, and advance the common good. The undergraduate experience at its best will move the student from competence to commitment." [7]

For Franciscans, this "larger vision" goes back to the commitment of Francis' first friars to study and eventually teach in the University of Paris where Theology and Philosophy were the principle fields of study. The Friars Minor were seen by the Pope as those "suitable men, powerful in word and work," envisioned by the decrees of the Fourth Lateran Council. [8]

However, Franciscan education for elementary and grammar school was not provided by the Friars Minor, except in the secondary level gymnasia of Germany and Austria, as required by the local governments. In Ireland, however, the "Third Order Regular" Brothers "devoted themselves to educating the youth of the surrounding districts; the liberality of the native princes enabled them to diffuse learning among the poorer classes." [9]

ST. FRANCIS PREPARATORY SCHOOL

Similar to St. Francis College, St. Francis Preparatory School is a separate, legal educational corporation administered by its own Board of Trustees composed of laymen and brothers. The present, over two-acre school, had modest beginnings from its original "academy" status in Brooklyn, first on Baltic Street in Cobble Hill and then at

North 6th Street in Williamsburg. Limited to a totally male enrollment until 1974, it moved to Fresh Meadows in Queens and became co-educational. One constant, however, remained in each location, its Franciscan heritage.

At St. Francis Prep the tradition of service is continued through the dedication of a diocesan priest chaplain, 12 brothers, 21 sisters from six different communities, and 131 lay professionals on staff. Their primary focus is to implant the gospel message of love of God and neighbor, the message so eloquently preached by St. Francis' life. So committed is this faculty that 45 members have been with the Prep for over 25 years, and 92 for over 15 years. In addition, many of their graduates return to teach at their Alma Mater. To recognize longevity of service, the school awards the Canticle Citation (a medallion and stipend), each year, to those completing the plateaus of 15 and 25 years.

Starting each school day, the entire student body, under the guidance of the Campus Ministry team, joins in reflective prayers (frequently composed by the students), which stress the importance of the individual, the beauty of the world around them, and God's special love - all themes beloved by our Franciscan founder. Patriotism is also encouraged through the recitation of the flag salute.

The current enrollment includes 2,739 young men and women who follow the rigorous college preparatory program offered. Incoming freshmen, who have the desire and ability, are able to enroll in a special Science Research Track which they follow for their four years, culminating in research internships at colleges and laboratories, often resulting in significant scholarships. An appreciation of natural resources, and the relevance of faith to science, promote awe of God's creation as lived by Francis.

"REBUILD MY CHURCH"

Undoubtedly, it is in the realm of service where the mandate given to Francis, to "rebuild my church," is so clearly recognized. Students at St. Francis Prep serve in many capacities as they care for the economically poor. Each Easter vacation, a van heads for Appalachia with volunteers who pitch in to paint houses, rebuild sagging porches, clean out gutters, plant gardens, and generally bring hope and comfort to a forgotten segment of America's poor. On a regular basis, all during the school year, 150 seniors sacrifice a free period to serve as role models for the young children in PS 4, the Special Education Public School behind the Prep. Weekly, different students work at the Presentation Parish soup kitchen, serving meals to those whose lack of income cannot supply their need for nourishing food.

Through the Service Program, junior students may opt to devote several hours, after school, in the evenings, or on weekends, to serve in shelters, work in hospitals, and nursing homes, assist parish athletic programs, teach CCD classes, and supervise elementary homework programs. Other students work with the mentally, or physically handicapped at the Bernard Fineson Developmental Center. All students assist in making the annual Christmas Party for handicapped adults a joyous occasion.

In school, religious activity service takes many forms. Fifty-four Eucharistic Ministers, 40 already installed and 14 in the process of training at St. Paul's Center, serve the six Special Liturgies held during the school year, in addition to being available for the 7:45 Mass celebrated daily in the School Chapel. At the four Masses in the beginning of the school year, students of each class level are officially welcomed and introduced to the Franciscan tradition.

Student Eucharistic Ministers help out in their parishes and bring Communion to nursing home and hospital patients, with the blessing of their pastors. They also attend vocation programs given by the Vocation Office and attend the diocesan youth leadership, "Let Your Light Shine," program. School dances and athletic events are held to raise money for particular causes, such as combating cancer or muscular dystrophy.

Each week, one section of the sophomore class journeys to the Franciscan Brothers' Mount Alvernia in Centerport, Long Island, to make one of 19 school retreats conducted there. One hundred forty student retreat leaders, previously trained in after-school sessions, have their turn as group facilitators. They lead the retreatants and give the two main talks: on relationship with God and relationship with others. They also give talks to freshman religion classes and provide information about the value of a retreat. Some have helped give Confirmation or Graduation retreats in parishes. Seniors and juniors have the opportunity to sign up for a retreat, geared to them, during the course of the academic year.

By providing over 100 sport and club interests, the Prep promotes holistic growth with special attention to fostering self-esteem, working as a team member, showing respect for the individual, and learning tolerance. One particular club focuses on concern for the environment, so that "Sister Earth" will not be mistreated. As St. Francis preached by simply walking through the town of Assisi, the Prep's Guidance Department provides beneficial lessons, with the many groups created for the perceived needs of teenagers.

From 7:00 a.m. until 11:00 p.m., St. Francis Prep is a hubbub of activity, a home away from home for its almost 2,800 students which it's administration, faculty and staff serve in caring surroundings permeated with hospitality and friendliness. "St. Francis would be well-pleased if he should drop by." [10]

ST. ANTHONY'S HIGH SCHOOL

As another school administered by the Franciscan Brothers, St. Anthony's High School gives its students, through its curricular and unique extracurricular activities, a superior academic experience in a Faith-filled, nurturing institution. Located in South Huntington, Long Island, St. Anthony's is a college preparatory school for young men and women. With its own Board of Trustees, the school is under the direction and ownership of the Franciscan Brothers of Brooklyn. Conducted by dedicated lay and religious men and women, the school works in close cooperation with parents, who the faculty believe, are the primary educators of their children.

As the Statement of Philosophy of the high school makes clear, St. Anthony's recognizes that "true education is directed toward the formation of the whole person. This education emphases the primacy of faith in God, the teachings of Jesus Christ, an understanding of the role of the Church, and a practical application of Franciscan ideals. These principles foster an awareness of the end for which each person is created, the good of the society to which each belongs, and the rights and responsibilities which each, as an adult, will share."

The Board of Trustees, Administration and Faculty believe that "such an environment fosters the spiritual values of the Catholic faith and the physical, moral, intellectual and aesthetic development of their students which develops a capacity for sound judgement, promotes an appreciation of the student's cultural heritage, and prepares each of them to take an active role in society."

Student service for their colleagues can be best seen in the "Saint Anthony's Leadership Team, known as "S.A.L.T., whose members welcome incoming students to the high school. Each S.A.L.T. member is assigned four incoming freshmen and contact them first by letter, then phone calls and meetings to help make their transition to high school as comfortable as possible by introducing them to other students and answering their questions. S.A.L.T. members wear a distinctive yellow shirt so that freshmen can find them through the beginning of the school year. The S.A.L.T. board and faculty moderators meet throughout the year to plan and organize events such as the Frosh Dance and the Christmas Toy Drive for poor children. Service to the neighboring community is provided by the TAU Fraternity, a Franciscan Secular Third Order community of upperclassmen. Members can be found babysitting after school at St. Elizabeth's Church, next to the school, tutoring young children at Our Lady of the Miraculous Medal in Wyandanch or visiting the elderly at local nursing homes. The TAU members also help in the transportation of the many bags of food collected during the annual Thanksgiving food drive. They are also responsible for organizing the Christmas Tree Sale and Lenten Soup Day.

Of the 40 clubs, 78 athletic teams, five academic honor societies, two theatrical productions yearly, and four school publications at St. Anthony's, their famous School Chorus is the largest activity with nearly four hundred talented students. These dedicated young women and men, freshmen to seniors, practice three times a week under the direction of Brother Joshua and Sister Marilyn, as they prepare choral works ranging from Handel's "Messiah" to Broadway's "Oliver". Talented junior and senior chorus members form the "Gregorian Schola"

which sings music from Latin hymns to contemporary
songs.

The School Orchestra, consists of nearly 100 musicians,
who practice daily under the direction of Mr. Bruce Engel.
These orchestral musicians perform with the Chorus in a
stunning performance of Handel's Hallelujah Chorus at
the Christmas Concert each year. Talented instrumentalists
form the Symphonic Band, a group of elite musicians who
have mastered an outstanding repertoire. The service of
music in promoting the Faith is shown each year in the
Liturgies which are enhanced by the Chorus and
Orchestra. This is most evident in the annual tours of these
talented students where they have performed, to great
acclaim, in churches and concert halls in Italy, France and
Spain. Music at St. Anthony's is a unique gift which truly
promotes the faith of its students and faculty.[11]

"THE GOOD WORK"

Continuing the long tradition brought from Ireland, the
Franciscan Brothers, as we read in the Introduction of this
history, still provide free education today to a significant
number of their students as they did in 1860 to: "assist a
numerous class to better their mental condition is worthy
of all praise, and will, we hope, be co-operated in by all
who can aid in the good work." [12]

In recent years, the Franciscan Brothers initiated a
program to send a delegation of administrators, trustees,
faculty, and staff in all of the Brothers' schools to
participate in a Franciscan Assisi Pilgrimage to enable
them to study and introduce into their schools the
Franciscan Spirit they experienced in St. Francis of Assisi's
Umbria and Rome.

The "good work" of the Franciscan Brothers was acknowledged at the 140th Anniversary of the Community. Bonaventure Midili, TOR, the Minister General Third Order Regular, wrote:

> *The General Council and I join you in thanking God for the wonders He has wrought in and through you and those who have come before you. You have touched the lives of many young men and women with the works of mercy in the ministry of education, and in social and pastoral services. We are united to you by a special bond in our profession of the same rule and our sharing of the same charism. We feel particularly one with you because of our common roots in the pioneer Franciscan brothers who came to Brooklyn in 1858 and in the providence of God gave rise to the TOR's in the United States of America.*

As the Homilist of the Franciscan Brothers 140th Anniversary Mass of Celebration, Most Reverend Roland Faley, TOR, former Minister General of the Third Order Regular, praised the Brothers' history in Brooklyn over the last fourteen decades. "It is the Franciscan Brothers as a community of dedicated men, who have served the church well for 140 years, that we celebrate today." He stated that "the title 'The Franciscan Brothers of Brooklyn' evokes many memories of labor, holiness, sacrifice, and dedication to education. It bespeaks a legacy that has truly enriched the church of New York, indeed the church of the United States."

In concluding, Father Roland prayed that the Franciscan Brothers "continue on a path of sound instruction, especially in the faith, and that there will always be an atmosphere that is 'student friendly'. We pray earnestly that young people of today will see your vocation as vital to the church, and that some will join your ranks."

Speaking directly to the Franciscan Brothers, he said that "You mean more to the church than even you imagine. Each of you is of inestimable value before God. In the Words of Francis in his *Letter to the Faithful*, the First Rule of the Third Order: 'You are the children of the heavenly Father whose works you do. You are the spouses, brothers, and mothers of Christ.' May your lives continue to praise the Lord for He who is mighty has done great things through you."

At the conclusion of this History of the Franciscan Brothers, may the Franciscan Spirit of this Congregation continue to be evident in the "faith, humility, poverty, and fraternal charity" of the Franciscan Brothers who continue to "seek their sanctification by the perfect manner" shown in the tasks they perform in the classrooms, offices, and ministries, which, by their "fervent piety and zeal, may become extraordinary in their nature. "

Pace e Bene!

Notes

[1] Franciscan Brothers of the Brooklyn Congregation of the Regular Third Order of St. Francis, "Constitutions of the Brothers of the Regular Third Order of St. Francis of the Diocese of Brooklyn," Brooklyn, 1924, p. 1.

[2] "Spirit of the Congregation," Jonathan Ringkamp, O.S.F., c. 1965, St. Francis College Faculty Residence.

[3] Frank Macchiarola, Ph. D. "Education With a Franciscan Twist," *The*

Tablet, Nov. 18, 2000.

4 "St. Francis College 2000-2001 Annual Report," pp. 7-8.

5 Guy Carlsen, Director of Student Financial Services, St. Francis College.

6 Frank J. Macchiarola, Ph. D. "An Open Invitation to Visit St. Francis College," *The Tablet,* November 3, 2001, p. 20.

7 Ernest Boyer, *College, The Undergraduate Experience in America,* New York; Harper & Row, 1987, p. 284.

8 Dominic V. Monti, O. F.M., "Franciscan Higher Education: A 750 Year Tradition," *Spirit and Life: A Journal of Contemporary Franciscan Life,* [The Franciscan Charism in Higher Education], Vol 2, 1992, p 64.

9 *Ibid,* p. 72.

10 Eileen Harrigan, S.C.H., member of the faculty and Honorary Alumna of St. Francis Prep, shared her thoughts on the Franciscan Spirit and Heritage of St. Francis Preparatory School, *The Canticle,* Fall 2000, pp. 1-2.

11 John Mark Minicozzi, O.S.F.and Joshua DiMauro, O.S.F., *The Canticle,* Spring, 2001, pp. 1-2

12 *The Irish News,* June 2, 1860, p. 4.

SELECTED BIBLIOGRAPHY

Andrews, Hilary, *Lion of the West: A Biography of John MacHale*, Veritas, Dublin, 2001.

Bayor, Ronald H. and Timothy J. Meagher, editors, *The New York Irish*, Johns Hopkins University Press, Baltimore, 1996.

Brady, Ciaron, Editor, *Interpreting Irish History; the Debate on Historical Revisionism, 1938-1994*, Irish Academic Press, Dublin, 1994.

Conlon, Patrick, O.F.M., *Franciscan Ireland*, Lilliput Press, Mullingar, County Westmeath, 1988.

Connolly, Sean J., *Priests and People in Pre-Famine Ireland, 1780-1845*, Gill and Macmillan, Dublin, 1982.

Corish, Patrick, *The Irish Catholic Experience, a Historical Survey*, Michael Glazier, Inc. Wilmington, Delaware, 1985.

Corkery, Daniel, *The Hidden Ireland, A Study of Gaelic Munster in the Eighteenth Century*, Gill and Macmillan, Dublin, 1924.

Corry, Emmett O.S.F., "Researching a Franciscan Identity in the Church, Rules and Constitutions Influencing the History of the Franciscan Brothers of Brooklyn, " *ANALECTA, TOR, XXX/163*, (1999): pp. 229-269.

_____, "The Franciscan Brothers of Brooklyn's Rules and Constitutions: The Evolution of a Charism in the Church," *Greyfriars Review*, 15: 1, (2001): pp. 101-135.

_____, "Franciscan Brothers of Brooklyn Respond to a Pope's 'Yes' and a Bishop's 'No,'" *ANALECTA, TOR, XXXII,* 167, (2001), pp. 177-207.

Cowan, Bernardine, O.S.F., "The Story of the Irish Franciscan Brothers" (manuscript), Mountbellew, Galway, 1955.

Deane, Seamus, General Editor, *The Field Day Anthology of Irish Writing,* 3 volumes, Field Day Publications, Derry, 1991.

Donnelly, James S. and Kerby A. Miller, editors, *Irish Popular Culture, 1650-1850,* Irish Academic Press, Dublin, 1999.

Dowling, P.J., *The Hedge Schools of Ireland,* Mercier Press, Dublin, 1968.

Florentz, Christopher J., Ed., *St. Francis College: The First Hundred Years,* St. Francis College, 1984.

Fox, Declan, O.S.F., "History of the Irish Franciscan Brothers" (manuscript) , Mountbellew, Galway, 1980.

Gabriel, Angelus, F.S.C., *The Christian Brothers in the United States, 1848 - 1948,* McMullen Co., New York, 1948.

Harvey, Karen, *The Bellews of Mount Bellew, A Catholic Gentry Family in Eighteenth-Century Ireland,* Four Courts Press, Dublin ,1998.

Jordon, Vincent, O.S.F., "The Order of Penitents, The Third Order Regular of Saint Francis in Ireland" (manuscript), Mountbellew, Galway, 1995.

Keogh, Daire, *Edmund Rice, 1762-1844,* Four Courts Press, Blackrock, Co. Dublin, 1996.

Kissane, Noel, *The Irish Famine, A Documentary History*, National Library of Ireland, Dublin, 1995.

Kowalsky, N, O.M.I. and J. Metzler, O.M.I., *Inventory of the Historical Archives of the Congregation for the Evangelization of Peoples, or "De Propaganda Fide"*, 3rd enlarged edition, Pontificia Universitas Urbaniana, Roma, 1988.

Larkin, Emmett, *The Historical Dimensions of Irish Catholicism*, The Catholic University of America Press, Washington, D.C., 1997.

_____, "Myths, Revisionism, and the Writing of Irish History ," *New Hibernia Review*, 2:2, (Summer, 1998), pp. 57-70.

McCaffrey, Lawrence J, *The Irish Catholic Diaspora in America*, Catholic University of America, 1997.

Miller, Kerby A. *Emigrants and Exiles, Ireland and the Irish-Exodus to North America*, Oxford University Press, 1985.

Nagle, Roger, O.S.F., "The Historical Growth and Development of the Franciscan Brothers of Brooklyn," M.A. Thesis, St. John's University, New York, 1943.

O Clabaigh, Colman N., OSB, " The Franciscan Third Order in Medieval Ireland," pp. 80-105 in *The Franciscans in Ireland, 1400-1534, From Reform to Reformation*, Four Courts Press, Dublin, 2002.

O'Day, Alan and John Stevenson, *Irish Historical Documents Since 1800*, Gill and Macmillan, Dublin, 1992.

O Grada, Cormac, *Black '47 and Beyond, The Great Irish Famine in History, Economy, and Memory,* Princeton University Press, Princeton, New Jersey, 1999.

Pazzelli,, Raffaelle, T.O.R., *St. Francis and the Third Order, The Franciscan and pre-Franciscan Penitential Movement,* Franciscan Herald Press, Chicago, 1989

Quinn, Patrick, T.O.R., "The Third Order Regular of St. Francis in Ireland," *ANALECTA, TOR,* XXIV/153, (1993): pp. 247-263.

St. Francis of Assisi: Writings and Early Biographies; English Omnibus of the Sources for the Life of St. Francis, Third Revised Edition, Franciscan Herald Press, 1972.

Francis of Assisi; Early Documents, 3 volumes, New City Press, New York, 1999.

Sharp, John K. *History of the Diocese of Brooklyn, 1853-1953, The Catholic Church on Long Island,* Fordham University Press, New York, 2 volumes, 1954.

Tanner, Marcus, *Ireland's Holy Wars: the Struggle for a Nation's Soul, 1500-2000,* Yale University Press, New Haven and London, 2001.

United States Documents in the Propaganda Fide Archives, a Calendar, editors: Finbar Kennelly, OFM, and William J. Short, OFM, Academy of American Franciscan History, Washington, D.C., 1966 - 2002+, 12 volumes.

Vatican Archives, An Inventory and Guide to Historical Documents of the Holy See, Francis X. Blouin, Jr., General Editor, et al, Oxford University Press, New York, 1998.

Watt, John, *The Church in Medieval Ireland,* University College Dublin Press, 2nd Edition, 1998.

Whelan, Irene, "Evangelical Religion and the Polarization of Protestant - Catholic Relations in Ireland, 1780-1840," (Ph.D. Dissertation), University of Wisconsin-Madison, 1994.

_____"The Stigma of Souperism," *The Great Irish Famine*, edited by Cathal Poirteir, Mercier Press, 1995, pp. 135-154.

Whelan, Kevin, *The Tree of Liberty; Radicalism, Catholicism and the Construction of Irish Identity, 1760-1830*, University of Notre Dame Press, in Association with Field Day, Notre Dame, Indiana, 1996.

_____, "The Catholic Parish, the Catholic Chapel, and Village Development in Ireland, " *Irish Geography*, Vol. 16, (1983), pp. 1-15.

ABOUT THE AUTHOR

Emmett Corry, O.S.F., a Franciscan Brother of Brooklyn, has examined archives in Rome, Ireland, California and Brooklyn, and in the tradition of an Irish *shanachai*, has prepared a unique story of the rich tradition of the Brothers who traveled from the West of Ireland to America a century-and-a-half ago.

Retired as Professor and Director of the Division of Library and Information Science of the Graduate School of Arts and Sciences of St. John's University, Brother Corry is active in the New York Irish History Roundtable which he served as President from 1993-1995. This History is the result of his current work as Research Archivist of the Franciscan Brothers.